British government policy
in Northern Ireland, 1969–2000

MANCHESTER
UNIVERSITY PRESS

British government policy
in Northern Ireland, 1969–2000

Michael Cunningham

MANCHESTER UNIVERSITY PRESS

MANCHESTER AND NEW YORK

distributed exclusively in the USA by Palgrave

Published by
Manchester University Press
Oxford Road, Manchester M13 9NR, UK
and Room 400, 175 Fifth Avenue, New York, NY 10010, USA
http://www.manchesteruniversitypress.co.uk

Distributed exclusively in the USA by
Palgrave, 175 Fifth Avenue, New York,
NY 10010, USA

Distributed exclusively in Canada by
UBC Press, University of British Columbia, 2029 West Mall,
Vancouver, BC, Canada V6T 1Z2

British Library Cataloguing-in-Publication Data
A catalogue record for this book is available from the British Library

Library of Congress Cataloging-in-Publication Data applied for

ISBN 0 7190 5766 3 *hardback*
     0 7190 5767 1 *paperback*

08 07 06 05 04 03 02 01   10 9 8 7 6 5 4 3 2 1

Typeset by
Action Publishing Technology Ltd, Gloucester
Printed in Great Britain by
Bookcraft (Bath) Ltd, Midsomer Norton

Contents

Preface and acknowledgements

Despite the huge number of texts devoted to the Northern Ireland 'question', there is no single account that provides a comprehensive account of the legislative and institutional initiatives of the British government over the period of direct rule. This is the aim of this book. The introductory chapter provides the context of direct British re-intervention in the late 1960s and the subsequent chapters chart developments chronologically in four policy areas: constitutional; security; economic; and social. These areas are considered as successive governments have argued that a multi-dimensional approach is necessary to the resolution of the 'question'. The conclusion explores the issues of bipartisanship and interpretations of British policy making.

I would like to thank the University of Wolverhampton for sabbatical support which enabled this book to be written, the University of Birmingham for its excellent library facilities and the anonymous reader for his/her comments. My principal release from the pressures of writing was to head for the hills, so my thanks go to all my walking companions including Alan Apperley, Richard Kelly, Michael Kenny, Steve Kibble, Clare Smedley, Angharad Thomas, Gordon Wilson, Kate Woodhead and Nick Woodhead. Most of all, thanks to Pauline Anderson for her love and support.

List of abbreviations

ACE	Action for Community Employment
AIA	Anglo-Irish Agreement
BIC	British Irish Council
CCRU	Central Community Relations Unit
CDU	Campaign for Democracy in Ulster
CRC	Community Relations Council
CSJ	Campaign for Social Justice
CWP	Community Work Programme
DPPB	District Policing Partnership Bodies
DSD	Downing Street Declaration
DUP	Democratic Unionist Party
ECHR	European Convention on Human Rights
ECST	European Convention on the Suppression of Terrorism
ECtHR	European Court of Human Rights
EPA	Emergency Provisions Act (NI)
EZ	Enterprise Zone
FEA	Fair Employment Agency
FET	Fair Employment Tribunal
GOC	General Officer Commanding
HRC	Human Rights Commission
IDB	Industrial Development Board
IGC	Inter-governmental Conference
IRA	Irish Republican Army
IRTU	Industrial Research & Technology Unit
JFD	Joint Framework Document
LEDU	Local Enterprise Development Unit
LEP	Local Enterprise Programme
NIAO	Northern Ireland Audit Office
NIDA	Northern Ireland Development Agency
NIFC	Northern Ireland Finance Corporation
NIHE	Northern Ireland Housing Executive
NIO	Northern Ireland Office
PAFT	Policy Appraisal and Fair Treatment
PCA	Parliamentary Commissioner for Administration

PTA	Prevention of Terrorism Act(s)
PUP	Progressive Unionist Party
RUC	Royal Ulster Constabulary
SACHR	Standing Advisory Committee on Human Rights
SDLP	Social Democratic and Labour Party
SFA	Selective financial assistance
STV	Single transferable vote
TEA	Training and Employment Agency
TSN	Targeting social need (areas)
UDR	Ulster Defence Regiment
UKU	United Kingdom Unionists
URIC	Urban and Rural Improvement Campaign
USC	Ulster Special Constabulary
UUC	Ulster Unionist Council
UUP	Ulster Unionist Party
UUUC	Ulster United Unionist Council
UWC	Ulster Workers' Council
YOPS	Youth Opportunities Programme Scheme
YTS	Youth Training Scheme

1

The background to British re-intervention

1920 to 1969

The constitutional relationship between Britain and Northern Ireland, which was to prevail for fifty years, was enshrined in the Government of Ireland Act 1920. The Act was the conclusion of years of abortive legislative initiatives which had attempted to forge a new relationship between Ireland and Britain, and established bicameral parliamentary institutions for Northern and Southern Ireland with provision for their eventual unification. However, the balance of political forces within Ireland made this extremely unlikely. Under the Anglo-Irish Treaty of December 1921 the Irish Free State was established as a dominion within the British Empire with formal authority over all Ireland. The Northern Ireland government, with jurisdiction over the six counties of Armagh, Antrim, Fermanagh, Tyrone, Londonderry and Down, was given the right to opt out of this arrangement and remain part of the United Kingdom, which it promptly exercised.

The significance of the 1920 Act is threefold with respect to Westminster's direct re-intervention in the late 1960s. First, in constitutional theory, if not political practice, section 75 of the Act was the most significant. It reserved the sovereign right of Westminster to legislate on any matter and states: 'Notwithstanding the establishment of the Parliaments of Southern and Northern Ireland ... the supreme authority of the Parliament of the United Kingdom shall remain unaffected and undiminished over all persons, matters and things in Ireland and every part thereof.'

Secondly, although section 75 enshrined the indivisibility of parliamentary sovereignty, the Act did not put in place adequate checks on the Northern Ireland administration, short of abolition. There was no machinery for detailed parliamentary or executive scrutiny of Northern Ireland affairs; unlike Scotland and Wales there was no Secretary of State answerable to Westminster and no Northern Ireland Committee was established. Northern Ireland was formally the responsibility of the Home Office but was relegated to the general department.

Thirdly, a matter of fundamental importance was the division of responsibility between the two parliaments. In particular, included within the category of 'transferred' matters (those for which the Northern Ireland parliament had legislative competence), were electoral arrangements and responsibility for law, order and internal security. This is significant because concerns about discriminatory practices in these areas persisted for the duration of the Northern Ireland administration and were central to the civil rights campaign of the mid-1960s onwards.

It would be an over-simplification to argue that by the early 1920s the British government took no interest in the affairs of Northern Ireland or the activities of the administration there. Concerns were expressed in the Cabinet and Colonial Offices regarding the legality of the establishment of the security apparatus in this period, particularly the Ulster Special Constabulary (USC) and the use of British money for this, and there were also reservations about electoral practices.[1] The complexities of financial arrangements between the two governments and the question of Northern Ireland's 'imperial contribution' were largely dealt with at official level rather than by ministers.[2]

Despite concerns such as those, by 1923 a convention had been established at Westminster whereby MPs were barred from asking questions about subjects and areas which were the competence of the Northern Ireland government. This symbolised both the degree of autonomy and the lack of detailed scrutiny which Westminster was generally to extend to Stormont. Indeed, there was little incentive to do otherwise; partition and the settlement of the early 1920s was advantageous to Britain in that it maintained a territorial foothold in Ireland to safeguard strategic interests (and access to three ports in the South under the 1921 Treaty), while at the same time it removed the Irish 'question' from mainstream British politics where for forty years it had proved highly contentious. It was not until the mid-1960s that consistent lobbying within Westminster for closer scrutiny of the administration of Northern Ireland was to occur.[3]

From the 1920s, the Conservative Party and governments were generally content to leave Unionist hegemony in Northern Ireland unchallenged, given their historical alliance and support for the Conservatives within the Commons. The Labour Party was, however, ideologically more disposed towards Irish nationalism; many of its members had adopted the Gladstonian concept of self-determination based on the thirty-two counties and some individual MPs were mindful of their Irish Catholic constituency support. However, Ireland was not a significant issue for the party, and the improbability of radically different policies evolving was signaled when the first Labour government of 1924 accepted that Ulster could not be coerced and that it would not attempt to renegotiate the 1921 treaty. This marked the beginning of a broadly bipartisan policy. In the 1930s the issue was largely dormant for Labour except for a visit by Stafford Cripps, a leading party member, in 1937 to canvass for a united Ireland and to mobilise the working class against the Ulster Unionist Party. The visit was a failure and Canning comments that 'henceforth, British Labour would rail against partition from afar, primarily in the Labour press'.[4]

De Valera, who became Taoiseach in 1932, attempted to renegotiate aspects of the 1921 Treaty which resulted in a trade war between the United Kingdom and Ireland. In an attempt to reach agreement in 1938 and head off de Valera's complaints concerning Unionist discrimination of the Catholic minority, in the North, the Home Office carried out an investigation into the allegations. It was, however, largely a token gesture which accepted uncritically Unionist reassurances of the even-handedness of the administration. Although some in the Dominions Office were more sympathetic to Catholic grievances they were marginalised by the well-established policy of keeping the problem at 'arm's length' and by the pro-Unionist sympathies of Hartington, Under-Secretary in the Dominions Office.

The period of the Second World War served to strengthen the tendency not to interfere with the administration of Northern Ireland and to rein-force a bipartisan approach opposed to the coercion of Northern Unionists. This was reinforced by Eire's neutrality during the conflict, which many contrasted with the sacrifices made by Northern Ireland. According to Canning, by 1941 Bevin, Attlee and Morrison shared Churchill's resentment of Eire's neutrality and had become increasingly sympathetic to unionism.[5] This helps to explain the response of the Labour government to the decision taken by Costello, Taoiseach of the Irish coalition government, in 1948 to declare a Republic and take Ireland out of the Commonwealth.[6] The advent of a Labour government had caused apprehension in the Northern Ireland government, which feared the implementing of socialist policies and a more pro-Nationalist orienta-tion.[7] This was fuelled by a pressure group within the parliamentary Labour Party, the Friends of Ireland, which agitated for a more rigorous supervision of the Stormont administration and was largely pro-Nationalist.[8]

However, the Ireland Act 1949 indicated that the Stormont administra-tion had little to fear from British legislation. The Act codified relations with the new Irish Republic and clarified the status of Northern Ireland. The guarantee to Northern Ireland, which was to become section 1(2) of the Act, stated:

> It is hereby declared that Northern Ireland remains part of His Majesty's dominions and of the UK and it is hereby affirmed that in no event will Northern Ireland or any part thereof cease to be part of His Majesty's dominions and of the UK without the consent of the Parliament of Northern Ireland.

Such reassurances provoked a large-scale rebellion by Labour back-benchers. It was argued that Labour had adopted a pro-Unionist position and the wording of the clause led to two specific concerns. One was that if a particular county had, or was to develop, a nationalist majority it would not have the option of joining the Irish Republic because of the 'any part thereof' formula. This had the effect of reinforcing the six-county expedient of 1920. The second concern was that consent was invested in the parliament of Northern Ireland rather than in the people. It was feared by critics that if a majority favouring a united Ireland were to come about, this would not be reflected in the composition of Stormont because of gerrymandered constituency boundaries. Various amendments were presented at committee stage and a total of sixty-six Labour MPs voted against the government during the passage of the bill.

Furthermore, Morrison rejected demands for closer supervision of Stormont and made clear his commitment to the constitutional convention. With respect to law and order, he stated 'it would be unconstitutional and improper, if not impossible, for this Government to take on responsibilities in this respect'.[9] He also expressed a desire that the issue should not become a 'disturbing and bargaining factor' in British politics.[10] With the subsequent collapse of the Friends of Ireland and the long period of Conservative dominance of British politics there were even fewer groups in British politics with either the desire or the capacity to raise the question of partition or the lack of Westminster supervision of the Northern Ireland government.

The Labour victory in the 1964 general election raised various hopes and fears that this situation would change. Harold Wilson, who became leader in 1963, was sympathetic to Irish nationalism and his supportive letter to the Campaign for Social Justice (CSJ), a Northern Ireland pressure group formed to combat discrimination and to promote civil rights, indicated that Westminster might undertake a closer scrutiny of Northern Ireland affairs. Such scrutiny was also being pressed for by the Campaign for Democracy in Ulster (CDU), a Labour Party pressure group which had a nominal membership of 100 MPs though far fewer activists.

The CDU campaign included repeated attempts to challenge the convention that precluded discussion of Northern Ireland affairs at Westminster, advocating the extension of the race relations legislation of 1967 to cover religious discrimination in Northern Ireland and calling for a Royal Commission to investigate conditions there. However, recent research has confirmed the lack of success of the campaign.[11] Up until the outbreak of violence in Londonderry in October 1968 the convention was consistently upheld in the Commons and supported by Labour Home Office ministers. The attitude of the three successive Labour Home Secretaries of this period is instructive. Frank Soskice visited Northern Ireland only once and praised the Unionist administration; Roy Jenkins, influenced it seems by his historical knowledge, considered Ireland a diversion for reforming governments and a dissipater of their energies;[12] and James Callaghan did not visit the province until the eruption of serious violence in August 1969. Wilson himself hinted at putting pressure on the O'Neill administration (Terence O'Neill, a UUP MP, who had come to power in 1963) by periodically raising the issue of reducing the voting rights of Northern Ireland MPs at Westminster and scrutinising the financial relationship between the two governments, although nothing concrete came of these ideas.

As Rose reveals, even after warnings of the possibility of IRA violence in 1966 to mark the fiftieth anniversary of the Easter Rising, the British government was content to leave intelligence gathering to the RUC rather than employ MI5.[13] This fits with the overall policy between 1966 and 1968 of bolstering O'Neill's tentative reformism and granting him autonomy in this policy. It is still a matter of contention whether O'Neill was committed to the ending of discrimination or was concerned with a technocratic modernisation with a liberal veneer; with most commentators holding to the latter position. The more crucial issue for the British government was that the pace of mooted reform was insufficient to satisfy the civil rights movement and yet was provoking tensions within Unionism with right-wing opposition to O'Neill mounting.[14]

In November 1968 Wilson and Callaghan met with O'Neill and his senior ministers to discuss a five-point plan of reform. This comprised a points system for public housing allocation, though this was not to be mandatory, the creation of a Parliamentary Commissioner for Administration (PCA), reform of local government including the abolition of the company vote, revision of the Special Powers Act to conform to international obligations and the replacement of Londonderry Borough Council with a non-elected Development Commission.

By the end of 1968 it appears that contingency plans for direct rule had been drawn up, including draft legislation, although Labour ministers differ on how seriously the option was considered.[15] The escalation of sectarian violence led to the deployment of British troops in August 1969 and Callaghan made it clear to the Commons that Westminster would take an active interest in all areas of policy and not only law and order.[16] However, rather than this resulting in direct rule, the government hoped that firm supervision of a (formally) jointly determined reform programme would restore stability and intervention could be short term.

From re-intervention to direct rule, 1969–72

The plans for reform and the division of responsibility between the two governments were set out in three communiques. The first addressed the question of control of the security forces. In effect, it subordinated the

Ulster security forces to the control of the General Officer Commanding (GOC (NI)) who was responsible to the Minister of Defence; both the Royal Ulster Constabulary (RUC) and USC were to come under his control when deployed in riot control. This was essentially a compromise as Westminster was not prepared to give operational responsibility to Stormont, although they were accorded a formal input. An accompanying declaration to the communique sought to reassure both Unionists by stating there would be no change to the status of Northern Ireland without the consent of its people and Nationalists by a commitment to equal treatment of all citizens.

The second and third communiques, issued after meetings in August and October 1969, outlined the reforms being undertaken or planned. These included the setting up of the Scarman and Hunt reports, establishing a Community Relations Commission (CRC) and a Ministry of Community Relations, legislation prohibiting incitement to religious hatred, reform of local government and the establishment of a centralised housing authority responsible for all public sector housing provision. Joint working parties of officials were to oversee the programme of reform and the Northern Ireland government undertook to take into the fullest account the views of the British government.

The Labour government remained in office until June 1970. In the ten months between the deployment of troops and that date, the strategy was to monitor and implement joint reforms which, it was hoped, would bolster the Stormont administration and satisfy the demands of the civil rights movement. The principal developments can be summarised as follows. The activities of the police had become central as violence escalated and in response the Stormont government established the Hunt committee in summer 1969.[17] Among the concerns of the civil rights movement and others was the close relationship between the police and the executive, its overwhelmingly Protestant complexion and its paramilitary nature. The Scarman report into the disturbances of 1969 rejected the claim that the RUC was, in general, a partisan force siding with Protestant mobs,[18] but it was clear that reform was necessary if the Nationalist population was to be reconciled with the Northern Ireland state.

The Hunt report was published in October 1969 and its recommendations were based on the 'consensus' model of policing, based on the theory of the British model. As part of the force's 'normalisation', it was to be relieved of the task of combating paramilitary and guerilla activity and the general issue of firearms would be phased out. The second major recommendation was the establishment of a police authority to redress the lack of public accountability and monitoring of the RUC, which had emphasised the close relationship between the police force and the executive. It was hoped that such a reform would lessen the identification of the RUC with the Unionist government. The third element of reform was the revision of the complaints procedure which had no provision for the proper recording of complaints and had reinforced concerns that the RUC was free from effective legal restraint. The changes were incorporated into the Police Act (NI) 1970, although the RUC continued to be armed as violence worsened.

The report also recommended the disbanding of the USC; a reflection of its paramilitary nature and almost total rejection by the Catholic community. It was to be replaced by the Ulster Defence Regiment (UDR), a locally recruited part-time force. Its principal responsibility would be as 'back up' for the army in security operations. The form, strength and equipment of the new force were to be decided by Westminster in consultation with the Northern Ireland government. The UDR was established by the UDR Act 1969 and instituted on 1 April 1970 as a regiment of the British army.

The other reforms enacted were of two broad types: those which extended British policy to Northern Ireland and those which were specific to the province. The O'Neill administration had pledged to create a PCA in its five-point plan of late 1968 and this office was established by the Parliamentary Commissioner Act (NI) 1969. In addition to investigating allegations of maladministration by central government departments, the PCA was given the responsibility for monitoring companies tendering for government contracts to ensure they did not practise religious discrimination.

The creation of the PCA was paralleled by that of the Commissioner for Complaints by the Commissioner for Complaints Act (NI) 1969. The Commissioner's role was that of ombudsman for local government and other public bodies not within the remit of the PCA. These two posts (held by the same person) marked an improvement in redress for the individual citizen but, as they did not have the power to investigate more general patterns of disadvantage and discrimination, their contribution to reducing grievances and disorder was limited.

Four reforms which were specific to Northern Ireland had their genesis in the 1969–70 period. These were the establishment of the Community Relations Commission (CRC) and its ministry, legislation prohibiting incitement to racial hatred, the centralisation of housing responsibilities and the centralisation of local authority functions.

The Ministry of Community Relations Act (NI) 1969 established the Ministry and an independent Commission was established by the Community Relations Act (NI) 1969. The concept of 'community relations' was vaguely defined but had two basic elements. One was to provide financial support for 'grassroots' projects and groups in an attempt to improve amenities and reflected a perceived link between social deprivation and violence, and the other was to combat sectarian attitudes and promote cross-community activities. However, the activities of the Commission were hampered by worsening sectarian violence, the lack of a clear strategy and under-funding.[19]

Another attempt to improve community relations was the introduction of the Prevention of Incitement to Hatred (NI) Act 1970. It was made an offence, with a maximum of two years' imprisonment, to publish or distribute written or other matter which was threatening, abusive or insulting or likely to stir up hatred or arouse fear in any part of the population. It is likely that the Act was introduced principally for presentational reasons. Prosecutions were difficult to secure for two reasons: intent had to be demonstrated against the accused; and the offence had to be committed against a specific person or persons – a general attack on a church or institution etc. was not an offence.[20]

Concerns over the unfair allocation of public housing by local authorities had been one of the catalysts of the civil rights movement. The decision to remove housing from local control was contained in the communique of October 1969. It should be noted that discrimination was only one and not the principal stated reason for such a change.[21] It was argued that various efficiencies and economies of scale would accrue from centralisation. Therefore, local authority and Development Commission responsibilities were handed to the Northern Ireland Housing Executive (NIHE). This policy was concluded under the Conservative government through the Housing Executive (NI) Act 1971, which made the NIHE responsible to and funded by the Ministry of Development. Other functions of local authorities were centralised for similar reasons: for efficiency and rationalisation of service delivery and in response to claims of discrimination. A review body was established in December 1969 with its conclusions being published in 1970.[22] It recommended the abolition of the existing structure of urban and rural district councils and county councils and their replacement with twenty-six single-tier authorities which were to retain only the functions carried out by 'lower-tier' authorities in the rest of the UK. Four area boards were to be created to administer health and social services and five area boards to administer education and library services. Other functions were to be controlled by the Ministry of Development. These proposals were premised on the continuation of a devolved administration and consequently, after direct rule was introduced, concern was expressed about the 'democratic deficit' that centralisation had created.

This policy of reform initiated by Stormont under the supervision of Westminster had been supported by the Conservatives, and their victory in the 1970 general election was not likely to result in a change of policy. Before the election, Quintin Hogg, the Conservative spokesman, had indicated his support for bipartisanship and Callaghan records Hogg's support for Labour policy in the preceding two years.[23] Despite its historic link with unionism, there was no significant lobby in the parliamentary party proposing any significantly different policy toward Ireland.

The period of just under two years between the Conservatives coming to office and the introduction of direct rule was marked by increased violence, the resurgence of the IRA and the centrality of security policy. The reform programme looked increasingly inadequate to halt the slide to large-scale communal disorder. The frustration felt by the government was articulated by the Home Secretary, Reginald Maudling, in February 1971 when he attributed the violence to insurrection and alleged that such actions no longer related to legitimate grievances of an oppressed minority.[24]

The accession of Brian Faulkner to the Northern Ireland premiership in March 1971 was an indication of a hardening of Unionist attitudes, and in August 1971 internment was introduced. Faulkner himself claimed to be a late convert to the idea and that he had opposed it in cabinet in the last government.[25] However, other commentators saw Faulkner's elevation as an indication that internment was almost inevitable.[26] While internment could not have been introduced without at least the acquiescence of Westminster, the policy indicated a shift towards greater influence for Stormont in what were previously jointly determined security decisions.

Labour voiced such concerns in the Commons debate on internment in late September 1971. However, Callaghan rejected a call for censure on the grounds that it might encourage extremism in Northern Ireland and appealed for the maintenance of bipartisanship. The opposition thus abstained, although sixty-eight Labour MPs voted against the government.

On 29 November 1971, for the first time since the revival of the 'troubles', the opposition voted against the government. However, the differences between the front benches were more a question of detail than of substance and the vote was as much to placate the rank and file as to signal the end of bipartisanship. The motion, presented by Callaghan, included a disinclination to support the continuation of internment, called for the transfer of security responsibility to Westminster, a constitutional commission to consider political advance and an end to 'interrogation in depth' (see p. 10 below). Despite Roy Hattersley's claim that if Labour had been in office Wilson would not have countenanced internment there seems to be little evidence to support this assertion.

The introduction of internment, used exclusively against Nationalists and Republicans, had alienated the whole of the Catholic community from the Stormont administration.[27] Furthermore, the Compton report,[28] set up to investigate allegations of ill-treatment of those interned, was seen as a 'whitewash', particularly with its semantic distinction that physical ill-treatment of internees did not constitute brutality. The government subsequently set up another inquiry and, in November 1971, Edward

Heath stated that the 'five techniques' constituting 'interrogation in depth' were no longer in use but did not rule out their re-introduction.[29]

The deaths of thirteen civilians, shot by the army on 'Bloody Sunday' in January 1972, marked the beginning of the end of the Stormont administration. On 1 February 1972 Labour divided the House over both security policy and the lack of political progress and on 24 March Heath announced the suspension of Stormont for one year as it refused to accept the transfer of law and order powers to Westminster.

The factors pushing the British government towards at least temporary direct rule are clear. At least since the introduction of internment reforming the Stormont administration to allow some form of minority representation looked a lost cause.[30] The British government was increasingly concerned about its image on the international stage with the deployment of troops and the lack of clarity about the legality of their actions until legislation of February 1972 added to the government's concern about the division of security responsibility with Stormont. However, there were two reasons why direct rule was reluctantly adopted. First, it breached the conventional wisdom that Irish affairs should be kept at 'arm's length' from British politics, secondly, the IRA would see the ending of Stormont as a victory and this was a factor in the delaying of direct rule.[31]

Notes

1 Proportional representation for local elections was abolished in 1922 by the Northern Ireland government. Because of the possible discriminatory implications of this, royal assent for the legislation was delayed. This was the only major constitutional conflict between the two governments.

2 The lack of knowledge concerning the financial arrangements between Stormont and Westminster in the late 1960s was remarked upon by Richard Crossman, *The Diaries of a Cabinet Minister: vol. 3. 1968–70* (London, Hamish Hamilton, 1977), p. 187.

3 A consideration of the establishment and practices of the Northern Ireland state are beyond the scope of this work. For a pro-Unionist interpretation of the establishment see B. Follis, *A State under Siege: the Establishment of Northern Ireland, 1920–1925* (Oxford, Clarendon Press, 1995). A representative of the nationalist critique of the state is M. Farrell, *Northern Ireland: the Orange State* (2nd edn, London, Pluto, 1980). P. Bew, P. Gibbon and H. Patterson, *Northern Ireland 1921–1994: Political Forces and Social Classes* (London, Serif, 1995) provide a left-wing, anti-Nationalist account. See T. Hennessey, *A History of Northern Ireland 1920–1996* (Basingstoke, Macmillan, 1997) for a recent summary.

4 P. Canning, *British Policy Towards Ireland 1921–1941* (Oxford, Oxford University Press, 1985), p. 232.

5 Canning, *British Policy*, p. 311. For a detailed account of wartime relations see R. Fisk, *In Time of War: Ireland, Ulster and the Price of Neutrality 1939–45* (London, Andre Deutsch, 1983).

6 For more details see R. Fanning, 'The response of the London and Belfast

governments to the declaration of the Republic of Ireland 1948–49' *International Affairs* 58, 1981–82.

7 See B. Barton, 'Relations between Westminster and Stormont during the Attlee premiership', *Irish Political Studies* 7, 1992.

8 See B. Purdie, 'The Friends of Ireland: British Labour and Irish nationalism 1945–49', in T. Gallagher and J. O'Connell (eds), *Contemporary Irish Studies* (Manchester, Manchester University Press, 1983). This was also a period of renewed anti-partition agitation in Ireland.

9 HC debates: vol. 464, col. 1956, 11 May 1949.

10 HC debates: vol. 464, col. 1961, 11 May 1949.

11 For a detailed account of Labour policy in these years see P. Rose, *How the Troubles Came to Northern Ireland* (Basingstoke, Macmillan, 2000).

12 Rose, *How the Troubles Came,* p. 89.

13 Rose, *How the Troubles Came,* p. 100.

14 The history of the civil rights movement is to be found in B. Purdie, *Politics in the Streets* (Belfast, Blackstaff, 1990).

15 Rose, *How the Troubles Came,* p. 169.

16 HC debates: vol. 788, col. 48, 13 October 1969.

17 'Report of the advisory committee on police in Northern Ireland', Cmd 535, Belfast, 1969.

18 'Violence and civil disturbances in Northern Ireland in 1969', Cmd 566, Belfast, 1972, p. 15.

19 See the account of the first chairman in M. Hayes, 'The role of the Community Relations Commission in Northern Ireland', *Administration* 20(4), 1972. The CRC was abolished in 1974 and the Ministry merged with the Department of Education.

20 The Act was consolidated in public order legislation in 1981.

21 Callaghan intended to 'take the politics out of housing' (H. Simpson, 'The Northern Ireland Housing Executive', *Housing Review* 22(3), 1973, p. 95).

22 Macrory report, 'Report of the review body on local government in Northern Ireland', Cmd 546, Belfast, 1970.

23 Quintin Hogg cited in P. Dixon, '"A house divided cannot stand": Britain, bipartisanship and Northern Ireland', *Contemporary Record* 9(1), 1995, p. 165. J. Callaghan, *A House Divided* (London, Collins, 1973), p. 64.

24 HC debates: vol. 811, col. 1320, 15 February 1971.

25 B. Faulkner, *Memoirs of a Statesman* (London, Weidenfeld and Nicolson, 1978), p. 117.

26 Sunday Times Insight Team, *Ulster* (London, Andre Deutsch, 1972), p. 260; J. Bardon, *A History of Ulster* (Belfast, Blackstaff, 1992), p. 683.

27 Apart from the moral and legal questions surrounding internment, it was largely ineffective in security terms because of inadequate intelligence.

28 'Report of the inquiry into allegations against the security forces of physical brutality in Northern Ireland, arising out of events on 9 August 1971', Cmnd 4823, London, 1971.

29 HC debates: vol. 826, col. 1009, 25 November 1971. The 'five techniques' were the hooding of suspects, deprivation of sleep, subjection to high-pitched noise, long periods of standing and a bread and water diet.

30 The SDLP had withdrawn from Stormont in July 1971 in protest at the lack of an inquiry into the deaths of two men shot by the army in Londonderry.

31 P. Bew and G. Gillespie, *Northern Ireland: Chronology of the Troubles 1968–1999* (Dublin, Gill and Macmillan, 1999), p. 50.

2

From direct rule to the Thatcher government, 1972–79

Constitutional policy

Direct rule was introduced on 24 March 1972 when the division of responsibility concerning security became increasingly untenable to Westminster as violence worsened. At a meeting on 22 March Faulkner had refused to relinquish formal Stormont control over security and had resigned.

The suspension of Stormont was designed to be a short-term measure. Under the terms of the Ireland Act 1949, Stormont was to be prorogued initially for one year and Westminster was to take full responsibility for administration until a new political solution could be engineered. Constitutionally, this suspension was uncontroversial in that both the Government of Ireland Act 1920 and the Ireland Act 1949 subordinated the Northern Ireland parliament to that of Westminster. The administrative and legislative arrangements necessitated by prorogation were dealt with by the Northern Ireland (Temporary Provisions) Act 1972. The main feature of this was that most legislation for Northern Ireland was to be enacted by Order in Council, which meant that it was not amenable to parliamentary amendment.[2]

This arrangement, by which Northern Ireland was excluded from the 'normal' legislative procedure, indicated that the re-introduction of devolution was the constitutional preference of the British government. Neither the unification of Ireland nor the closer integration of Northern Ireland into the UK were considered practical options by the government.[3] Therefore, the parameters of policy were quickly established with the government hoping for reconstituted devolution with cross-community support for the new institutions.

British government talks with the IRA in the summer of 1972 confirmed the latter's commitment to the 'armed struggle', and this ensured that the government's focus switched to the constitutional parties. After a conference on constitutional initiatives held at Darlington in September, boycotted by the Democratic Unionist Party (DUP) and the nationalist parties, a Northern Ireland Office discussion paper 'The

Future of Northern Ireland' was published in October 1972. The prospects for progress appeared slender as the majority of unionists, supported a majoritarian form of democracy in any future assembly, while the Social Democratic and Labour Party (SDLP) advocated proportionality within the executive and the development of joint sovereignty. Given the lack of consensus between the parties, the government laid down the minimum requirements and parameters for political development. The main emphasis was on a revised form of assembly. Attlee's pledge in the 1949 Act concerning the consent principle ruled out joint authority or the repartition of Northern Ireland, and independence was rejected on the grounds that Britain could not maintain financial or military support while conceding virtual sovereign status. Integration was not seriously entertained in the discussion paper; it was noted that it had little support in Northern Ireland, would make relations with the Republic more difficult and increase the legislative burden on Westminster. Devolution was established as the favoured option in which cross-community support would be necessary and 'real participation should be achieved by giving minority interests a share in the exercise of executive power' (paragraph 79).

The second major element of the paper was concerned with the Irish dimension. Interdependence between North and South in the areas of security and economic policy, and impending common membership of the EEC were cited as reasons for a closer relationship, although the paper was vague and non-specific about what institutional form this might take. This recognition was significant because it was the clearest indication since the abortive Council of Ireland of the early 1920s settlement that the British government did not see Northern Ireland as a solely 'internal' matter, and the question of links with the Republic was to be central to the fate of the Sunningdale proposals of the following year (see p. 15 below).

Before the proposals were fashioned into a White Paper, a referendum was held on the constitutional position of Northern Ireland. With the introduction of direct rule, Heath had committed the government to a plebiscite to reassure the people of the province that the consent principle would be respected. The Border Poll, as it was termed, was held on 8 March 1973 under the provisions of the Northern Ireland (Border Poll) Act 1972. Labour had questioned the value of such a poll when first announced, fearing that it would heighten community tensions and that it should not precede the publication of the White Paper.

The Poll was of limited value as it did not canvass opinion on possible internal arrangements but simply asked the electorate to choose between Northern Ireland remaining part of the UK or joining the Republic of Ireland. Nationalist parties advocated a boycott and so on a turn out of 58.5 per cent there was an overwhelming majority for maintaining the

British link of 591,820 votes to 6,463.

The White Paper 'Northern Ireland Constitutional Proposals' was published in March 1973. It reiterated the points made in the 1972 Discussion Paper and outlined the five principal areas on which the government hoped political advances could be made. These were some form of devolved institution, a unicameral legislative assembly of between eighty and 100 members, an important role for a committee structure within the executive, a codification of human rights and freedoms and institutional arrangements for co-operation and consultation on an all-Ireland basis. To digress from the chronology, it is interesting to note that these are all elements of the Good Friday Agreement reached twenty-five years later, though that agreement has additional elements not developed in the early 1970s.

Three concerns informed government thinking about the form and competence of a future assembly. First, it should have substantial devolved powers, legislative and executive, as an incentive for the Northern Ireland parties to participate and make it work. Secondly, a single-party executive (or one composed of parties from only one community) would not provide stability and simple majoritarianism was rejected. Thirdly, various powers that had been the responsibility of Stormont and the source of controversy would be reserved to Westminster.[4] Therefore, the principal areas of responsibility devolved would be education, housing, social services, industrial development, agriculture and the environment. However, the ultimate sovereignty of Westminster was underlined in that it could overrule any assembly decision concerning transferred matters.

With respect to the Council of Ireland the government stated that '. . . it favours and is prepared to facilitate the development of such a body'.[5] The details of the remit and operation of the Council were not included in the White Paper, or the subsequent bill, since these would of necessity follow tripartite discussions between the assembly and the two governments.

The proposals were given legislative effect in the Northern Ireland Constitution Act 1973, which was passed in July so post-dating the elections to the assembly. The Labour Party had given broad support to the legislation; indeed, Callaghan's warning that should Unionist opponents try to sabotage the assembly Britain should reconsider its position was interpreted by some as implying that Labour in the future might not be bound by the principle of northern majority consent.[6]

The election for the assembly took place on 28 June 1973 under the Northern Ireland Assembly Act passed in May. Seventy-eight seats were contested using the single transferable vote (STV) system within the twelve Westminster constituencies.[7] The Official Unionists who supported the White Paper provisions gained twenty-four seats and twenty-six were won by Unionists opposing the proposals. The remaining twenty-eight seats were won by parties supporting the White Paper, including nineteen for the SDLP which had a monopoly of Nationalist representation. Therefore, supporters of the government's proposals had fifty-two seats, although the fluidity of Unionist politics raised the possibility of defections from the Faulkner camp to that of the opponents of the White Paper.

By November agreement had been reached between the Official Unionists, the SDLP and the Alliance Party on the formation of the executive. This allowed the next stage of discussions, which included the Council of Ireland, to take place. This was scheduled prior to the executive taking office on 1 January 1974 and the three parties and the two governments met at Sunningdale from the 6 to 9 December 1973.[8] At this meeting the Irish government formally accepted that there would be no change in the status of Northern Ireland until a majority of people in the province desired such a change.[9] However, this did little to bolster Faulkner's position within unionism as Cosgrave, the Taoiseach, would not undertake to hold a referendum on removal of Articles 2 and 3 of the Irish Constitution which claimed jurisdiction over the whole of the island.[10] For its part, Britain added nothing to its position enshrined in the 1973 Act with the corollary to the majority consent principle that it would not oppose unity if a majority in the North were to vote in favour.

The final form of the Council of Ireland was to depend upon further discussions between northern and southern representatives but these never materialised. An initial projection formulated at Sunningdale was for a two-tier structure. This would consist of a fourteen-member executive Council of Ministers, seven appointed by the Dail and seven by the assembly, and a sixty-member consultative and advisory assembly with equal representation from the two legislatures. Decisions taken by the Council of Ministers would have to be unanimous and areas of possible competence included trade, energy, agriculture, tourism and transport.

As in the contemporary period, the extent and competence of cross-border bodies was a contentious issue. The ambiguity surrounding the possible evolution of such bodies – the notion of process in the talks – served only to fuel Unionist fears that they were a staging-post to a united Ireland, and Nationalist emphasis on their importance added to Unionist concerns.[11] The need for unanimity in ministerial decisions would have provided a check on the development of the competence of the Council and its composition was premised on the maintenance of partition. Nevertheless much of unionism interpreted the process as one biased against them and indicative of a British desire for disengagement.

The final principal subject of the Sunningdale talks was security and possible future joint initiatives. Britain's main concern was to make easier the extradition of terrorist suspects from the Republic by the removal of the claim of political motivation as grounds for exemption. The constitutional and legal complexities precluded an immediate decision on extradition reform or on other possible changes such as the creation of all-Ireland courts or the right of courts to try offences committed in the other part of Ireland. Therefore, a Joint Law Enforcement Commission was established which reported in May 1974.[12]

It is questionable whether a majority of Unionists would have accepted power-sharing if the 'Irish Dimension' had been de-emphasised; the SDLP set much store on the latter because reforms to policing and an end to internment had not been forthcoming. However, essentially the vagueness of the Sunningdale agreement which was necessary to fuse together the newly-created executive and the two governments only served to allow its opponents to focus on the parts that confirmed their suspicions. As one commentator remarked 'quintessentially, the Sunningdale Agreement refracted and obscured debate to the point that each participant could draw conclusions favourable to his own particular political stance'.[13]

The prospects for the executive looked bleak when Faulkner resigned as leader of the Unionist Party on 7 January 1974 following the Unionist Council rejection of the Council of Ireland proposals. This was to add strength to the claims of opponents that the executive did not fulfil the criterion of popular support in the province. At the general election of February 1974, Unionists opposed to Sunningdale stood under the umbrella title of the United Ulster Unionist Council (UUUC) and won eleven of the twelve seats with 50.8 per cent of votes cast.

The Labour Party won the general election, though without gaining an overall majority, and Wilson appointed Merlyn Rees Secretary of State for Northern Ireland.[14] Labour was faced with the problem of being committed to the power-sharing executive which was subject to both external pressure and suffering from internal divisions over policy priorities. On 14 May the assembly voted 44 to 28 against renegotiating constitutional arrangements and thus to proceed with the establishment of the Council of Ireland. This precipitated a strike by the Ulster Workers' Council (UWC), an umbrella grouping of loyalist trade unionists and paramilitaries. Rees refused to negotiate with the UWC and, following failed attempts to slow the implementation of the Council of Ireland, Unionists resigned from the executive on 28 May.

To oversimplify somewhat, there are two broad positions concerning the importance of the UWC strike and the British response to it. Some members of the executive, including John Hume and Paddy Devlin (SDLP), blamed the government for not defending the agreement and acting more forcefully against the UWC. If this had been done, then the executive could have prospered. The second position argues that divisions within the parties forming the executive and the unresolved detail of policy, meant that Sunningdale was effectively doomed by the end of 1973.[15] The first interpretation depends in part on the assumption that early action against the strike would not have hardened Loyalist resolve and provoked an escalation of violence; as indicated below, the British government was not prepared to take that risk. The result of the general election in February indicated to the British government that the executive did not have the legitimacy necessary for its maintenance.

Additionally, Rees had been advised by the Defence Secretary, Roy Mason, that the army did not have the expertise to take over the running of power stations in which support for the strike was solid and the government was concerned about the possibility of open conflict with Loyalist paramilitaries. Fisk has argued that another factor was Wilson's concern about 'contagion'; that the collapse of the executive would contaminate the stability of his own administration if he continued to support it and this made its abandonment inevitable. This fits with the view of Bew and Patterson that power sharing was a desirable but not an essential part of the structure of British administration and, therefore, there were limits to the support the executive would be given.[16]

In the Commons debate following the executive's collapse, the British parties presented a united front. Rees announced the prorogation of the executive under the terms of the Northern Ireland Constitution Act 1973 and defended his decision not to negotiate with the UWC. Integration was rejected on the grounds that it would overburden Westminster and would run counter to what Rees perceived to be the development of a nascent Ulster nationalism manifested by the UWC strike. Conservatives and Labour concurred on what was to be a dominant theme in the Constitutional Convention of 1975; agreement in Northern Ireland was more likely to be forthcoming if the role of Westminster and Dublin was downplayed and if there was more flexibility in potential institutional frameworks.[17]

There was a dual motivation here. The failure of Sunningdale lent credence to the belief that a less ambitious strategy developed principally by the Northern Ireland parties might prove successful and, in the event of failure, their intransigence rather than the inadequacy of British policy might be focused upon.[18] Thus, the constitutional policy of the Labour Party from 1974 to 1979 was marked by a scaling down of ambition compared with other periods under review.

A White Paper, 'The Northern Ireland Constitution', was published on 4 July 1974 to make provision for a Constitutional Convention. Its remit was to consider 'what provision for the government of Northern Ireland is likely to command the most widespread acceptance throughout the community there.'[19] The Convention was to be purely consultative with no legislative or administrative powers. The White Paper included the term 'power sharing' and it was clear that the government would not countenance devolution with an executive composed of representatives of only one community. The 'Irish Dimension' was included but the form it might take was left purposely vague.

The Convention was to have seventy-eight members elected by STV within the twelve Westminster constituencies. It was to sit for six months or until it submitted recommendations, whichever was earlier. If agreement had not been reached in this period it could be extended for three months, subject to parliamentary approval, or recalled within six months of dissolution. On receipt of the report, the government might choose to devolve both legislative and administrative powers if it considered that the 'widespread acceptance' criterion had been met.

The White Paper was closely followed by the Northern Ireland Act of July 1974 which made provision for the election to and operation of the Convention and clarified administrative responsibilities following the collapse of the executive. It also reintroduced direct rule, which was to be renewed annually if devolution was not effected. The Conservatives supported the proposals though some on the right argued for a firmer commitment to the union and less mention of the 'Irish Dimension'.

With the legislative framework in place, the government left time for discussion between and within the Northern Ireland parties to develop and produced three discussion papers to facilitate the work of the Convention.[20]

The election was held on 1 May 1975. The UUUC, which had maintained its unity since the 1974 general elections, exploited the STV system efficiently and gained forty-seven of the seventy-eight seats and 54.8 per cent of votes cast on a platform of opposition to mandatory power sharing and to an institutionalised Irish Dimension. The other thirty-one seats were gained by four parties which supported power-sharing, with the SDLP winning seventeen. On 7 November the Convention voted 42 to 31 to submit a draft report based on the policies outlined above with a rejection of guaranteed ministerial positions for members of any but the majority party in the assembly. Under the terms of the Northern Ireland Act 1974, the Convention was then dissolved.

The report was debated in the Commons on 12 January 1976. It was clear that the report did not fulfil the remit of 'most widespread acceptance' and Rees ordered the Convention to reconvene on 3 February to consider the possibility of progress. However, positions struck were largely adhered to and the UUUC proposal of 50 per cent of committee representation going to opposition parties did not satisfy SDLP and Alliance conceptions of power sharing. The last meeting of the Convention took place on 3 March and two days later Rees announced its dissolution.

Governmental options were now limited. Indefinite direct rule was the most likely outcome, although in this period there was much speculation about British disengagement and withdrawal.[21] Although Rees denies in his autobiography that he seriously contemplated this, it appears that the government deliberately hinted at the possibility during the period of the truce between the IRA and the security forces between February 1975 and January 1976 (during which Republican violence continued under 'flags of convenience' and Loyalists continued to attack Catholics). The intention was to promote confusion in Republican ranks over strategy and to encourage the rundown of IRA capabilities. Increasingly vocal discontent in government circles about economic subventions to Northern Ireland helped to create a sense that disengagement was a serious possibility.

Rees was replaced by Roy Mason as Secretary of State in September 1976. This was widely perceived as indicating a greater emphasis on economic and security policy and a relegation of political initiatives.[22] However, the government was still formally committed to devolution and in early 1977 Mason conducted a series of bilateral meetings with the four principal political parties but no progress was made.

Following a further series of talks, in late November 1977 Mason announced a 'five-point plan'. As the lack of inter-party agreement in Northern Ireland precluded full devolution, Mason favoured a unicameral assembly elected by proportional representation (point one) which would have a consultative role regarding legislation (point two). Although a temporary measure, it was envisaged that this structure could form the basis for further devolution (point three) and, therefore, interim arrangements had to be durable and demonstrate parties' willingness to make them work (point four). Therefore, any arrangements had to be administratively sound (point five).

Mason emphasised the open-ended nature of his proposals and stressed that they did not have to replicate those emerging from Sunningdale.[23] Earlier in the year the UUUC had fragmented but there was no indication that a significant fraction of unionism was prepared to accept 'partnership' government of a form acceptable to the SDLP. This stalemate increased Conservative scepticism about pursuing a devolutionary path, and Airey Neave, the shadow spokesman, advocated the establishment of regional councils which would restore the responsibilities of local government to Northern Ireland. Neave's statement that his party no longer supported the attempts to resurrect power sharing did signal a breach in overt bipartisan commitment to it. Although the late 1970s did see an 'integrationist' shift within Conservatism the significance of this should not be overestimated. Neave and the other Conservative spokesman, John Biggs-Davison, claimed that the regional council proposals were not significantly different from Mason's ideas to signal the demise of bipartisanship and that they wanted to maintain it.[24] The Conservative position was partly informed by parliamentary arithmetic which encouraged the cultivation of Ulster Unionists and also by the impasse around power sharing. However, it is unlikely that if successful power sharing had been launched by Labour between 1977 and 1979 that the Conservatives would have opposed its implementation.

In late 1978 Callaghan (who became Prime Minister in 1976) accepted the recommendation of a report by the Speaker's Conference for increased Westminster representation for Northern Ireland.[25] This was seen as an implicit retreat from devolution which had previously been considered a compensation for under-representation and some Labour backbenchers denounced the policy as a move towards integrationism and as a sop to the Ulster Unionists.[26]

In January 1979, Mason wrote to the leaders of the main Northern Ireland parties reiterating the proposals of November 1977 but there was insufficient common ground for any progress. On 28 March the government lost a vote of no confidence by one vote. Gerry Fitt, the sole SDLP MP, who normally supported Labour abstained in protest at what he saw as the drift towards integrationism and the findings of the Bennett report on the ill-treatment of suspects (see 'Security policy' below).

Security policy

At the beginning of the direct rule period, security policy underwent tactical shifts. The negotiation of a cease fire with the IRA and engagement in exploratory talks in July 1972 had been facilitated by the granting of special category status for prisoners, a reduction in the numbers interned and a low army presence in Nationalist areas. The failure of the talks and a renewal of the IRA bombing campaign led to an army offensive and the ending of nationalist 'no go' areas in August 1972.

However, this stronger line did not imply a renewed emphasis on internment. The government was keen to find alternatives since internment had three major disadvantages. First, a settlement involving constitutional Nationalists was unlikely while it continued, secondly it damaged Britain's international reputation and made relations with the Republic more difficult, and thirdly, it emphasised the political nature of the conflict whereas normal legal procedures would allow the government to present the violence as criminal in origin.[27]

To this end, in September 1972 a commission was established to 'consider legal procedures to deal with terrorist activities in Northern Ireland'.[28] To bridge the gap between its report in December and new legislation to replace the Special Powers Act, the Detention of Terrorists (NI) Order was introduced on 7 November 1972 and received parliamentary approval on 11 December. Essentially, detention was a modified form of internment. Within twenty-eight days of arrest, a suspect's case had to be referred to a commissioner by the Chief Constable. The commissioner could recommend further detention if the suspect were involved in terrorist activity. The use of a commissioner, a senior legal figure, was designed to emphasise the quasi-judicial nature of the process and act as a check on executive power. Although the suspect was allowed to prepare a defence to be presented at the commissioner's hearing, the procedures and the test of admissibility fell short of normal legal practice. Concerns raised by critics included the fact that there was no judicial or external intervention in the initial twenty-eight-day period and that there was no time limit between the referral of the case and the commissioner's hearing; thus people could be detained for months with no consideration of their case. Despite some back bench reservations, Labour did not oppose the Order since its rejection would leave the internment provisions of the Special Powers Act in force and because it was a temporary measure pending forthcoming legislation.

The Diplock report was published in December 1972. Its significance can scarcely be overestimated. First, it marked the advent of a policy in which prosecution through the courts was gradually to replace executive detention in an attempt to bury the distinction between political violence and 'normal' crime. Secondly, the report laid the basis for legislation which, though amended, was to remain in force for almost thirty years. Thirdly, it revealed the relative ease with which long-established judicial procedure could be jettisoned when expedient.

Diplock's first major recommendation was to introduce the trying of cases involving certain offences by judge only because of the problem of witness and jury intimidation and the possibility of perverse acquittals by juries. These offences became known as 'scheduled' offences as they were listed as a schedule to the 1973 Act based on Diplock's recommendations.[29] A plurality of judges hearing a case was considered and rejected by Diplock as being unsuited to the adversarial procedure employed in UK courts and also because this would place too much pressure on the resources of the judicial system.

The second major recommendation related to the admissibility of suspects' confessions. Difficulty in securing convictions could undermine the move to judicial primacy and the lack of witness evidence in many cases meant confessions were heavily relied upon. Judges had tended to apply strictly the 'voluntary' concept of giving information and making confessions, thus ruling inadmissible the applying of pressure or building of an atmosphere in which the suspect was likely to co-operate or confess. Diplock considered that this interpretation of procedures led to the acquittal of guilty persons[30] and recommended that the applying of psychological pressure should be deemed admissible practice. Any admission should be given in evidence unless proved on the balance of probabilities that it was obtained through the use of torture or inhuman or degrading treatment.

Other recommendations included reversing the onus of proof relating to the possession of proscribed articles, such as firearms, ammunition and explosives. As the law stood the defendant was not required to prove that she/he had no knowledge of such items on his/her property etc., and the prosecution had to prove there was such knowledge. Bail restrictions were to be tightened partly because it was granted more freely than in England and such leniency increased the likelihood of witness intimidation between the initial hearing and the trial proper.[31]

These recommendations were designed to remove impediments to the securing of confessions, witness evidence and convictions. The other main area to be addressed to secure successful prosecution of offenders was that of arrest. The powers of the RUC were covered by the Special Powers Act, which was still in force, but the position of the army was less clear cut.[32] Diplock sought to codify the legal basis of army action and recommended that the army should have the power to hold a suspect for a maximum of four hours for the purpose of identification. If necessary, further holding after this period would be the responsibility of the police. Searches for explosives and wanted persons were also to be within the army's powers.

It was implicit in Diplock that the army should take a secondary role as the report was geared towards prosecution and the reduction of 'exceptional' forms of law enforcement. Therefore, the provisions did not allow for the mass house searching and 'screening' of the population that had underpinned the use of internment between 1971 and 1974.[33]

The majority of Diplock's recommendations were incorporated into the Northern Ireland (Emergency Provisions) Bill which received its second reading in April 1973. William Whitelaw (who became Northern Ireland Secretary in 1972) promised that, if the bill were passed, the whole of the Special Powers Act would be repealed and the new legislation would be subject to annual renewal. Labour was to abstain on all stages of the bill as the front bench accepted the need for emergency powers but hoped that amendments would be accepted in committee.[34] One of these related to the lack of compelling evidence concerning perverse jury decisions and actual, rather than potential, jury intimidation. Thus, Labour wanted trial by jury retained for scheduled offences unless a High Court judge believed that violence, intimidation or bribery would prejudice the chances of a fair trial. The government argued that it was unrealistic to expect a judge to be able to make such a determination in all cases and the amendment would add to the judicial workload. The amendment was defeated so that non-jury trial was to become the rule for terrorist offences and descheduling would be the exception. An earlier vote in committee had gone in favour of a plurality of judges; this was overturned by a government amendment which accepted the case put by Diplock.[35] Two safeguards were to be introduced to try to allay critics' fears: a convicted person would have reasons for the verdict explained; and there would be an automatic right of appeal. The Diplock recommendations concerning admissibility of confessions and the onus on the defendant in cases of possession were accepted.

Despite being premised on finding alternatives to detention, these powers were retained since the government, following Diplock, was not convinced that the courts alone could deal with the levels of terrorist violence. In respect of powers of arrest, the police could arrest on suspicion (with no 'reasonable' clause) of involvement in terrorism and detain for up to seventy-two hours before the preferring of charges. The armed forces could arrest and hold suspects for up to four hours. Both police and army were granted the power to stop and search for weapons and to stop and question to ascertain a person's identity and movements or knowledge concerning shooting incidents, explosions, etc.[36] The arrest powers of the army were framed in the context of retained detention powers which were used up to mid-1975, although the direction of policy was towards criminal conviction.

The remaining sections of the Emergency Provisions Act 1973 dealt with the proscription of the IRA, Sinn Fein, other smaller republican groups and the Ulster Volunteer Force. As well as membership it was an offence to solicit support for or contribute to proscribed organisations. The power to deproscribe organisations or add to the list of those proscribed was reserved to the Secretary of State for Northern Ireland.

The Northern Ireland (Emergency Provisions) Act (EPA) became law in July 1973 and provided the legislative framework for the move from extra-judicial anti-terrorism strategies to one based on criminal convictions. It repealed the Special Powers Act 1922, the Detention of Terrorists (NI) Order 1972 and the Criminal Justice (Temporary Provisions) Act (NI) 1970.[37]

Much of the security policy enacted by the Labour governments elected in February and October 1974 had its genesis in the previous administration. This included changes to the EPA, the development of 'criminalisation', and extradition policy following discussions at Sunningdale with the Republic of Ireland. These will be considered in turn and the passage of the Prevention of Terrorism Act 1974 (PTA) and the Bennett report on suspect ill-treatment will then be reviewed.

In April 1974 Rees had announced the setting up of a committee to examine the operation of the EPA.[38] Labour felt that the Diplock report had been too narrowly focused on legal and procedural matters and had not considered the wider civil liberties and human rights context. Pending changes to the legislation, the Act was to be renewed every six months (as opposed to annually in the 1973 Act). This was intended to placate back bench critics of the legislation who were also concerned about the retention of detention, which Rees was not prepared to abandon until violence declined.

The Gardiner report was published in January 1975. It recognised that progress in security had to be matched with that in the areas of political, social and economic activity; and that consideration should be given to the introduction of a bill of rights.[39] Despite an emphasis on community relations and the threat posed to them by emergency legislation, much of Diplock was endorsed. Its recommendations on the suspension of juries, single-judge courts, tighter restrictions on the granting of bail and the admissibility of confessions were all supported. However, in the last of these, it was emphasised that the judge had discretion to rule inadmissible any confession suspected of being obtained through inhuman or degrading treatment.

The report's position regarding criminalisation broadly matched government thinking as outlined by Rees in April 1974.[40] Special category status was condemned as it facilitated paramilitary organisation and emphasised the political nature of offences. Detention was criticised for falling short of proper legal standards and providing propaganda material to opponents. The committee concluded that detention could not be retained as a long-term policy as it helped to prevent reconciliation, was inimical to community life and created a sense of injustice.

As it was deemed a political decision, the committee made no recommendation for the date of the ending of detention. Various amendments were recommended for reforming the process. The most significant were the replacement of the commissioner system with a detention advisory board, independent of the executive, to consider cases against individuals and the placing of time limits on the process. A maximum of five weeks would elapse between the issuing of an interim custody order (the start of the process) and a decision by the Secretary of State whether to sign a detention order or to order the release of the detainee. Under the 1973 Act, there was no time limit between referral to commissioners and their recommendations.

These changes, and the abolition of appeal hearings, were incorporated into the Northern Ireland Emergency Provisions (Amendment) Act 1975 along with minor changes to the powers of search for security forces and to proscription. The removal of the quasi-judicial element in detention via the commissioner made the scheme more like pre-1973 internment, but as it was not to form part of the government security strategy this was of limited significance.

The Amendment Act 1975 remained in force until 1978 when a new EPA was passed. The 1978 Act consolidated that of 1973 and incorporated the amendments of 1975. There was no inquiry into the Act before its updating and the procedural arrangements were the same as for the 1973 legislation; it was subject to six-monthly renewal and sections of the Act could be allowed to lapse by order.

From the beginning of the administration the government had embraced the policy of criminalisation, which broadly meant the use of judicial processes to deal with terrorism and police primacy wherever possible. It was accepted that the army was ill-suited to a policing role and that its use tended only to emphasise the political nature of the conflict. This policy was endorsed in the White Paper of July 1974 which expressed the government's desire for community co-operation with the police as the best way to undermine the paramilitaries. This would then 'enable the Army to make a planned, orderly, and progressive reduction in its present commitment and subsequently there would be no need for the Army to become involved in a policing role.'[41]

While this strategy had various potential benefits, the short-term problems were evident. First, the police had little support in many of the Nationalist areas and the failure of the assembly in 1974 made such support harder to effect. Secondly, a reduction in the role of the army was likely to increase the role of the locally recruited UDR. This regiment was almost entirely Protestant and the involvement of some members in sectarian attacks gave it the appearance of a reconstituted 'B' Specials in the eyes of many Nationalists.[42] Thirdly, operationally police primacy was unrealistic in areas of high Republican violence, and army (including the SAS) activity in areas such as South Armagh was to remain the dominant presence.[43]

If incremental moves towards police primacy were to be effected, the efficiency of the RUC and the procedures for dealing with complaints and accountability had to be addressed. The first of these areas was dealt with by the Ministerial Committee on Law and Order of July 1976. It covered police numbers, the structure of the force, co-ordination with the army and the improvement of collecting and collating criminal intelligence. These reforms and the increased security role for the UDR and the RUC Reserve meant that by the end of 1976 operational changes had paralleled the ideological and legislative moves towards criminalisation and 'Ulsterisation'.[44]

It is difficult to judge what reforms would make the RUC acceptable as a community-based force. One problem that critics emphasised was the timid and uncritical attitude of the Police Authority which had not established an independent element in the monitoring of complaints despite a statutory power to do so. Additionally, complaints which did not allege a criminal offence by the police were dealt with internally without an independent element.

The report of the working party on police complaints came to similar conclusions to its British counterparts, upholding that initial investigations should remain in the hands of the police and that there should be no right of appeal against the Director of Public Prosecution's (DPP) decision about prosecution where a criminal offence was alleged. Its principal recommendation was the establishment of a Police Complaints Board, the main role of which was to monitor the investigation of complaints. If action were not taken, the Deputy Chief Constable would be required to justify the decision and, in the last resort, the Board could order disciplinary action to be taken.

Critics were concerned that the reforms were overly modest and reflected the views of the police establishment, in particular the Police Authority and the Police Federation. The Police Complaints Board was established by the Police (NI) Order 1976, but there is little evidence that it made much impact on police–community relations and it would not be until the Patten report of 1999 that more radical reform would be undertaken.

Emerging from the Sunningdale talks, a Law Enforcement Commission, composed of members of the judiciary of the UK and the Republic of Ireland, was established to consider the problem of suspects evading extradition to the North by invoking political motivation. Its report of July 1974 considered four possible solutions.[45] First, the extension of extradition powers, secondly, the establishment of an all-Ireland court and thirdly, the extension of jurisdiction of the courts of Northern Ireland and the Republic to cover both parts of Ireland. The fourth, a variant of the third, was to have a court with three judges in both parts of Ireland with jurisdiction over both parts, one judge being a member of the judiciary of the other state.

The second option would require constitutional change in the Republic and would thus take a long time to implement. The principal disadvantage to the third and fourth options was that the commission felt that it would not be possible to compel witnesses to give evidence across the border, although evidence could possibly be transmitted by a High Court judge between jurisdictions.

The commission's rejection of these left the option of extradition remaining.[46] The commission split over the issue as the Irish members upheld that the extradition of those whose crimes were politically motivated breached both domestic and international law. The British members argued that bilateral treaties could take precedence over international treaty obligations, and the latter could be overridden by the enormity of a particular crime. There was, therefore, no convincing legal impediment to stronger extradition law, rather, it was a matter of political sensibilities.

The failure to reach agreement on extradition meant a compromise was sought which resulted in the Criminal Jurisdiction Act 1975 and complementary legislation in the Republic, the Criminal Law (Jurisdiction) Act 1976. The British Act had three essential provisions: an offence committed in the Republic could be tried in Northern Ireland; the Republic would be requested to provide evidence for the trial; and evidence would be sought in Northern Ireland relating to prosecutions in the Republic. As this related to terrorist offences, the accused in such cases had to a fugitive and suspected of a scheduled offence and would thereby be tried in non-jury courts. Witnesses would not be compelled to cross the border, therefore, evidence could be taken on commission in the Republic. The reciprocal legislation had a difficult passage through the Dail, despite the fact that the British government saw the measure as a compromise which was unlikely to have a major effect on the terrorist campaign.

The other major change in security legislation, in addition to the EPA amendment, was the introduction of the Prevention of Terrorism (Temporary Provisions) Act 1974 (PTA). The immediate reason for its introduction was the death of nineteen people on 22 November in two bomb attacks on Birmingham pubs, although the proposals had been drafted earlier in the year in the event of the escalation of IRA attacks in Britain. The Bill was introduced by the Home Secretary, Roy Jenkins, on 28 November and had four main provisions. First, proscription of the IRA was to be extended to the rest of the UK (Northern Ireland was covered by the EPA). Secondly, the Home Secretary was to be empowered to exclude people from Britain to Northern Ireland. Thirdly, police powers of arrest and detention were to be extended. Fourthly, more rigorous checks would be made on those travelling between Ireland and Britain.

The powers of arrest were to be subject to a 'reasonable' suspicion clause but did not have to be related to a specific offence. Detention was to be permitted for up to forty-eight hours for the purpose of obtaining information and could be extended for up to five days subject to the approval of the Home Secretary. Any person suspected of membership of a proscribed organisation, of being subject to an exclusion order or of being involved in terrorist acts was subject to these detention powers.

The exclusion provisions were wholly executive in nature and not subject to judicial review. Those threatened with exclusion had the right to have their case referred to an adviser to the Home Secretary established under the Act, but this appeared to be of limited significance as, for security reasons, the advisers were not privy to the information on which exclusion was based. Exclusion orders could only be served if the suspected offence were related to the Northern Ireland situation. A citizen of the UK could not be excluded from Britain to Northern Ireland if she/he had been ordinarily resident in Britain for the previous twenty years or was born in Britain and normally resident there.

Jenkins himself described the powers as 'draconian' and, in recognition of this, the Act was to be subject to six-monthly renewal and restricted to terrorism related to Ireland. There was some back bench criticism of the measures; particular concerns included the executive nature of exclusion and that the Act was an emotive and ill-considered reaction to the bombings.[47] However, these were minority concerns against the background of the bombings and the second reading passed unopposed.

Various amendments were introduced in an attempt to mitigate the more severe elements of the bill. They included limiting the Act's duration to three months, the establishment of a tribunal with the power to confirm or revoke an exclusion order and reducing the residential qualification for exemption from exclusion from twenty to five years. These were either withdrawn or defeated by the government.

The Act was passed unopposed with the principal sections relating to arrest and exclusion as above. Proscription was limited to the IRA though other groups could be added by supplementary order. As well as extending police powers, immigration and customs and excise officers were given authority to board planes and ships to search for evidence relating to suspected offences or to search for those served with exclusion orders.

As critics of the Act were to point out over the years, it was difficult to demonstrate that it was effective in preventing 'mainland' activity by the IRA. The government appeared to recognise this and justified the Act on the tenuous grounds that it was necessary to prevent the deterioration of relations between the Irish community in Britain and the 'indigenous' population.[48]

Because of back bench concerns, particularly over the lack of a judicial element in exclusion, Jenkins pledged that the legislation would not be renewed beyond November 1975 unless substantial sections could be dropped. Instead new primary legislation would be presented by the government. The government accepted police and adviser advice that there should be no major changes to the Act. Therefore, in November 1975 the second reading of a new act was held concurrently with the renewal order to bridge the gap until new legislation could take effect.

The government rejected any independent or quasi-judicial element in the exclusion system and it remained unclear exactly how much information was given to advisers. Two changes in what became the 1976 PTA did improve the rights of those threatened with exclusion. The period in which written representation against exclusion could be made was extended from forty-eight hours under the 1974 Act to ninety-six hours. Secondly, the right to a personal interview with an adviser was made absolute; under the 1974 Act it could be refused if it was considered 'frivolous'. However, two alterations tended to reinforce the stringency of the Act. Renewal was to be annual rather than six-monthly and the provisions relating to support for terrorism were widened.[49]

Eleven Labour members voted against the third reading, forming a 'hardcore' who were gradually to move the party towards a more critical position. Opponents were concerned not only with the detail of the legislation but the dangers of a drift to permanence. The implication of this would be that the onus would be on opponents to demonstrate that the Act was not effective rather than on the government to justify the maintenance of what had been introduced as short-term, 'draconian' legislation.

In 1978, the Home Secretary, Merlyn Rees, set up a committee under Lord Shackleton to review the PTA within the remit of 'accepting the continued need for legislation against terrorism'. Opponents were angered about this circumscription since they felt this need had to be demonstrated by review and not taken for granted. The Shackleton report[50] was published in August 1978 and endorsed the bulk of the existing provisions. No changes were recommended in powers of arrest or detention, though Shackleton conceded that his defence of the Act was subjectively based and it was largely fruitless to look for conclusive proof of the effectiveness of the Act. Detention for up to seven days and the power of exclusion were upheld with minor recommendations concerning the comfort and rights of those held. Proscription was endorsed, although Shackleton conceded that its practical significance was limited but it reflected public feeling that terrorist groups should be outlawed.

In conclusion Shackleton expressed the hope that the temporary concept of the legislation would not diminish and that it would be regrettable if support developed for such powers to slide into permanent legislation.[51] However, it was to become clear in the subsequent years that such warnings were not heeded. Governments tended to employ a 'Catch 22' nature of justification. If terrorism in Great Britain continued the Act would be deemed necessary for public safety; if terrorism declined or stopped the Act would be deemed effective and thus the government would not risk repeal.[52]

The final development in security policy during the Labour administration to be considered is the Bennett report into police interrogation methods.[53] This report, published in March 1979, had its genesis in the continuation of the 'criminalisation' policy discussed above. The ending of detention made the need to obtain evidence for convictions in court paramount. The difficulty in obtaining witnesses to give evidence, either because of intimidation or because of lack of support for the regime, meant that confessions were an important means of securing convictions.[54]

Concern about abuses, including physical ill-treatment, existed among elements of the RUC and the Police Authority and could not therefore be dismissed as IRA propaganda. This led to the government setting up the inquiry chaired by Bennett in June 1978. This was done with some reluctance and a public inquiry was refused after an Amnesty International report concluded that suspect abuse had occurred. In his 1979 report, Bennett found that abuses had taken place, although Mason emphasised that this was only a small part of the report which also recorded evidence of a campaign to discredit the security forces.[55]

Bennett highlighted the lack of codification of rules governing interrogation and a lack of clarity about what practices would render an admission inadmissible. Given that the government recognised that assaults had occurred, three verdicts of guilty and nineteen prosecutions in total between 1972 and 1978 was a suspiciously low figure.[56] Bennett recommended the introduction of a formal code of conduct to govern interrogation procedure. The code should specifically prohibit threats of physical or sexual abuse, the use of insults or obscenities and the carrying out of unnecessarily physically demanding actions. The duration of interviews should be regulated and they should normally only take place between 8 am and 12 pm with regular breaks. Only two officers should be engaged in interviewing at any one time and only three groups of two should be engaged on any one case.

The other principal area of reform was the provision of suspects with a written record of their rights and improvement in solicitor access. Denial of access was directly related to the securing of confessions and this denial had never resulted in evidence or confessions being ruled inadmissible. The report also recommended a greater role for the Police Authority in the investigation of complaints.

The fact that Bennett rejected independent supervisors at interrogation and looked for reform to be implemented by senior officers suggests that he did not believe that abuses were sanctioned at higher levels or were part of a strategy. The thoroughness of the report and its many positive recommendations was exploited by Mason who emphasised these elements and played down the fact that it concluded that abuses had occurred and that nothing had been done by the government to reveal any determination to punish the perpetrators of past offences. A Commons statement was made on the same day as publication which prevented careful consideration by MPs and the government rejected a demand by Gerry Fitt, supported by Ian Paisley, for an emergency debate on the report. However, Mason did accept the Bennett proposals for the installation of TVs for monitoring interviews, improved access to solicitors and the limitation on the numbers of officers involved in each case. The incidence of complaints did decline in the period following the report, probably as a result of a combination of better supervision, procedural reforms of interrogation and government sensitivity to the adverse publicity that accusations and the Amnesty report had produced. On the debit side, the position of the Police Authority and the Police Complaints Board remained weak and critics were sceptical about relying overmuch on the police service to reform itself.

Economic policy

Prior to the more direct involvement of Westminster in Northern Ireland in 1969, an important element of economic policy had been efforts to attract external manufacturing investment to the province. This was underpinned by infrastructural development which included the designation of many of the larger towns as 'growth' or 'key' centres and a high level of government inducement to private capital. Although Northern Ireland remained disadvantaged compared with the UK average in unemployment and living standards, its economy performed relatively well in the second half of the 1960s. This was due to the general emphasis on regional policy in the UK, the amount of internationally mobile capital in circulation and the relatively high rates of government support administered by the devolved government compared with those available to depressed regions in Britain.[57]

However, by the period of direct rule this policy was experiencing two major problems. First, the international recession of the early 1970s had reduced the amount of manufacturing capital locating in Northern Ireland and, secondly, the violence and civil disorder gave rise to an 'image' problem which deterred investors. A major report on the economy noted that by late 1971 inward investment had all but dried up.[58] It is difficult to give a weighting to these two disincentives to investment; however, it seems that the impact of violence was greater in terms of discouraging new investment than on those companies already operating in the province.[59]

The transition from devolution to direct rule did not mark a break in the general policy of industrial support (see p. 33 below). The principal measures taken can be broadly divided into three categories. These were support for commercial and industrial enterprises, measures designed to retrain the workforce or employ it in direct labour schemes and measures directly related to the effects of violence and these will be considered in turn.

There were two major agencies of industrial support created in the early 1970s. The Local Enterprise Development Unit (LEDU) was established in 1971 by the Ministry of Commerce of the devolved administration and retained under direct rule. It was charged with responsibility for financial and other support for the small-business sector – defined as firms employing fewer than fifty people. One reason for its establishment was the decline of inward investment and the reduction in jobs created and it sought both to help increase employment and address the spatial imbalance in industrial location which led to the uneven spread of unemployment. The latter remit was reflected in the exclusion of the Belfast region from the scope of LEDU projects.

The LEDU was formed as a company and four of the directors chaired the four area panels established to cover the province. The area panels liaised with local businesses to promote the incentives offered. To further encourage a policy of dispersal, grants were in part related to distance from Belfast with higher grants being available in peripheral regions.

A feature of the LEDU was the emphasis it put on non-financial support. As well as grants of between 30 per cent and 40 per cent for premises, plant and machinery, the government stressed the availability of 'back-up' facilities. Examples included advice and practical help with design, marketing, research and development, exporting and related services. It was hoped that this form of cost subsidisation would allow small-scale craft and artisan operations to be commercially viable, for it was at these low capitalised sectors producing high value goods at which LEDU was principally aimed (although its remit was later revised to include the service sector).

The second institutional change related to financial support for industry was the creation of the Northern Ireland Finance Corporation (NIFC) by the Finance Corporation (NI) Order 1972. Its origins preceded direct rule and it would have been established by Stormont had not suspension taken place. The Cairncross report of 1971 had recommended a body which could offer financial support to companies adversely affected by violence and civil disorder but which had sound long-term economic prospects. The report recommended that industrial grants remain the responsibility of the Ministry of Commerce and the NIFC could, for example, provide loans or purchase shares in companies to offset liquidity problems. As the *direct* effects of violence within the province were less than anticipated, the NIFC functioned more as a development bank and supporter of new investment than as a salvager of companies threatened with closure because of civil disturbance.

The second major area of economic initiatives was employment training and publicly-funded labour-intensive schemes to address the problem of the unskilled and often long-term unemployed. Retraining was premised partly on the hope of attracting new investment and as a response to the shedding of labour by traditional industries and agriculture. As well as direct economic benefits, there were the hoped for social benefits of reduced unemployment including a reduction in the incidence of disorder.

In response to these considerations, government sponsored training centres were expanded and, by 1975, provided 3,300 places, ten times pro rata the number in Britain. Two schemes were designed to tackle unemployment among the unskilled who often worked in industries prone to recession and job insecurity, construction being a prime example. The Urban and Rural Improvement Campaign (URIC) employed 4,500 in labour-intensive schemes mainly on environment improvement projects such as reclamation and landscaping work. Enterprise Ulster (EU) was set up in 1973, initially for a five-year period, for those who had been unemployed for two years or longer. It was also labour-intensive and in any scheme at least 75 per cent of the cost had to consist of the labour component.

The original rationale of the scheme was to provide a bridge between the dole and employment and help to 'rehabilitate' those who had experienced long-term unemployment. However, as unemployment increased, the criterion of a place was reduced to one year's unemployment and the 'rehabilitation' concept declined as it became more of a holding operation.

The third category of support for industry and commerce was short-term measures specifically designed to counter the direct effects of violence on commercial viability. In 1971 the Counter Redundancy Scheme was introduced as a direct subsidy to labour costs, under which companies received financial support to prevent laying-off workers during short-term downturns in business. By late 1974 it was estimated that 9,500 jobs had been retained by operation of the subsidy. In 1972 a temporary rent rebate scheme was introduced whereby commercial premises in Belfast, Derry and Newry, areas among the worst affected by violence, were entitled to receive grants equivalent to 75 per cent of one year's rates if it could be demonstrated that revenue and profitability were seriously affected by the security situation. A third measure, the Security Staff Grant Scheme, was introduced in September 1972. The government paid 75 per cent of the cost of employing full-time security staff if a company employed more than ten people. It is difficult to assess whether these measures made much difference to employment maintenance, although they may have contributed to the low closure rate of companies as a result of physical damage.

As indicated above, the political and administrative changes involved in the introduction of direct rule made little impact on industrial policy.[60] Although the Conservative government had been elected with an ideological hostility to state intervention and regional policy, by the introduction of direct rule the period of 'U-turns' was already in operation. Additionally, violence and Northern Ireland's relatively weak economy were strong incentives to adopt a pragmatic approach. David Howell, the first minister under direct rule with responsibility for industrial policy, embraced such pragmatism and indicated that the state would bear all the capital costs of projects in employment 'blackspots' such as parts of west Belfast.[61]

In the early years of the 1970s unemployment, an important indicator of government policy, declined slightly. Paradoxically, in the short term, the troubles may have helped reduce unemployment. Higher rates of migration, increases in government support schemes and jobs created through civil service reorganisation, public sector house building and security employment were all contributory factors. The longer-term problem was a growing reliance on public expenditure which depended on the health of the UK economy as a whole and the ability of the Secretary of State to sell Northern Ireland's case to the cabinet and Treasury.

On coming to office in 1974, Labour inherited the tripartite institutional arrangement for industrial support composed of the Department of Commerce, the NIFC and the LEDU. This structure remained until April

1976 when Stan Orme, the minister responsible for commerce, introduced the Industries Development (NI) Order. The main purpose of the order was to replace the NIFC with a new body, the Northern Ireland Development Agency (NIDA).

The NIDA was intended to have a more positive and interventionist role than the NIFC. It was to have a dual role of setting up state industry on its own or jointly with private capital and supporting existing firms by providing loans or services, such as advice on improving marketing and research and development. The power to award grants was to remain with the Department of Commerce. The NIDA was to operate on commercial criteria, although it was clear there was a latitude to allow social considerations to influence decisions.[62] The NIDA had a certain congruence with wider British policy, for example, the Welsh and Scottish Development Agencies; however, it was envisaged that it would play a greater role in providing risk capital than its British counterparts. Despite Conservative reservations about the degree of state intervention in the economy, the corporatist representation on the NIDA was not markedly different from that of the NIFC established under the Conservatives.

The small business agency, LEDU, was left largely unchanged. However, in 1974 its operations were expanded to include the Belfast region which had been excluded on its establishment in 1971. This was part of a wider policy shift away from the growth-centre strategy of the early 1960s and an attempt to limit industrial development in the greater Belfast region. However, LEDU was able to provide capital grants of up to 50 per cent in peripheral areas compared with up to 40 per cent in the Belfast region.

The difficulties facing the government were highlighted by a major report published in September 1976.[63] It identified three main problems confronting the Northern Ireland economy: the erosion of manufacturing jobs; the collapse of inward investment; and the poor prospects for public sector job creation when the government was trying to limit public expenditure. Despite the problems of attracting foreign investment and the concerns over 'branch plant syndrome'[64] the report endorsed the maintenance of this policy and also that of the role of the state as entrepreneur and the retention of existing levels of employment in the public sector.

The proposals for tax 'holidays' for investors were not adopted, probably as a result of Treasury pressure over cost-per-job limits laid down for industrial support and the potentially adverse effect on other UK regions.[65] Overall, the government response to the report was modest, with the two main changes not being introduced until August 1977. The first was improvement in support for industry. Selective capital grants for machinery and equipment were raised from the level fixed in 1971 of 30 to 40 per cent to between 40 per cent and 50 per cent. However, in practice, individually negotiated packages between companies and the

Department of Commerce and NIDA could result in government agencies providing the bulk of capital necessary for a project.

The second part of the policy was a more aggressive approach to the marketing of Northern Ireland. To this end, Mason became personally involved in high-profile public relations exercises and Northern Ireland opened its own promotional offices in Japan and the USA and, following a review in 1978, Department of Commerce officials were seconded to posts in the USA specifically to counter the poor image of Northern Ireland. This strategy did revive the interest of potential investors but the subsidisation of inward investment was a risky policy. The inability of indigenous industry to provide sufficient employment meant inward investment had to be pursued. However, there were often problems in controlling the cost of a project once it was established and job promotions (that is, those forecast) were not always realised. The sponsoring agency then faced the dilemma of whether to pull out of the venture or extend financing in the hope of some future return.

These problems were shown in sharp relief in the DeLorean case, where £77 million of public money had been spent by the time of the collapse of the luxury car project in 1982 (a venture which had previously been rejected by the Republic of Ireland and Puerto Rico). Critical reports on this case and others concerning the cost of job promotions were to result in a later revision of support for large capital intensive ventures.[66]

As well as the general legislation for industrial support, specific measures were introduced to aid the shipbuilding and aircraft industries. Northern Ireland companies had been excluded from British nationalisation legislation and this had fuelled fears of British economic disengagement. The government claimed that this exclusion would make for administrative simplicity in the event of devolution when responsibility would be with the relevant minister in the Northern Ireland executive. Thus, the shipbuilders Harland and Wolff became wholly owned by the Department of Commerce under the Shipbuilding Industry (No. 2) (NI) Order 1975, and Shorts and Harland, the aircraft company, became jointly controlled by the Department of Commerce which held 91 per cent of the shares and the Department of Industry the remainder.

Separate legislation had been introduced because of the huge subventions needed to modernise and allow the orderly run down of the shipyards. The slow decline and loss making of Harland and Wolff would have almost certainly resulted in closure had it not been for social considerations and the symbolic importance of the industry to the Unionist community. This highlighted the tensions of an industrial support policy which tried both to stress commercial criteria and be mindful of the political and social implications of economic outcomes.

The underlying state of the Northern Ireland economy in the latter half of the 1970s was poor.[67] Unemployment rose over this period but would have been higher without the scale of government intervention, and the leveling off toward the end of the period may be attributed to a revival in inward investment, an increase in real terms in public expenditure and the introduction of the Youth Opportunities Programme Scheme (YOPS) in 1977.[68]

Social policy

The two years of Conservative administration from the advent of direct rule to the Labour election victory of February 1974 saw innovations in two areas: consideration of measures to prevent discrimination in employment; and the safeguarding of human rights. It was largely a period of consolidation following the flurry of reforms in the period 1969 to 1972 (see chapter 1 for summary) and governmental attention was fixed most firmly on constitutional proposals (see pp. 12–16 above).

A working party was set up in August 1972 under Paul Channon, the Minister of State (who was succeeded by William van Straubenzee in November) to consider ways of preventing discrimination in private sector employment.[69] This marked a continuity with pre-direct rule policy as the Stormont administration had been considering such an inquiry pending further discussions with employers and trades unions, and it was these corporate interests which composed the working party.

The working party rejected the use of 'quotas' for a number of reasons; principally that they conflicted with the principle of equal opportunity and would perpetuate, rather than lessen, community divisions. Instead, the concept of 'affirmative action' was advocated. In the working party's use of the term it meant that any agency set up to counter discrimination should have a wider role than the investigation of individual complaints. It should, for example, formulate programmes under which equality of opportunity could be achieved. Examples included reviewing recruitment practices to ensure that they did not, albeit unintentionally, favour one community.[70] The prospective agency was to have three broad functions. First, the investigation of individual complaints of discrimination, secondly, to advise and exhort organisations to ensure that their recruitment and promotional practices were not inadvertently discriminatory and thirdly, the agency would undertake research into factors, such as educational achievement, relevant to the creation of full equality of opportunity. While hoping there would be voluntary support for such action and that conciliation and persuasion would settle disputes, the report argued that legal sanctions might be necessary and advocated making discrimination a legal offence.

Legislation was to be phased in, with firms employing less than twenty-five people exempt for the first two years and those with fewer than ten employees exempt for three years. The report was aware that attempts at reform were not isolated from the wider context and that an increase in employment opportunities would be the single biggest influence towards eradicating discrimination. The bulk of the report's proposals were incorporated into the legislation of 1976.

A pledge to increase the safeguards against discrimination and to monitor the implications of legislation for the rights of the citizen was made in the White Paper of 1973. Sections 17–19 of the Northern Ireland Constitution Act 1973 which followed the White Paper declared that any law or subordinate instrument passed by the assembly would be declared void if it discriminated against a person on political or religious grounds. If the Secretary of State considered that proposed legislation was discriminatory he could refer it to the judicial committee of the Privy Council for consideration. It was also to be unlawful for Northern Ireland ministers, members of the executive or any body within the remit of the PCA or the Commissioner for Complaints to discriminate or 'aid, incite or induce' another to do so in the discharge of their functions.[71]

An innovation was the establishment of a Standing Advisory Commission on Human Rights (SACHR). Its functions were twofold: one was to advise the Secretary of State 'on the adequacy and effectiveness of the law for the time being in force in preventing discrimination on the grounds of religious belief or political opinion and in providing redress for persons aggrieved on either ground'[72]; and the other related function was to co-ordinate the activity of other agencies involved in this area and make recommendations to the Secretary of State. To facilitate inter-agency co-operation, the PCA, the Commissioner for Complaints (usually one person held both offices) and the chair of the Community Relations Commission were to be *ex officio* members of the SACHR. The absence of reference to a Bill of Rights in the White Paper and the narrow statutory remit of the SACHR raised questions about its likely effectiveness and this would become a concern for the SACHR itself.[73]

Partly due to the establishment of the executive and its subsequent collapse, it was not until 1976 that the recommendations of the working party on discrimination were given legislative effect in the Fair Employment (NI) Act 1976. The Act, supported by the Conservatives, established the Fair Employment Agency (FEA) which became operative in September 1976. It consisted of a chairman and eleven other members appointed by the Department of Manpower Services, three of whom were nominees of the Northern Ireland CBI and three nominees of the Northern Ireland Committee of the Irish Congress of Trades Unions.

The FEA's functions were to be the three recommended by the 1973 working party (see p. 36 above) and the additional one of monitoring public sector recruitment policy. The provision of redress in the case of individual complaints relieved the PCA and the Commissioner for

Complaints of responsibility in this area. To deal with the three main areas in turn.

The FEA was empowered to investigate individual complaints of discrimination. Findings of direct discrimination against individuals were few. In the first four years of the FEA six findings of discrimination were made and four of these were overturned by the courts which tended to rehear the case rather than, as the FEA anticipated, restrict themselves to a review of the FEA's findings and the reasons for them. Cases of direct discrimination were probably fairly limited and it seems likely that those who did practise it could put an objective 'gloss' on their activities so that proof was hard to obtain.[74]

The second function of the FEA was the promotion of equality of opportunity. This was to be effected, wherever possible, by voluntary action by companies, agencies, etc. To this end, section 5 of the Act required the Department of Manpower Services, after consultation with interested parties, to publish a 'manpower policy and practices' guide. This would advise employers how to improve recruitment and promotion policy so as to avoid potential discrimination.

Those bodies, in the public or private sector, which accepted the manpower policy directives were invited to sign a 'Declaration of Principle and Intent' which would allow them to advertise themselves as equal opportunity employers. The value of this provision was questionable since it was largely self-regulatory and did not require any further action by the signatory.[75]

Section 12 of the 1976 Act gave the FEA legal sanctions against bodies which failed to implement recommendations concerning the institution or improvement of equal opportunities. If voluntary agreements on procedures were unsuccessful and companies ignored or breached FEA recommendations the FEA could make an application to the county court which could grant injunctions or award damages.

The third major role of the FEA was research into possible barriers into the attainment of equality in employment opportunities and by 1979 three papers had been published dealing with the occupational profile of the population, a comparison of attitudes towards work of the two communities and educational achievements. The broad picture which emerged was one of Catholic over-representation among the unemployed and in low status jobs which could not be adequately explained by educational performance or attitudes to employment which did not indicate any difference between the two communities.

There were concerns that both the FEA and the SACHR were not given wholehearted support by the government. The FEA was both under-staffed and under-funded compared with the government's own projections on establishment and the Northern Ireland civil service itself paid no attention to the 'manpower policy and practice guide' and later resisted an investigation by the FEA into its practices. The SACHR continued to express its concern over its limited statutory remit.[76] In August 1978, Mason informed the SACHR that he endorsed it having a wider scope for considerations made on its own initiative but there was no official redefinition of its role. Its overall influence on government policy remained slight, particularly in relation to reservations about aspects of security legislation and advocacy of the adoption of a Bill of Rights.

By the end of the 1970s hopes that direct rule would be a short-term policy had been dashed and the prospects for devolution and an 'Irish dimension' along the lines of Sunningdale were slim. Although the government had not abandoned constitutional initiatives, there was a sense of a 'scaling down' of expectations and an emphasis on incremental security and economic reforms. The change of administration in 1974 had not resulted in any major shifts in policy; however, by the late 1970s there were groupings within both the Conservative and Labour Parties which felt the Unionist or Nationalist cause, respectively were not being prosecuted with sufficient vigour.

Notes

1 For a more detailed account of this period see chapters three and four of M. Cunningham, *British Government Policy in Northern Ireland 1969–89: its Nature and Execution* (Manchester, Manchester University Press, 1991).
2 Executive responsibility was invested in the new Secretary of State for Northern Ireland, William Whitelaw. Other departmental responsibilities were shared among three junior ministers.
3 Callaghan thought that integration would be 'an historic blunder of the first magnitude', HC debates: vol. 834, col. 251, 28 March 1972.
4 The main examples were security policy and responsibility for electoral and legal arrangements.
5 'Northern Ireland Constitutional Proposals', Cmnd 5259, para. 110.
6 Clause 1 of the Act pledged that Northern Ireland would remain a part of the UK as long as a majority desired it. The 1949 Act had invested the decision in the Northern Ireland parliament.
7 The reason for employing STV was not explicitly stated by government but the hoped for effects included greater representation for smaller and non-confessional parties.
8 See I. McAllister, 'The legitimacy of opposition: the collapse of the 1974 Northern Ireland Executive', *Eire–Ireland* 12(4), 1977 and P. Power, 'The Sunningdale strategy and the Northern majority consent doctrine in Anglo-Irish relations', *Eire–Ireland* 12(1), 1977.
9 For the text of the communique, and the position of the British government, see HC debates: vol. 866, col. 37, 10 December 1973.
10 A High Court judgment in the Republic ruled that the communique was not repugnant to the Constitution as it did not acknowledge that Northern Ireland was part of the UK.
11 Faulkner believed the powers would be residual and thought the cross-border

structures 'necessary nonsense' to maintain SDLP support for the executive (cited in P. Bew and G. Gillespie, *Northern Ireland: a Chronology of the Troubles 1968–1999* (Dublin, Gill and Macmillan, 1999), p. 74).

12 'Report of the Law Enforcement Commission' (Cmnd 5627), London, 1974.

13 McAllister, 'The Legitimacy of opposition', p. 32.

14 Rees's account of his tenure is M. Rees, *Northern Ireland: a Personal Perspective* (London, Methuen, 1985).

15 This argument is to be found in G. Gillespie, 'The Sunningdale Agreement: lost opportunity or an agreement too far?', *Irish Political Studies*, 13, 1998. A detailed account of the UWC strike is to be found in R. Fisk, *The Point of no Return* (London, Andre Deutsch, 1975).

16 Fisk, *The Point of no Return*, p. 198. P. Bew and H. Patterson, *The British State and the Ulster Crisis* (London, Verso, 1985), p. 68.

17 See HC debates: vol. 874, cols 878–1021 and 1038–83, 3/4 June 1974.

18 Rees, *Northern Ireland*, p. 107.

19 'The Northern Ireland Constitution', Cmnd 5675, 1974 para. 50.

20 Subjects included guidance on procedures, the formation of committees and comparative examples of mechanisms for minority representation.

21 For example, see the *Sunday Times* article cited in P. Bew and G. Gillespie, *Northern Ireland*, p. 104.

22 Mason's emphasis on security and somewhat 'gung ho' style was to make him popular with Unionist politicians.

23 HC debates: vol. 939, col. 1834, 24 November 1977.

24 See P. Dixon, '"A House divided cannot stand": Britain, bipartisanship and Northern Ireland', *Contemporary Record*, 9(1), 1995, pp. 171–2 and more generally for the argument of the persistence of bipartisanship.

25 It was recommended that representation be increased from twelve to between sixteen and eighteen seats.

26 See, for example, McNamara (HC debates: vol. 959, col. 306, 28 November 1978).

27 The granting of special category status, which the government soon regretted, was a *de facto* recognition that paramilitary violence was politically motivated.

28 'Report of the Commission to consider legal procedures to deal with terrorist activities in Northern Ireland' (Diplock report). Cmnd 5185, London, 1972.

29 These were offences most commonly associated with terrorist activity including arson, murder, riot, robberies and assaults involving firearms and explosives and membership of proscribed organisations. In specific cases, the Attorney-General could direct that an offence be descheduled.

30 Diplock, para. 59.

31 Diplock, para. 54.

32 The Northern Ireland Act of March 1972 had retrospectively indemnified the actions of troops engaged in searching and making arrests.

33 For internment statistics see K. Boyle, T. Hadden and P. Hillyard, *Ten Years on in Northern Ireland: the Legal Control of Political Violence* (London, Cobden Trust, 1980), table on p. 28.

34 The second reading was approved by 155 votes to eighteen. Fifteen Labour members opposed, principally over concerns about the erosion of civil liberties.

35 Arguments for plurality included the balancing of religious representation on the Bench, the reduced risk of judicial error and that three judges sat in special courts in the Republic of Ireland.

36 These clauses did not make legal general information gathering or 'trawling'

divorced from knowledge of or involvement in terrorist activity.

37 This had been passed to provide mandatory sentences on those involved in civil disorder.

38 'Report of a committee to consider, in the context of civil liberties and human rights, measures to deal with terrorism in Northern Ireland' (Gardiner report), Cmnd 5847, London, 1975.

39 Gardiner, paras 12 and 21.

40 HC debates: vol. 871, col. 1466, 4 April 1974.

41 'The Northern Ireland Constitution', Cmnd 5675, 1974, para. 42.

42 Catholic membership of the UDR was estimated at 2 per cent in 1979 (L. O'Dowd, B. Rolston and M. Tomlinson, *Northern Ireland: Between Civil Rights and Civil War* (London, CSE Books, 1980), p. 185).

43 There is some anecdotal evidence that professional rivalry and tensions existed between different sections of the security forces.

44 The use of local forces had the benefit for government of reducing domestic controversy over the death of British troops. Opposition to British involvement from service personnel families is discussed in P. Dixon, 'Britain's "Vietnam Syndrome"? public opinion and British military intervention from Palestine to Yugoslavia', *Review of International Studies* 26(1), 2000, pp. 108–13.

45 See note 11, above.

46 For more details on the extradition question see M. McGrath, 'Extradition: another Irish problem', *Northern Ireland Legal Quarterly* 34, 1983.

47 These points were made by Labour backbenchers Litterick, Abse, Hooley and Thorne. For critiques of the PTA see C. Scorer and D. Hewitt, *The Prevention of Terrorism Act: the Case for Repeal* (London, NCCL, 1981) and J. Sim and P. Thomas, 'The Prevention of Terrorism Act: normalising the politics of repression', *Journal of Law and Society* 10(1), 1983.

48 HC debates: vol. 892, cols 1153–4, 19 May 1975.

49 These included withholding of evidence related to terrorism and measures aimed at 'front' organisations suspected of funding terrorism.

50 'Review of the operation of the Prevention of Terrorism (Temporary Provisions) Acts 1974 and 1976', Cmnd 7324, London, 1978.

51 Cmnd 7324, para. 159.

52 Later versions of the Act established its permanence and covered both domestic and international terrorism.

53 'Report of the committee of inquiry into police interrogation procedures in Northern Ireland', Cmnd 7497, London, 1979. See P. Taylor, *Beating the Terrorists?* (Harmondsworth, Penguin, 1980) for a more detailed account of ill-treatment of suspects.

54 Cmnd 7497, para. 30.

55 Cmnd 7497, para. 19.

56 In twenty-six cases of officers being found at fault in civil proceedings over this period, no disciplinary action was known to have taken place (Cmnd 7497, para. 154).

57 From June 1970, selective capital grants would provide between 45 per cent and 60 per cent of capital depending on the rate of unemployment in the area where investment was to take place. This replaced the flat rate 50 per cent which had been available since October 1969.

58 'Review of economic and social development in Northern Ireland: report of the joint review board' (Cairncross report), Cmd 564, Belfast, 1971.

59 L. McClements, 'Economic constraints', in D. Watt (ed.), *The Constitution of*

Northern Ireland: Problems and Perspectives (London, Heinemann, 1981), p. 103.

60 R. Hogwood, 'The regional dimension of industrial policy', in P. Madgwick and R. Rose (eds), *The Territorial Dimension in United Kingdom Politics* (London, Macmillan, 1982), p. 57.

61 *Fortnight* 71, November 1973.

62 Orme: HC debates: vol. 908, col. 1724, 1 April 1976.

63 'Economic and Industrial strategy for Northern Ireland: report by the review team' (Quigley report), HMSO, Belfast, 1976.

64 This describes the tendency of multinationals to locate branch plants in peripheral areas which are the most vulnerable to closure or contraction in periods of recession.

65 *Fortnight* 152, August 1977.

66 See Committee of Public Accounts 14th report, HC 612, 1980 and Committee of Public Accounts 25th report, 'Financial Assistance to DeLorean Motor cars Ltd', HC 127 (1) and (2), 1984.

67 This is reflected in the title of the review by R. Rowthorn, 'Northern Ireland: an economy in crisis', *Cambridge Journal of Economics* 5, 1981.

68 Unemployment figures for the six years 1974–79, respectively, were 6.4 per cent, 8.3 per cent, 10.2 per cent, 11.3 per cent, 12 per cent and 11.6 per cent.

69 It was published in 1973 as 'Report and recommendations of the working party on discrimination in the private sector of employment', (van Straubenzee report), HMSO, Belfast.

70 Informal and 'word of mouth' practices are examples of such forms.

71 Formal legal safeguards were contained in the Government of Ireland Act 1920 so some scepticism may be in order about the effectiveness of such provisions.

72 Northern Ireland Constitution Act 1973, section 20(1).

73 These reservations about its remit are contained in various annual reports.

74 One reason direct discrimination may have been limited is because of the widespread segregation in the labour market; many people did not apply for jobs in companies dominated by the 'other side'. See R. D. Osborne, 'Fair employment in Cookstown? A note on anti-discrimination policy in Northern Ireland', *Journal of Social Policy* 11(4), 1982.

75 It was not until 1982 that an employer seeking a government contract was required to sign the declaration.

76 See 3rd Annual Report, 1976–77, HC 199, Belfast, 1977/8.

3

The Conservative administrations, 1979–90

Constitutional policy

The Conservative general election manifesto of 1979 stated that 'in the absence of devolved government, we will seek to establish one or more elected regional councils with a wide range of power over local services'. This reflected the failure of devolution initiatives over the previous five years and the influence of the 'integrationist' lobby which included the Conservative spokesman, Neave. He had been killed by the INLA in March and thus integration lost a leading advocate.

There were, however, broader reasons why under Secretary of State, Humphrey Atkins, the government embarked on a devolution strategy. The most significant of these was international opinion, particularly that of the USA. Guelke argues that it 'seems reasonable to conclude that US pressure was the main reason for the initiative'.[1] An integrationist approach would have been unpopular with the USA and the UK was concerned to prevent Northern Ireland from becoming an issue in the American presidential election and wanted to defuse criticism which had resulted in an arms embargo on the RUC following the revelations of the Bennett report (see Chapter 2). The second important international actor was the Republic of Ireland. Integrationism would strain relations and make the improved security collaboration that Margaret Thatcher was seeking more difficult to realise.

An indication of the importance of the American connection is that the new initiative was 'leaked' by the British Ambassador in Washington in September 1979. Towards the end of October, Atkins announced that he was inviting the four main Northern Ireland parties to a conference at Stormont to discuss a possible solution.[2] On 20 November the White Paper containing the government's proposals was published.[3] The paper ruled out discussion of options which the government would not accept or which were not practicable. These included independence, Irish unity, confederation and a return to a Stormont-type administration. This narrowed the options to some form of devolution in which there would have to be 'reasonable and appropriate arrangements to take account of the interests of the minority'. Six years after Sunningdale the term 'power sharing' was still excluded from official discourse.

The White Paper was marked by much flexibility. The government expressed a preference for legislative and executive devolution, as in 1974, but more limited executive devolution would be acceptable if inter-party agreement could be reached.

Provisions and safeguards for minority representation were similarly flexible. If the executive were to be formed on a 'cabinet' system there were three possible methods of representation. The Secretary of State could appoint members of the executive as in 1973, places could be filled in proportion to party strengths in the assembly or by direct election in parallel elections. Alternatively, the executive could be formed by a committee system, in which case a proportion of chairs and/or seats on committees would be guaranteed to representatives of the minority. Other possible safeguards included the use of 'weighted' votes either in committees or in the assembly and the power of the Secretary of State or provisions of a Bill of Rights to block legislation if it were opposed by a certain proportion of the assembly. An appendix to the White Paper outlined the various options available. Amid the detail, it was clear that the parameters for government were the administrative feasibility of and broad-based support for any settlement.

The White Paper was debated on 29 November and received support from Labour for the broad framework. Criticism focused largely on the open-ended nature with the opposition arguing that Atkins should play more of a steering role rather than adopt a neutral position towards the various options in the appendix.

The Conference first met on 7 January 1980 and thirty-four half-day sessions of talks occurred between that date and 24 March when it was indefinitely adjourned. No progress was made. The Ulster Unionists, under new leader James Molyneaux, were becoming increasingly integrationist and had boycotted the talks, the DUP rejected power sharing in a paper submitted in February and the SDLP had only attended after Atkins had broadened the scope of discussion to embrace the Irish dimension.

A second White Paper was published in July 1980 which presented the results of the conference and suggested possible ways forward.[4] Its tone was cautious and somewhat pessimistic, revealing that the government had not expected agreement to be reached. It reviewed the possible mechanisms for minority representation either within the executive or through a council of the assembly created to balance the power of the executive through blocking, delaying or referral powers. If neither of these basic models was acceptable, direct rule would continue. As with the first White Paper, Labour endorsed the broad principles and sentiments. Opposition spokesman Brynmor John indicated that Labour favoured minority representation within the executive as the council structure would be largely negative and thus encourage polarisation rather than accommodation.[5]

More trenchant criticisms of the government came from a group of its own backbenchers, which accused it of reneging on the manifesto commitment and suspected that the reason for the devolutionary attempts was to establish a body which could provide members for an all-Ireland institution.[6] The government denied this and argued that local government reform would raise the same problems in relation to minority representation and that there was general support for devolution in Northern Ireland. However, by November 1980 Atkins admitted that there was insufficient agreement for progress and integrationists' fears were increased by the second Anglo-Irish summit of the year held in December (see p. 47 below). Atkins' swansong was a proposal for an advisory council composed of about fifty elected representatives in Northern Ireland to consider legislation and scrutinise the functioning of government departments. This received a cool response and Atkins was replaced by James Prior in September 1981.

The likelihood of agreement between the Northern Ireland parties had receded further in the atmosphere surrounding the hunger strikes of spring and summer 1981.[7] Despite this unpromising background and his own pessimism, Prior announced new proposals in April 1982 following three months of discussions with the Northern Ireland parties.

The supposedly novel element in the proposals was popularly termed 'rolling devolution' though Brian Mawhinney, a Conservative MP, had suggested something similar in the White Paper debate of July 1980 and elements of it had existed in Mason's proposals in the previous administration. The basic idea was that an assembly would be established and if agreement could not be reached on devolution, it would retain a scrutinising and deliberative role with respect to Northern Ireland departments through 'shadowing' committees.

The 'rolling' concept meant that devolution could proceed on a stages basis; some responsibilities could be devolved if agreement were reached while others could be retained by the Secretary of State. Therefore, devolution did not have to be 'all or nothing'. If a department's functions were not devolved, the relevant committee would continue to fulfil its advisory and scrutinising role.[8] Security and law and order were initially to be reserved powers but could be transferred later if the assembly operated successfully.

As with all initiatives since 1973, power sharing was a taboo phrase and it was not considered necessary to have guaranteed places for minority representatives within the executive. Prior stressed that he was willing to leave the workings of the assembly to those elected to it. However, there were specific rules governing the move to devolution itself. For this to occur there had to be cross-community support reflected by 70 per cent or more of the assembly voting in favour or other convincing evidence. In such an instance, the Secretary of State had a statutory duty to lay the proposals before Parliament.

The prospects for the proposals were poor. The SDLP was moving towards an all-Ireland consideration of the problem and was angered by the lack of emphasis on the Irish dimension and the Ulster Unionists and Conservative integrationists repeated their positions struck at the time of Atkins' proposals.[9] Prior did not receive support from his own government as Thatcher was at best lukewarm about the initiative.

Given the balance of forces, it remains to be explained why such a path was followed. One reason was that Prior and his deputies felt that to do nothing was unacceptable and to risk accusations of passivity, especially among the international community.[10] Another was that the proposals had the broad support of the Labour opposition and thus helped to maintain bipartisanship, despite the fact that the Labour Party conference of September 1981 had formally adopted a policy of 'unity by consent'.

Provision for the establishment of the assembly was made in the Northern Ireland bill which had a second reading on 10 May 1982. A group of Conservative integrationists was opposed and were to fight a rearguard battle in committee, with three members of the government resigning and Labour abstaining, arguing for a greater emphasis on the Irish dimension and guaranteed minority representation in any future executive. The third reading was passed by a majority of 137 to 29 on 29 June 1982.

The elections to the assembly took place on 20 October 1982 on the well-established formula of seventy-eight seats to be filled by STV using the electoral boundaries of the twelve Westminster constituencies. The chances for movement toward devolution appeared to be nil as the SDLP was to contest the election on an abstentionist platform. Of greater concern to the government was that Sinn Fein, contesting its first assembly elections in an attempt to capitalise on the mobilisation of support around the hunger strikes, gained 10.1 per cent of first preference votes. This was approximately one in three of what may be assumed to be the Catholic vote.[11] This made it difficult to maintain that there was no support for the politics of violence and if Sinn Fein were to establish itself as a significant party the chances of reviving power sharing looked even slimmer.

The SDLP and Sinn Fein won nineteen seats between them, so the assembly met with fifty-nine members participating and embarked upon its scrutinising and deliberative functions, including reviewing draft Northern Ireland legislation.[12] This role for the assembly could continue indefinitely since there was no time limit placed on its existence and there was no prospect of devolution while the Nationalist and Republican boycott continued.

The stalemate in the assembly added impetus to initiatives which transcended the internal dimension and focused on the development of Anglo-Irish relations. In May and December 1980 Thatcher and Charles Haughey, the Taoiseach, had held meetings. At the first of these the 'unique relationship' between the two countries was recorded and at the second, to reflect the 'totality of relations', the two delegations agreed to consider citizens' rights, security matters, economic co-operation and possible new institutional arrangements. This was cemented in the Anglo-Irish Intergovernmental Council which was established in November 1981.

Given Thatcher's supposed visceral unionism and the risk of widespread Unionist opposition to an increased role for Dublin, it needs to be explained why the Irish dimension was extended in the early 1980s, resulting in the Anglo-Irish Agreement of 1985 (see p. 49 below). An important internal factor was the entry of Sinn Fein into electoral politics. In the general election of June 1983 it gained 13.4 per cent of the vote compared with 17.9 per cent for the SDLP. While the chances of Sinn Fein becoming the dominant nationalist party were probably slim, this increase of support from 1982 was an incentive for the British government to bolster constitutional nationalism which increasingly emphasised the all-Ireland dimension of any settlement. A related issue was that Sinn Fein support was interpreted by many commentators as an indication of 'alienation' among the Nationalist community, reflecting the continuation of material disadvantage and lack of cultural parity. This notion of alienation was used by John Hume in an effort to establish an all-Ireland Forum to discuss possible structures in which to accommodate the two dominant traditions in Ireland.

The balance of international forces also pointed towards the likelihood of the extension of the Irish dimension. The USA was likely to look favourably on such a development and, as discussed above, international concern made it more difficult to pursue a passive policy. Also, the European Community, partly as a result of Hume's lobbying, had began to take a more active interest in Ireland and in March 1983 the political committee of the European parliament proposed to prepare a report on the Northern Ireland question.[13] It was approved by the Political Affairs Committee in February 1984 and later by the European parliament. Although it respected UK sovereignty and refrained from advocating any particular constitutional blueprint, it did endorse an all-Ireland dimension in social and economic development, supported the Intergovernmental Council and advocated the establishment of a parliamentary tier. To summarise, interested international observers tended to view the question in a way that was more in tune with Nationalist rather than Unionist perceptions.[14]

The New Ireland Forum met for a year between May 1983 and May

1984 without official Unionist or British representation. The report considered three possible frameworks for a future Ireland: joint authority; a federal/confederal state; or a unitary state. Neil Kinnock, the Labour Party leader, welcomed the report since it endorsed 'unity by consent' and Prior diplomatically welcomed the positive aspects of the report, including the condemnation of violence, while arguing that all three options appeared to be ruled out since none fulfilled the criterion of Northern consent. At an Anglo-Irish summit at Chequers in November 1984 Thatcher bluntly rejected all options: 'I have made it quite clear . . . that a unified Ireland was one solution. That is out. A second solution was confederation of the two States. That is out. A third solution was joint authority. That is out. That is a derogation of sovereignty.'[15] Thatcher's dismissive tone annoyed the Irish delegation and at the press conference following the summit she rejected the imposition of a settlement from London. She also appeared to be increasingly sceptical of the 'alienation' thesis which had been pushed by Garret FitzGerald, the Taoiseach and Fine Gael leader, and Hume, possibly influenced by the fact that Sinn Fein's vote in the European election of 1984 was marginally lower than that of 1983. It thus appeared at the end of 1984 that the Anglo-Irish process was being slowed and downplayed by the British government. However, by November 1985 the Anglo-Irish Agreement (AIA) had been signed indicating that countervailing tendencies were stronger.

There are various ways to explain why a supposedly Unionist Prime Minister put her name to an agreement which virtually the whole Unionist community opposed. One is that she adopted a 'minimalist' reading of the agreement whereby Ireland's role and influence in Northern Ireland would be residual, and in return the UK would benefit from increased co-operation in security matters and the suppression of terrorism. Although its effect is difficult to quantify, the bombing of the Conservative conference in Brighton in October 1984 may have reinforced the impetus for such co-operation. Therefore, British sovereignty was not diluted or at least such a claim could be made. Secondly, it seems that Thatcher's unionism (or perhaps, patriotism) was fundamentally constructed from an English perspective in which the sensibilities and sensitivities of Ulster unionism were of secondary importance.[16] Despite her famous claim that Northern Ireland was as British as her own constituency, the acceptance of different structures of governance for Northern Ireland suggests this not to be the case. Thirdly, commentators have pointed to her own executive style which made her sceptical about well-established policies and the agencies which constructed them which allowed for potentially new departures.[17]

An indication of the direction of policy was the importance in negotiations of the Cabinet Secretary Robert Armstrong and David Goodall of

the Cabinet Office and the relative lack of input of Northern Ireland officials, who were either more sceptical or more likely to be aware of
Unionist hostility to any such developments.[18]

Negotiations took place through much of 1985 at both ministerial and
official level. In May and June it appeared that the prospects were poor
because the Irish negotiators favoured reforms to the security forces and
judicial system to combat 'alienation' which were unacceptable to some
of the British contingent, including the disbanding of the UDR and the
possibility of three judges sitting in Diplock courts.[19] The absence of such
changes in the AIA indicates that the balance moved in the UK's favour
in the period leading to the signing of the AIA on 15 November 1985.

The AIA established an Intergovernmental Conference to be jointly
chaired when meeting at ministerial level by the Secretary of State for
Northern Ireland and an Irish minister designated as the permanent Irish
ministerial representative. This position was filled by Peter Barry, the
Foreign Affairs Minister. There was also provision for meetings to be
held at official level and for other ministers and advisers to be included if
the topic under discussion fell within their area of responsibility.[20]

The role of Dublin in the conference fell short of the three options of
the Forum report and Article 2(b) stated that there was no derogation
from the sovereignty of either government within its own jurisdiction.
The conference recognised the right of the Irish government to be
consulted on matters relating to Northern Ireland and the British government's commitment to listening are contained in the same article and
'determined efforts' were to be made to resolve differences.[21]

The conference was to consider four principal areas: political matters;
security matters; legal matters, which included the administration of
justice; and cross-border co-operation, which included economic,
cultural, social and security matters. Political matters involved efforts to
accommodate the two traditions in Northern Ireland, to ensure the avoid-
ance of economic and social discrimination and to consider the possibility
of a bill of rights. To help promote equality, the Irish government was to
be consulted on the role and composition of the relevant agencies. These
included the Police Authority, the Police Complaints Board, the FEA, the
SACHR and the Equal Opportunities Commission. Security matters were
concerned with three principal areas: security policy in general; relations
between the security forces and the nationalist community; and prison
policy. Issues mentioned under Article 8 on legal matters included the
possibility of mixed courts, extradition and extra-territorial jurisdiction.
A commitment to enhanced cross-border co-operation was made in
Articles 10 and 11, although specifics were not mentioned. The conference was subject to review after three years or earlier if requested by
either government.

As with both earlier and later initiatives, the possibility of adaptation and the sense that the AIA was part of a *process* rather than an endpoint allowed diametrically opposite interpretations to be placed upon it. Unionists were not reassured by Dublin's acceptance that the status of Northern Ireland could only be changed with the consent of the Northern majority since the status was not defined in the relevant article. Neither did the possibility of a reduction in Dublin's input in the event of devolution offer them solace. Conversely, British statements concerning Dublin's recognition of partition led Republicans to denounce it.[22]

Having summarised the role and scope of the conference, it would be instructive to locate it within the context of previous initiatives. It can be differentiated from these in three ways. First, the recognition of the right of the Irish Republic to be consulted over Northern Ireland policy and act as *de facto* advocates for the Nationalist community extended the Irish dimension beyond that envisaged in 1973 and can be contrasted with the downplaying of the dimension between the mid-1970s and the early 1980s. Secondly, the Unionist community was excluded from consultation and its consent and participation was not necessary for the conference to function. This circumvented the problems of boycotts and the unwillingness to engage in power sharing structures. Thirdly, the rights and identity of the Nationalist community were emphasised more than in previous initiatives, with the possible exception of the Sunningdale period.

However, there were also important continuities. As O'Leary has noted, a two-track approach had informed policy making within the Northern Ireland Office; the internal track of trying to secure the broadest possible support within Northern Ireland and the external track of maintaining good relations with the USA and the Irish Republic to avoid international embarrassment.[23] The AIA was consistent with both of these, and by effectively tying the Republic into the process but without conceding executive authority British policy was largely 'fireproofed' internationally.

The remaining years of the 1980s after the AIA witnessed little positive movement. Unionism was united in its hostility to the AIA but the many forms of protest undertaken failed to result in its suspension or abandonment. Gradually tensions developed between the main two parties over the boycotting of government business and the violence associated with protest.[24] Unionist politics became marked in this period by a lack of consensus about possible ways forward and preferred constitutional arrangements. A myriad of ideas was thrown up in this period including various forms of devolution, integration, independence and new structures for North–South relations, and the increasingly vocal campaign for equal citizenship reflected growing disenchantment with the policies and tactics of the Ulster Unionists and the DUP.

Particularly with hindsight, it is clear that there were significant developments within nationalism. Between January and August 1988 there was a series of seven meetings between John Hume and Gerry Adams. In September, the end of the talks was officially announced and the SDLP regretted being unable to persuade Sinn Fein to have the IRA call off its campaign of violence and Sinn Fein declared itself perplexed by the SDLP's perception of the neutrality of Britain's role in Northern Ireland. It took over ten years for the end-game of this process to be played out; in the short term it made Unionist and Nationalist co-operation in renewed devolution less likely.

The constitutional stalemate led to the suspension of the Northern Ireland assembly in 1986. In protest at the AIA, normal business was suspended in December 1985 and a committee formed to consider opposition to it. By March 1986 the assembly was refusing to carry out the scrutiny of draft legislation. Being in breach of its statutory responsibilities put the assembly's future in jeopardy and twice in May 1986, Secretary of State Tom King warned of the possibility of suspension. On 19 June the Northern Ireland Assembly (Dissolution) Order 1986 was approved by the Commons with Labour supporting the government. The Order dissolved the existing assembly but did not abolish the legal basis for the establishment of a possible future assembly.

The Commons debates on the renewal of direct rule reveal three main features of government constitutional policy: devolution as a long-term aim; the rejection of integration; and adherence to the AIA. Labour broadly supported these, although it tended to emphasise the potential of the AIA as part of a process leading to unification and was developing the concept of 'harmonisation' whereby it was argued that functional cross-border co-operation would lead to closer political linkages.[25] With respect to the AIA, the government was prepared to play the 'long game'. As critics pointed out, in the short term the AIA had not improved relations between the two communities, violence had increased and relations between the two governments had been far from harmonious.

However, both governments remained committed to the more formalised structures put in place in 1985. This was apparent when the review of the AIA, published in May 1989, concluded that no fundamental change was required. In light of the disagreements between the governments, procedural changes were recommended to forestall the development of disputes. These included a regular schedule of meetings (as had developed in 1988) which would allow a more systematic consideration of forthcoming developments, an informal ministerial meeting at least once a year and scope for widened ministerial participation to increase the range of topics of mutual interest covered in conference.[26] To emphasise the positive work of the conference, it was undertaken to publicise more effectively the discussions which took place.

The other points covered in the review included a commitment to devolution by the two governments, recommendations for greater recognition of the rights and identities of the two traditions in Northern Ireland, progress in fair employment legislation and towards the establishment of an Anglo-Irish parliamentary tier which had been recommended in the joint studies of 1981.

It was clear by the end of the 1980s that the bi-governmental approach was mutually beneficial and would not be laid aside, although the form it took might evolve over time. If the British government gambled that sections of unionism would come to a *modus vivendi* with such structures over time it was proved right, although such a development was to take almost a decade from the signing of the AIA.

Security policy

This section will deal in turn with the principal security legislation, 'supergrass' trials, and, lastly, miscellaneous security provisions. The main pieces of legislation, the PTA 1976 and EPA 1978, were passed under a Labour administration with Conservative support and when the Conservatives came to office they saw no need for further changes in the provisions.

A small group of Labour members had consistently opposed the legislation and this opposition grew in the early 1980s. At the same time, a leftward shift in constituency associations led to a more critical position concerning bipartisanship in both security and constitutional policy.[27] In the debate on PTA renewal, the Labour front bench position in 1981 was still was one of abstention, although it tabled a motion calling for an inquiry into the Act to consider its operation and possible amendments. Roy Hattersley argued that this was a modest request focusing mainly on the desire for more comprehensive information about the use and possible abuse of exclusion provisions. Whitelaw, the Home Secretary, refused an inquiry on the grounds that it was only two and a half years since the Shackleton report. A total of forty-four MPs voted against renewal and this rose to fifty-three in 1982, despite Whitelaw conceding to demands for a review. He did not specify why, although it was probably an attempt to bolster an unsteady bipartisanship. The review, chaired by Lord Jellicoe, was published in February 1983.[28] Statistics presented in the report revealed that nearly 90 per cent of those arrested under the Act were not subsequently charged or subject to an exclusion order, which indicated to its critics that the Act was being used for intelligence gathering and/or harassment.

Jellicoe conceded that it could not be proved that the arrest powers made a significant difference in preventing terrorism but erred on the side of caution. Extended detention was endorsed but with certain safeguards. These included the provision that the maximum five-day extension beyond the initial forty-eight hours should not be granted automatically and then only on the grounds of anticipated results and, where possible, such extensions should be only granted by the Home Secretary and not by junior ministers. Jellicoe also recommended improved rights and conditions of those held, including access to a solicitor every forty-eight hours, a printed notice of rights to be retained, improvements in the holding accommodation and financial support for those detained for more than forty-eight hours. Exclusion orders were also endorsed but recommended that their use should be subject to regular review with a view to possible abolition. Three principal changes to the 1976 provisions were recommended. First, the normal period of residence which indemnified a person from exclusion should be reduced from twenty to three years. Secondly, exclusion should be for a fixed three-year period rather than indefinite and the onus shifted onto the Home Secretary to justify its extension, rather than the excluded person providing grounds for its revokation. Thirdly, the period in which representation against exclusion could be made should be extended from four to seven days. There would also be the right to a personal interview with an adviser after exclusion had occurred. This was to remedy the problem whereby people often did not make representations as this had the effect of prolonging detention before exclusion.

Despite improvements to exclusion provisions, the report as a whole confirmed the fears of critics that exceptional legislation was becoming more acceptable and permanent. Jellicoe advocated the dropping of the 'Temporary Provisions' section in the title of the Act and also that its provisions should be extended to cover international terrorism and not just that associated with Northern Ireland. As a countervailing safeguard, it was recommended that annual renewal should be retained and any new Act should be of a maximum five years' duration, but the trend was towards permanence.

In the renewal debate of March 1983 Whitelaw announced that a new bill would be introduced based on Jellicoe's recommendations. Labour opposed the renewal of the 1976 Act for the first time. Hattersley argued that it had not been demonstrated that the Act was necessary for the nation's safety and, given the infringement of civil liberties, this was essential. He also located the decision to produce a new Act covering international terrorism within a deeper illiberal trend in government law and order policy.[29] The government's defence was based on the preventative nature of the Act, which meant that how few charges were brought was of little significance in assessing the Act's worth. The new bill received its second reading in late October 1983. In tabling an amendment opposing the bill, Hattersley argued that it was wrong in principle as it involved arbitrary arrest and detention and in practice as it could not be shown to be effective and could increase support for terrorism.

Labour's change of position since 1974 was not inconsistent, he argued, because the justification had changed from preventing a 'backlash' against the Irish community in Britain to intelligence-gathering, which Leon Brittan, the Home Secretary, seemed to endorse.[30]

The new Act became law in March 1984. It incorporated the Jellicoe recommendations on exclusion, the extension of arrest powers to international terrorism, it was limited to five years' duration and subject to both annual renewal and review by an independent figure. Contrary to Jellicoe, the 'Temporary Provisions' section of the title was retained. Sections relating to arrest, detention and proscription were left unchanged from the 1976 Act.

In the years leading up to the next Act in 1989 Labour continued to vote against renewal on the grounds outlined above of both principle and of practical objections. They criticised the government's maintenance of exclusion powers despite the recommendations of the independent reviews and the rejection of the recommendation that detention beyond the initial forty-eight hours should be the responsibility of the courts rather than the Home Secretary.

The new PT bill, which had to become law by March 1989 to prevent the powers lapsing, received its second reading on 6 December 1988. Many of the provisions of the 1984 Act were retained. The main changes were as follows. First, the Act was to be of indefinite duration and not limited to five years. Secondly, remission in Northern Ireland was reduced from a maximum of one-half of the sentence to one-third for those sentenced to more than five years for a scheduled offence. Thirdly, and most significantly, measures designed to prevent the flow of money or property to terrorist organisations by 'laundering' via legitimate businesses were introduced. These gave the courts greater powers to investigate accounts and to seize assets, and moved the onus of proof to the defendant to explain the source of such monies. Douglas Hurd, the Home Secretary, had announced such changes in September 1988 in response to RUC concerns that a significant proportion of paramilitary funding came from ostensibly legitimate companies.

The passage of the bill was marked by acrimonious disputes between government and opposition and by a confused stance from Labour which strained relations between its front bench and some backbenchers. Labour was critical of the arrest powers, executive control of extended detention, and that the government had ignored recommendations to end exclusion orders and to drop the offence of withholding information which might be of assistance in preventing the commission of terrorism by another person.

In consequence, Hattersley moved an amendment declining a second reading for the bill. However, when it was defeated the Labour front bench chose to abstain on the second reading on the grounds that it supported the clauses which were designed to curtail terrorist funding. This provoked protest from the left of the party which failed to understand the policy of abstention in the light of party policy of opposition to the PTA. Forty-three Labour members voted against the second reading and two of the rebels, Clare Short and Andrew Bennett, resigned from their junior shadow cabinet positions. The second reading was given by 305 votes to forty-five.

Inter-party disputes continued in committee. Labour accused the government of reneging on a commitment to bring in a judicial element to extended detention in response to a European Court of Human Rights (ECtHR) ruling; in turn the government accused Labour of obstructing the passage of the bill, although Labour denied it had agreed a timetable for the committee stage. Labour amendments to limit detention to a total of four days, to end exclusion orders and to restore remission of sentences to one-half were either withdrawn or defeated. After the use of the guillotine on committee, the third reading was passed on 30 January 1989 with Labour opposing. The new PTA came into force in March 1989.

The other principal piece of security legislation was the EPA. The annual reports of the SACHR highlighted concerns over its operation, including the lack of a 'reasonable' suspicion clause in relation to arrest powers and the government's claim that the burden of proof lay with those wishing to change the Act.[31] Partly informed by these concerns and the lack of publicity given to them, Labour called unsuccessfully for a judicial review in 1980 and 1981. Specific areas Labour wanted considered were the introduction of a plurality of judges in 'Diplock' courts, a reduction in the number of scheduled offences and changes to the wording of the section relating to admissibility.

In July 1982 James Prior announced an inquiry into the EPA was to be established; a response to consistent Labour pressure and an attempt to reduce bipartisan strains. The review, to be chaired by Baker, did not start until April 1983 and Labour's position was gradually hardening. It abstained on both renewal orders of 1983 but in July 1984 voted against the continuation of the EPA for the first time. This did not mark a repudiation of the Act *in toto* but was a protest over the lack of urgency shown by the government in arranging a debate on the Baker report which had been published in April.[32] Labour was also concerned by the limited scope of the report which had, prior to taking evidence, accepted the need for the continuation of emergency provisions.

The Baker report largely endorsed the provisions of the 1978 Act. It covered five major areas: provisions for bail; powers of arrest; suspension of juries; admissibility of confessions; and detention. These will be considered in turn. Baker argued that the initial onus for opposing bail should be on the prosecution. This would reverse the 1978 provision whereby it was the responsibility of the defence to demonstrate that bail could be granted without the risk of further offences being committed. Given that the judge had wide discretionary powers to deny bail if such concerns arose, Baker felt this change held little risk. He also recommended an automatic right of bail after twelve months' remand if the defendant had not been committed for trial.[33]

As the powers of arrest were different in the two pieces of emergency legislation, Baker felt that they should be rationalised and preferably incorporated into one new Act. The EPA did not, unlike the PTA, require 'reasonable suspicion' but only 'suspicion' of an offence which was of some legal significance. The 'reasonable' criterion should be extended to the arrest powers of both the police and army.

A return to jury trials was rejected because of the problems of intimidation and a plurality of judges was considered to slow the process and be of no practical use. Baker argued that the best way to reduce pressure on Diplock courts was to increase the number of descheduled offences, especially as many had no terrorist connections and to extend the power to 'certify out' to the Director of Public Prosecutions (DPP) rather than it remain the preserve of the Attorney-General.

Confessions were inadmissible under the 1978 Act if they were obtained by the use of 'inhuman or degrading treatment'. The SACHR had argued that the use of violence and the threat of its use should specifically be made illegal and this was endorsed by Baker. Finally, detention without trial had not been used since 1975 and had lapsed in 1980. However, it remained on the statute book and Baker recommended its repeal as it was not consistent with the policy of criminalisation and police primacy and was also an international embarrassment. Any new Act should be renewed annually and be of five years' duration to bring it in to line with the new PTA.

The report was debated in late December 1984 at the same time as the second annual renewal of the 1978 Act for 1984. The government response to it was broadly favourable, while Labour was to divide the House because of the delay in the holding of the debate, its dissatisfaction with the government response to the questions of the length of remand, the use of uncorroborated evidence in 'supergrass trials' (see p. 58 below) and the decline in the acquittal rate in Diplock trials. However, Labour did not commit themselves to opposing the new legislation as long as the government took seriously the concerns they had raised.

In June 1985 the government announced that a new Act was to be drafted, although no date was given for the legislation. In the interim, the government had rejected three of Baker's recommendations: the removal of detention; the delegation of descheduling to the DPP; and a mandatory right to bail after twelve months' remand. A minor change was contained in the Northern Ireland (Emergency Provisions) Act 1978 (Amendment)

Order 1985 which widened the category of offence that could be descheduled at the discretion of the Attorney-General to include kidnapping, false imprisonment and offences which carried a sentence of less than five years. The Order was approved in January 1986 with Labour support.

The second reading of the new EPA was held in December 1986, concurrently with the continuance order. The bill may be considered a 'mixed bag' and thus provoked an ambivalent response from the opposition and the civil liberties lobby. While it offered improvements to the rights of the arrestee and mitigated some of the more oppressive aspects of the legislation, this was informed by the increasing institutionalisation of the Act as its temporary nature receded further.[34]

The more liberal aspects of the bill included the requirement of 'reasonable suspicion' in the exercise of arrest and search powers replacing 'suspicion' only in the 1978 Act, the reduction of the maximum period of detention without ministerial authority from seventy-two to forty-eight hours and the statutory right of access to a solicitor within forty-eight hours of arrest. Other changes included changing the onus of proof in applications for bail to the prosecution and increasing the safeguards with respect to the admissibility of confessions. It was to be made explicit that confessions obtained by the use or threat of violence were not admissible and that confessions could be excluded by a judge in the interests of justice.

Lest it be thought that the government had embraced a new-found liberalism, there were countervailing tendencies in the legislation. Peter Archer, the Labour spokesman, stated that Labour would not oppose the second reading given the positive elements outlined above, but would press for amendments in committee. Specific concerns included the change from biannual to annual renewal, the retention of detention on statute and the refusal to introduce three judges in 'Diplock' courts.[35] Subsequently, amendments were moved to remove detention powers, to limit remand to a total of 110 days and to increase the number of 'scheduled' offences which could be 'certified out'.[36] All of these were defeated and on 8 April 1987 the bill received an unopposed third reading.

The combination of (formally) increased safeguards for suspects and defendants with additional police powers emphasised the similarity with 'normal' legislation, such as the Police and Criminal Evidence Act 1984. Therefore, although the new Act was of five years' duration, there were indications of a trend towards permanence. Labour felt the government was overly cautious and over-reliant on security measures and voted against annual renewal for the rest of the 1980s. The government was criticised for consistently ignoring the concerns raised by the SACHR and specific disquiet focused on the retention of detention powers, the problem of lengthy remand, the lack of a plurality of judges and incursions upon the suspect's right of silence (see p. 61 below).

Detention powers had not been used since the mid-1970s as successive governments had endorsed the policy of 'criminalisation'. The problem of securing convictions through the courts had been made more difficult by the adverse publicity surrounding the interrogation of prisoners and the implementation of the Bennett report (see Chapter 2). These factors help to explain the emergence of the use of accomplice evidence on a large scale from 1981; commonly known as the 'supergrass' strategy. Although there was recent precedent in British law, there were crucial differences in the operation of such trials in Northern Ireland. First, the judge had a duty to warn the jury of the danger of convicting on the basis of uncorroborated evidence; in the absence of juries in 'Diplock' courts this resulted in the rather dubious practice of the judge warning himself. Secondly, the majority of convictions in Britain were obtained with corroborated evidence and in 1977 the DPP issued a directive that no more cases should be brought on uncorroborated 'supergrass' evidence. Thirdly, it appears that in only one case in England was immunity from prosecution granted; in other cases a reduced sentence was the incentive to provide evidence.

The origins of the policy in Northern Ireland are unclear. Nicholas Scott, Under-Secretary of State at the Northern Ireland Office, stated that there was no executive decision to encourage the use of accomplice evidence and that it was an operational decision by the RUC.[37] The RUC position was that it merely encouraged those willing to give evidence, although lawyers cited cases of their clients being pressurised to provide information and to provide the RUC with names of those it wanted brought to trial. The scale of the activity provokes scepticism about both of these official lines; between November 1981 and November 1983 at least twenty-five 'supergrasses' were responsible for the arrest of nearly 600 suspects.[38] This was unlikely to have happened without at least tacit approval from the Attorney-General or other members of the executive.

As well as the moral questions around immunity and whether credence could be given to the evidence of those with a vested interest in implicating others, the actual process of the trials brought the system into disrepute. The sheer number of defendants and charges and the corresponding length of trials raised the question of whether any testimony could be relied upon to recall all the details of specific cases.

In response to both judicial disquiet and civil liberties and other pressure group concerns, the government issued guidelines about aspects of the trials. In a Commons statement in October 1983, the Attorney-General stated that all decisions concerning immunity from prosecution were taken by the DPP, after consultation with the Chief Constable.[39] In practice, the role of the police must have been decisive since they were the only body capable of judging the potential of the accused as a 'supergrass.' Despite the claim that immunity was not sought for those accused or guilty of murder, immunity was granted much more freely than it had been in British cases.[40]

The problem of corroboration was not resolved. It would be extremely difficult to make corroborative evidence necessary for prosecution since the *raison d' être* of the 'supergrass' strategy was that other evidence was frequently not available. The presence of a jury might have provided some safeguard but their reintroduction was not on the agenda.

In his review of the EPA, Baker argued that uncorroborated evidence was acceptable since judges were competent to assess the credibility of 'supergrasses' and reasons had to be given for verdicts in Diplock courts. He believed that such trials were likely to be a passing phenomenon but that if they continued there should be a limit of twenty defendants per trial and that bail should be mandatory after twelve months. The use of 'supergrasses' peaked by 1983 and a series of cases collapsed after this date, although they were not abandoned until 1986. It seems many within the judicial system became increasingly concerned about the damage being done to the reputation of the system and the need to stress its independence from executive control helped to foster a more critical stance.[41]

At the same period as the 'supergrass' trials increasing concerns were raised about the summary killing of suspected Republicans, commonly known as 'shoot to kill' cases. The shooting of suspects when security personnel were not themselves at risk breached both criminal law and 'yellow card' directives for army operations. By the nature of such incidents it is virtually impossible to determine if such occurrences constituted a predetermined policy and if so at what level it was sanctioned. What is clear is that the later inquiry into the shooting of seven unarmed men in 1982 by the RUC carried out by John Stalker, Deputy Chief Constable of the Greater Manchester Police, was consistently obstructed by the RUC. Prior to the release of important evidence to Stalker, he was sent on 'extended leave' pending an inquiry into alleged misconduct and possible disciplinary proceedings arising from his conduct as Deputy Chief Constable.[42] Stalker believed that his suspension was wholly connected to the Northern Ireland inquiry. Although the inquiry was to continue under Colin Sampson, the Chief Constable of West Yorkshire, the removal of Stalker might have been in part a 'delaying tactic' at a time (early 1986) when the maintenance of RUC morale in face of anti-AIA protests was a governmental imperative. Sampson presented his report in March 1987 in which he found evidence of conspiracy to pervert the course of justice and obstruction of the police investigation and recommended criminal charges. In the event, no criminal proceedings were brought since this was deemed not to be in the public interest or the interests of national security.[43] This decision and the refusal to detail the national security issues involved reduced Anglo-Irish relations to their lowest point since the signing of the AIA.[44] In June 1988, the Police Authority decided by a majority of one that no disciplinary proceedings should be instituted against the Chief Constable and two chief officers concerning accusations of obstructionism during the Stalker inquiry and a separate investigation recommended disciplinary action against twenty lower ranking officers. In March 1989 this resulted in eighteen reprimands and one caution. If the Stalker inquiry did not prove conclusively that there was a policy of 'shoot to kill', the leakage of information from RUC stations to Loyalist paramilitaries and the involvement of UDR officers in sectarian attacks demonstrated a disturbing incidence of 'low level' malpractice and illegality among the security forces.[45]

In addition to the established legislation described above, there was a series of *ad hoc* responses in the late 1980s to the failure of existing policy to deal with the incidence of terrorism and the well-entrenched political support for Sinn Fein. On 12 October 1987 the NIO published a discussion paper, 'Elected Representatives and the Democratic Process in Northern Ireland'. This was a response to the problem posed by Sinn Fein participation in local councils. Unionists councillors had complained of the inconsistency, not to say hypocrisy, of the government which expected Northern Ireland representatives to discharge functions in the council chambers with Sinn Fein members when it refused to meet them itself. The government was also concerned that Sinn Fein members were free to express generalised support for the 'armed struggle'.

The paper considered four options: proscription of Sinn Fein; an oath of allegiance; extended disqualification for prospective council members with convictions; and a declaration eschewing violence as a condition of taking office. The preferred option was for the declaration and this was incorporated into the Elected Authorities (NI) bill which received its second reading on 5 December 1988. Clauses 3–7 contained the details of the declaration which was to cover candidates for assembly and district elections and those co-opted to fill vacancies. If elected, members were not to 'express support for or approval of proscribed organisations or acts of terrorism ... connected with the affairs of Northern Ireland'. Such support was to be a civil offence with a penalty of five years' disqualification.

Unionists wanted it to be a criminal offence as the civil nature put the onus on councillors to bring cases and this made them vulnerable to attack. Labour attacked the proposals as unnecessary and ill-conceived. It was feared that such legislation would have propaganda value for Sinn Fein and be presented as an attack on free speech and that it would have little practical effect in stopping support for the IRA.[46] Labour moved an amendment to oppose the declaration which was defeated. It abstained on the second and third readings because it supported other clauses of the bill which extended the district council franchise.

A second measure aimed at curtailing publicity for the Republican cause was the broadcasting ban on Sinn Fein announced in October 1988.

This seems to have resulted from a more direct involvement by the Prime Minister, Margaret Thatcher, in Northern Ireland policy in this period which provoked intra-governmental tensions. To formulate responses to Sinn Fein and the IRA, she utilised a highly restricted ministerial committee which led to differences with Douglas Hurd, the Home Secretary, who had reservations about the measure.[47] On 19 October Hurd issued a notice to the chairmen of the BBC and IBA requiring them to refrain from broadcasting direct statements by representatives of proscribed organisations and also by persons whose statements supported or invited support for these organisations. Hurd argued that this was justified because of the offence caused to viewers and because of the support and sustenance gained by terrorists from such broadcasts.

On 2 November a motion was presented to the Commons to approve the October directive. Hurd added to his arguments by claiming that fear was spread via such broadcasts but, as a concession to balance, the ban would be lifted for the duration of election campaigns and in parliamentary proceedings. Labour opposed the ban and Hattersley argued that it was incompatible with a free society and would be a propaganda coup for the terrorists rather than a frustration of them. Other Labour members saw the genesis of the measure in a combination of Thatcher's authoritarian instincts and the ill-conceived need to be seen to be doing something. A Labour amendment opposing the ban was defeated by 244 votes to 183 and the motion approved by 243 votes to 179.

The third measure entailed the restriction of the suspect's right to silence. This was contained in the Criminal Evidence (NI) Order 1988 introduced by Tom King on 8 November 1988. He stated that the right to silence was not to be removed but that the courts would be allowed 'in certain carefully defined circumstances to draw such inferences as would be proper from an accused's silence'.[48] Under the existing law the judge in a 'Diplock' court had to direct himself that he may not draw inferences from a suspect's silence even when an innocent person may reasonably be expected to protest his/her innocence or provide evidence in support of establishing his/her innocence. King argued that the change was justified in light of the 'deliberate and extreme exploitation' of the present position by suspects trained to refuse to answer questions and had to be set against the background of improved suspects' rights under the EPA 1987.

Four circumstances were outlined in which the judge would be permitted to draw inferences from the suspect's silence. First, if the suspect offered an explanation at trial when it might have been given at the initial questioning. Secondly, if the suspect refused to give evidence when the prosecution had established that there was a case to answer. Thirdly, if the accused refused to explain to the police specific details, such as marks on clothing and, lastly, if the accused refused to account for his/her presence at a particular place.

Labour opposition reflected its criticism of the other measures considered above, including an over-reliance of short-term legal measures which revealed a political bankruptcy. It also accused the government of inconsistency in that it argued that the change was necessary to deal with paramilitary activity and also that the measure was not exceptional as it was later to be extended to England and Wales. Members also expressed concern that there was a lack of convincing evidence that the right to silence was an important obstacle to the securing of confessions. Despite disquiet among some government backbenchers about the erosion of a long-standing common law right, the Order was approved by 274 to 210 with Labour opposing.

The final area of security policy worthy of attention is that of extradition. The Irish government had committed itself, at the time of the AIA, to acceding to the European Convention on the Suppression of Terrorism (ECST). It was assumed that this would make extradition of suspects to Northern Ireland easier, particularly as a Supreme Court ruling of 1985 had reversed the conclusion of the 1974 Law Enforcement Commission and found that it would be unconstitutional to exempt from extradition those charged with terrorist offences relating to Northern Ireland. The Republic signed the Convention on 24 February 1986 but it was not implemented until December 1987.

Although there had been a move away from rejecting the political offence immunity, extradition remained a politically sensitive issue particularly within the more pro-Republican Fianna Fail Party. While there does not appear to have been a formal *quid pro quo*, the Irish government had hoped that accession to the Convention would lead to reforms in the administration of justice in Northern Ireland, including three judges in 'Diplock' courts.

Extradition was the subject which caused the most acrimony between the two governments in the late 1980s. A series of failed extradition attempts owing to defective warrants and procedural irregularities in the British requests led to heated exchanges between law officers and politicians of the two countries, British attacks on the Republic's resolution and Irish resentment of the colonial high-handedness of British attitudes.[49]

It can be argued that tensions over extradition were out of proportion to the overall role it had to play in the anti-terrorist campaign and security policy. However, for the government, and particularly for some Conservatives and Unionists opposed to the AIA, it became the litmus test of the Irish government's commitment to defeat the IRA. For Thatcher herself, one of the main attractions of the AIA was hoped for improvements in inter-governmental security co-operation. However, there was a certain irony about British complaints to the Irish government about judicial decisions in the Republic when it was keen to invoke the separation between executive and judiciary when expedient.

Economic policy

The advent of a Conservative administration in May 1979 with an ideological hostility towards public expenditure, corporatist representation and to regional policy mechanisms in general had grave implications for the Northern Ireland economy and the policies of the Rees/Mason period. However, despite the abolition of the Regional Employment Premium in 1979, three years later than in Britain, there was evidence that the Conservatives accepted the need for public support for private capital both in expanding areas and those in decline. For example, financial support for DeLorean and Harland and Wolff was maintained and Northern Ireland was accepted as a special case in as much as financial incentives were higher than in assisted areas in Britain.[50]

The rapid decline in manufacturing jobs in the early 1980s helped to consolidate an increasing emphasis on support for the service sector and hi-tech industries. However, the service sector tended not to be as labour intensive as manufacturing industry and this would preclude abandoning attempts to attract investment for the latter sector. An unpublished review for the government by Arthur Andersen, the accountancy consultants, in 1979 considered that support for industry was 'broadly cost effective'.[51] Standard Capital Grants were available at 30 per cent compared with 22 per cent for Special Development Areas in Britain and approximately fifty measures, both financial and 'back up', were available in the form of selective assistance, which were usually negotiated by companies on an individual basis with the Department of Commerce.

If incentives to companies were 'broadly competitive with those available in other countries',[52] a possible area of reform was the institutional arrangements for support. Concerns had been expressed about whether sufficient co-ordination existed between the three agencies involved (Department of Commerce, NIDA, LEDU) which may have been informed by the perception that the Republic of Ireland, through the Industrial Development Authority, had greater success in promoting economic development and incoming investment.

Changes were resisted by government in 1980–81 as Giles Shaw, the minister responsible for industry, argued that the agencies were performing well. Other factors may have been that as devolution talks were in progress, the government wanted to await the outcome given that industrial support would be a transferred matter. It has also been suggested that the civil service feared that restructuring would weaken its influence in industrial policy and pressed the Department of Commerce to resist such changes.[53]

In the absence of major changes the government announced its intention to create a consultative forum to co-ordinate policy of the three agencies. Three other measures were announced. There was to be a change of emphasis in NIDA operations, which was to concentrate on industrial development promotion in growth and especially hi-tech sectors. Its 'rescue' function was to be assumed by the Department of Commerce. The second measure was an increase in promotional staff for the Department of Commerce with two more based in USA and one each in France and Germany. The third change was to expand the Department of Manpower Services to enable it to play a leading role in industrial retraining and offering support for managerial training schemes.

In 1982, however, institutional change took place following a steering group recommendation of the previous year. Under the Industrial Development (NI) Order, presented to Parliament in July 1982, the Industrial Development Board (IDB) was established. It was to replace the NIDA and the section of the Department of Commerce concerned with industrial development, and was to operate at 'arm's length' from ministerial control. To facilitate this it was empowered to allocate up to £3 million to any company in selective financial assistance without prior approval from the Ministry of Finance and Personnel (which controls departmental expenditure) and up to £2 million in miscellaneous provisions, such as equity stakes, training assistance and factory leasing. The composition of the board of the IDB was to reflect commercial criteria rather than corporatist representation. However, there still existed a possible tension between granting autonomy to development agencies and the need for government supervision of the allocation of public funds. As the IDB was part of the newly-created Department of Economic Development, doubts were expressed by the Chamber of Commerce and the Northern Ireland Economic Council as to how autonomous it would be and how much difference the new arrangements would make.[54]

Towards the end of 1982, Prior announced that the IDB was to have senior personnel allocated to four specific sectors: robotics; electronic office equipment; medical electronic equipment; and service sector equipment. This change was in response to the hoped for, yet so far largely unrealised, hi-tech diversification which various agencies and reports had endorsed. In March 1983, Prior announced a new set of measures to stimulate industrial development in an attempt to offset the effects of recession. Corporation tax reimbursement of up to 80 per cent was to be offered on approved projects. As a profit-related concession, it would only be available to companies which had achieved viability. It would be administered in the form of a grant, related to employment creation, since differential tax policy would breach the uniformity of the UK fiscal structure. Other measures included an increase from 75 per cent to 100 per cent de-rating on industrial premises, grants towards energy conservation projects in an attempt to offset Northern Ireland's higher energy costs and a new advisory service to provide information on improved production processes and research and development.

By the mid-1980s there was little scope for reorganisation of the IDB or for significantly increasing the financial incentives available; indeed, the standard capital grant was reduced to 20 per cent in March 1985 following a review by the Department of Economic Development. Therefore, the IDB concentrated on other ways to try to attract foreign investment. One example was the establishment of the 'Northern Ireland Partnership' in late 1983; an informal group of over one hundred companies and organisations which attempted to counter the 'image' problem of Northern Ireland which was considered to be a major barrier to attracting overseas investors. A second example was the attempt to attract investment from previously under-exploited sources, particularly Japan and Singapore, to offset the number of closures by American-controlled companies. A third element in the strategy was the emphasis put on the development of joint ventures and licensing agreements between Northern Ireland and foreign companies. This reflected the difficulty there had been in attracting fully-integrated productive units, as opposed to branch plants, to the province.

An IDB report of 1985 endorsed the strategy that had been indicated in Prior's announcement of 1982 (see p. 64 above) with an emphasis on hi-tech sectors, including electronics and information technology and medical care and technology, as offering the best prospects for future activity.[55] The report also endorsed a policy of offering support services to companies and trying to move away from an emphasis on the provision of capital investment. The section on inward investment echoed the concerns of earlier reports in that priority was to be given to those companies locating key 'back-up' functions along with manufacturing facilities in an attempt to avoid 'branch plant syndrome'.

General government concern with value for money and the targeting of incentives was reflected in the reduction in the rate of the standard capital grant from 20 per cent to 12.5 per cent in November 1987. Peter Viggers, the minister with responsibility for economic development, stated that the system of automatic grants had two principal disadvantages: it did not take into account the question of the relationship between investment and jobs created; and had a possible displacement effect in placing competitors of those in possession of standard capital grants at a disadvantage in local markets. Subsequently, in March 1988, the General Assistance Grants (Abolition) (NI) Order 1988 abolished the provision for standard capital grants.

The changing emphasis of IDB operations was revealed in evidence given by its chief executive to the Public Accounts Committee in 1989.[56] In the period 1982 to 1984 many of its operations were geared to helping companies survive in a period of recession, whereas in 1987–88 some 80–90 per cent of projects considered were concerned with the promotion and creation of new employment. What is difficult to gauge is whether this relative recovery reflected the increased effectiveness of the development agencies or the knock-on effect of the relative improvement in the UK economy. IDB performance indicators were somewhat imprecise but it seemed clear that the allocation of large monies to risky projects was a thing of the past.

Having considered changes in the structure and operation of the main support agency, the rest of this section will examine the role of LEDU, job creation measures, miscellaneous economic measures and conclude with a review of economic policy in the 1980s.

The remit of the LEDU was extended at the end of 1980 to allow it to offer assistance to the service sector; prior to this it had been limited to manufacturing or related industries. Two new measures were introduced to assist those who had been made redundant to start up small businesses. The Small Business Development Programme was introduced in October 1979 aimed at those with previous large company experience with up to 80 per cent start up costs available and, in 1981, a new enterprise grant was introduced aimed at the unemployed who had no previous experience. As well as an expanded remit, the annual job creation targets were expanded from between 1,000 and 1,200 to 4,000 in 1980–81. This was the result of an internal decision in the face of rapidly growing unemployment and one attractive to government as the cost-per-job figures were relatively low.[57] In late 1983, the Local Enterprise Programme (LEP) was established and administered by the LEDU. The programme aimed to establish enterprise agencies in each of the twenty-six district council areas. Their function was basically twofold: to provide start up units in the form of vacant industrial premises or by financing the construction of purpose built units; and to advise on business plans, accounting and other company needs. Up to 50 per cent of funding would be provided by LEDU and the remainder by the client company. Three further incentives were introduced in 1985 covering grants for property development, marketing schemes and ones to subsidise small firms' borrowing costs.

The trend in LEDU operation reflected that of the IDB in trying to identify areas with high growth potential and to focus on 'back up' support more than capital injections. In February 1988 the areas of computer software, business services, advanced telecommunications, franchising schemes and leisure/tourism were identified as those on which to concentrate and the five-year corporate plan of 1989 planned 10, 000 annual job promotions by 1994.[58]

The provision of industrial training schemes and courses broadly reflected UK policy as a whole, although it tended to be more extensive reflecting higher levels of unemployment. In autumn 1982, the Youth Training Scheme (YTS) was introduced to replace the Youth Opportunities Programme (YOPS) which had existed since 1977 and had provided places for 10,000 people. YTS was introduced a year earlier than in Britain and was to be more comprehensive. It attempted to find work experience/college places/apprenticeships for 16 and 17 year olds, whereas in Britain the emphasis had been on work experience.

To deal with the problem of the longer-term unemployed Action for Community Employment (ACE) was introduced in April 1981 as a supplement to the Enterprise Ulster (EU) programme established in 1973. It was to provide full- or part-time employment for those who had been unemployed for twelve of the previous fifteen months. The sponsor of a project, often a community group or voluntary body, would be provided with up to 90 per cent of its labour costs by government. By comparison with the YTS, which was ostensibly to have a training scheme, ACE was a straightforward job creation scheme typically offering environmental or building repair work. By 1984 over 9,000 adults were placed on ACE, EU or various training and management schemes, and the severity of the unemployment problem was indicated by the three-year extension of EU in March 1983 and a doubling in ACE expenditure between 1982–83 and 1983–84.[59] ACE continued to expand throughout the 1980s and by 1989 some 8,670 people were placed on its schemes. Concerns were raised about the lack of a training element to the jobs provided, for example, by the Northern Ireland Assembly Economic Development Committee, and the government launched an enterprise pilot scheme in 1987 to facilitate the move from ACE schemes to self-employment. Although the EU was extended for a further five years in 1986, subject to periodic review, ACE was the principal scheme providing between six and seven times the places of EU. This was principally because the cost-per-job figures were significantly lower for ACE projects.

Two areas of policy in this period indicate that Northern Ireland was not a 'place apart' when it came to economic policy (see p. 68 below for a further discussion). One was the introduction of two Enterprise Zones (EZs) in Belfast in July 1980 and a third in Derry in November 1982. EZs had been announced in the budget of March 1980 and were premised on the assumption that freedom from bureaucratic restriction would allow the flourishing of enterprise. Therefore, firms locating in such zones would be granted 100 per cent de-rating, be exempt from keeping statistics for government purposes and be subject to simplified planning procedures. Critics were sceptical about their likely impact on employment creation and this was borne out by a Department of Environment (NI) report of 1988 which concluded that much of the employment in the zones was the result of relocation rather than additional jobs.[60] However, there were advantages to be gained apart from employment creation and the report concluded that the 'zoning' of areas contributed to their environmental and infrastructural regeneration and provided a boost to the commercial property market.

A second policy marking a degree of congruence was that of privatisation. Harland and Wolff and Shorts, two of the province's most important manufacturing companies, had been in government ownership since 1975. The former had received subsidies of over £1 billion between 1975 and 1988 despite attempts to diversify production and the cutting of the workforce from 8,000 to 3,800 over the same period.[61] Although the rate of public support was declining, the government formally announced its decision to privatise Harland and Wolff in July 1988. The Select Committee on Trade and Industry endorsed the policy in early 1989 and, after abortive attempts, the yard was sold in March 1989. The sale involved further public expenditure as the government provided £60 million of loan stock, repayment terms related to performance, and £38.75 million in grants to facilitate further rationalisation. The government control invested in the Aircraft and Shipbuilding Industries (NI) Order 1979 was revoked.

Details of plans to privatise Shorts were also announced in 1988. Shorts had been losing money, facing severe international competition and its image in the USA market was not helped by accusations of discrimination in employment practices. Following the Trade and Industry report of 1989, the government took over responsibility for Shorts' debts to commercial banks in an attempt to expedite the sale of the company. In June 1989 Tom King approved the sale to Bombardier, a Canadian company. As with Harland and Wolff, the sale involved the writing-off of much public money and government responsibility under the 1979 Order was revoked.

The most notable features of the Northern Ireland economy in the 1980s were the steep rise in unemployment and retraction in manufacturing in the first half of the decade.[62] In this, economic trends were not dissimilar to the UK as a whole. However, while aspects of 'Thatcherite' policies were applied to the Northern Ireland economy the picture is somewhat contradictory.[63] Attempts to reduce the emphasis on capital support for companies (through the ending of standard capital grants), the 'targeting' of resources in 'inner cities', scepticism concerning economic planning, the introduction of enterprise zones and the promotion of small business are evidence that aspects of Thatcherite neo-liberalism were implemented in Northern Ireland. This strategy co-existed with a greater emphasis on public expenditure than in the rest of the UK. Much of the greater per capita expenditure in the 1980s is accounted for by the economic and social problems of the province, its demography and compensation for relative underspend in earlier periods. However, even allowing for this, Northern Ireland was generously treated in terms of public expenditure. More than one commentator has remarked on the persistence of Keynesianism within the province; indeed Prior, Secretary of State from 1981 to 1984, remarked that 'we are all Keynesians here',[64] and towards the end of the Thatcher administrations, a journalist referred to the 'Keynesian Republic' of Northern Ireland.[65] In particular areas, for example, housing in the early 1980s, public expenditure was relatively high and related to hoped for 'spin off' effects in terms of improvements in the security situation. While public expenditure is probably the most important example, the belated introduction of privatisation and legislation to curb trade union activity indicate that Northern Ireland policy diverged from that applied to Britain. The conclusion of Gaffikin and Morrissey that pragmatism and flexibility were features of the Thatcher agenda in Northern Ireland is well-founded.[66]

Social policy

For most of the period in question, there was little institutional or legislative change in this area. The principal development was the response to cumulative evidence that the legislation of 1976 and the operation of the Fair Employment Agency (FEA) had not eliminated Catholic disadvantage which resulted in new legislation and institutional change in 1989.

In January 1985 the SACHR, which like the FEA had complained of under-staffing and resourcing, decided to undertake a major review of the agencies and legislation designed to safeguard citizens against political and religious discrimination and to ensure equality of opportunity. The 1981 census and research by the FEA had indicated that the Catholic community still suffered disproportionately from higher unemployment, poor housing and lower living standards and these findings were endorsed by a Continuous Household Survey of 1985.

Pressure for change came from both internal and external sources. The FEA had expressed concern over underfunding and lobbies from the United States were important in encouraging the government to reconsider fair employment legislation. Pressure from the United States was largely based around the MacBride principles, formulated in 1984 under the patronage of Sean MacBride, former IRA leader, Irish Minister for Foreign Affairs and founder member of Amnesty International. The principles had nine clauses, including better monitoring of the workforce composition, affirmative measures to increase the representation of under-represented groups, timetables for affirmative action, the development of training programmes to increase minority recruitment and the banning of provocative sectarian or political symbols in the workplace.

There are two crucial points to note in considering the MacBride principles. Much debate focused upon whether they advocated 'positive' or 'reverse' discrimination which was contrary to British legislation. According to the FEA, the drafting of the principles was confused and ambiguous.[67] Secondly, opposition to the principles was often linked to the status of their advocates. The government and other opponents felt that much of the American lobby was less concerned with improving the situation in Northern Ireland than with embarrassing the British government as part of a pro-Republican withdrawal campaign.

The principal tactic employed by MacBride lobbyists in the USA was to encourage state legislatures to pass legislation under which public and institutional investment funds would be invested in companies which embraced the principles, including their subsidiaries in Northern Ireland, and by 1989 thirteen states had taken such a course.

Although it was reported that Rhodes Boyson, Minister for Economic Development, initially supported the principles to demonstrate government commitment to fair employment, it was to launch a vigorous campaign against them.[68] Ministers and officials claimed that the principles advocated policies which contravened the 1976 Act and that they would be a deterrent to investors.

The American pressure was important in concentrating the government's mind and forcing it to formulate alternatives.[69] External pressure also came from the Irish government via the Anglo-Irish Conference. Along with the administration of justice, fair employment was one of the most frequently discussed topics, although Dublin did not present proposals of its own but was critical in the delay in firm proposals emanating from the British government.

To turn from the background of political pressure to the evolution of legislation. In September 1986 the Department of Economic Development (DED) published a discussion paper, 'Equality of opportunity in employment in Northern Ireland: future strategy options'. The main proposals were the advocacy of stronger affirmative action, the introduction of contract compliance possibly through the use of financial sanctions, a merger of existing agencies in the field of equal opportunities and the establishment of a government unit staffed by civil servants to promote equality of opportunity outside the structure of any new fair employment body.

These proposals went some way to addressing the problems of the 1976 legislation. These included the voluntary nature of staff monitoring, the lack of clarity about whether affirmative action was legal and if so, which forms of it and the lack of government sanctions against transgressors of those who breached equal opportunity codes. The FEA itself welcomed the possibility of contract compliance, a more effective Declaration of Intent and a new appeals procedure for individual cases. It expressed reservations about the government unit given the civil service's poor record in promoting equal opportunities and the proposed merger of agencies.

New legislation was unlikely to emerge quickly as the SACHR report was not due until 1987 and the government was keen to undergo a long consultation period with interested parties in Northern Ireland and build a bipartisan approach at Westminster. Interim measures announced in 1987 included a revamped guide for employers issued by the DED and an increase in funding for the FEA of just over 30 per cent and an increase in full-time staff from twenty to thirty-one.[70]

The SACHR report was published in October 1987 after two years in preparation. It reviewed the failings of the FEA, particularly in respect of the lack of employers' knowledge of the 'Guide to Manpower Policy and Practice', and the weakness of the Declaration of Principle and Intent. The merging of agencies and the establishment of a government unit as recommended by the DED paper were rejected and it was criticised for failing to consider the setting of targets and timetables and the use of affirmative action at the point of selection.

There were a total of 123 recommendations and only the principal ones will be highlighted here. Quotas and reverse discrimination were rejected. Indirect discrimination should be prohibited and targets for more equal representation in the workforce and timetables to achieve this should be encouraged as a way to evaluate affirmative action initiatives. Organisations on the register of holders of a revised Declaration of Practice would receive a certificate of three years' duration and renewal would be dependent on the monitoring of the workforce's religious composition in an attempt to avoid the failings of the previous system. Government grants and contracts should be limited to subscribers to the Declaration.

A new agency should replace the FEA. It would retain the power of company and sector investigations and research. It was recommended that individual cases of discrimination should be considered by industrial tribunals with the commission (the suggested title of the new body) empowered to assist complainants. This would avoid the potential conflict of interest whereby the FEA had brought complaints and also adjudicated in cases.

The report endorsed an emphasis on voluntary action to improve equality of opportunity with legal sanctions as a last resort, which marked a continuity with procedure established in 1976. The new body was to have the same committee structure as the FEA, and include employer and trades union representation. It was suggested that budget and staffing arrangements be removed from joint control of the Departments of Finance and Personnel and the DED and placed with the NIO. Other agencies, including LEDU and IDB, should improve the monitoring of the implications of their policies for equal opportunity.

The White Paper, 'Fair Employment in Northern Ireland' (Cmd 380) was published in May 1988. It was speculated that publication was brought forward in an attempt to placate the Republic after the strains of the Stalker affair and the refusal to reconsider the convictions of the 'Birmingham Six', although this was denied by Peter Viggers, the minister presenting the paper.[71] The preamble accepted the existence of discrimination, although it was argued that it was not the main reason for employment differentials. The use of quotas was ruled out and the merit principle was to remain paramount. The separation of individual case investigation and pattern/practice cases was endorsed; the former being the responsibility of a separate division of existing industrial tribunals and the latter being the principal role of the putative Fair Employment Commission.

Indirect discrimination was to be made illegal and to evaluate companies' progress in achieving more balanced workforces monitoring was essential. Therefore, employers with more than ten employees (twenty-five in the first two years of the legislation) were obliged to monitor annually the composition of their workforce and to submit returns to the commission. The most important factor in combating indirect discrimination was affirmative action defined as 'special measures taken to promote a more representative distribution of employment in the workforce and designed to give all sections of the community full and equal access to employment opportunities.'[72] Examples included outreach schemes, less informal recruitment, more schools used by employers for recruitment and a ban on flags and emblems in the workplace.

A code of practice was to be prepared by the commission. This would be a source of information for employers and a basis on which the commission could draw up voluntary undertakings for employers and impose directives for affirmative action. It would also be a guide for the tribunal in cases of individual discrimination and in appeals or enforcing orders of compliance from the commission. The code would be voluntary but measures would have statutory effect if incorporated by the commission into a directive.

The code would be prepared initially by the DED, considered in draft by Parliament in the forthcoming legislation and subject to revision by the commission once in operation. Areas covered would include, *inter alia*, the definition of key concepts, a summary of employer responsibilities, examples of good practice in recruitment and promotion procedures, illustrations of how indirect discrimination could be avoided and the reasons for the need for monitoring.

Failure to register with and to submit monitoring returns to the commission would be a criminal offence. On registration an organisation would be entitled to receive a certificate of co-operation which would be held unless it was found to be in breach of statutory obligations, *viz.* failing to submit or update monitoring returns or failing to comply with directives issued by the commission. A breach of the employers' duties would be a criminal offence; if directives were not complied with the commission could apply to the High Court for a contempt ruling which could result in fines or committal. Further penalties included the withholding of grants and contracts from companies which had lost certification.

The White Paper proposals were debated on 1 July 1988. Labour was critical of government policy arguing that the proposals were weaker than those recommended by the SACHR and that the government was not committed to the principles of fair employment but was largely responding to American pressure. Kevin McNamara outlined a series of criticisms, including that the concepts of merit and indirect discrimination were inadequately defined, affirmative action was too restrictive and weak, the code of practice was not included in primary legislation and could not, therefore, be scrutinised in committee and many agencies would be exempt from grant and contract compliance. The second reading of the Fair Employment (NI) Bill was given on 31 January 1989. Concerns expressed by employers, some of the Conservative Party and civil servants had led to the bill being 'watered down' compared with the White Paper provisions.[73] Labour was to register its dissatisfaction by moving an amendment to deny the bill a second reading. This was defeated and Labour opposed the second reading which was passed by 272 votes to 192.

Labour concerns, supported by the SDLP and various non-governmental organisations (NGOs), were varied. As the code of practice had not been included in the legislation, there were important matters of detail that could not be discussed including the definition of affirmative action, contract compliance and the operation of tribunals. Other concerns included the failure of the bill to impose a positive duty on employers to pursue equality in employment, inadequate redress for individuals discriminated against and that the commission would be the responsibility of the DED. Given the latter's close relationship with employers it was felt that this could lead to a conflict of interest.

After long and often acrimonious committee sessions, Labour supported the third reading on 25 May 1989. Improvements in committee which had allowed Labour support included clarification that affirmative action would not be subject to charges of reverse discrimination and would, therefore, be legal, the strengthening of goals and timetables and increased levels of compensation for individuals who were victims of discrimination. Tensions still existed between the two main parties after amendments introduced in the Lords were approved by the Commons in late July. The legislation was to take effect from January 1990 and the new Fair Employment Commission would replace the FEA at the same time.

Within a very complex area, broad divisions existed as the Conservatives were keen that legislation should not be used as a precedent for other anti-discrimination legislation within Britain and that employers should not be subject to continuous legal interference. Labour, generally, favoured a wider reading of what could constitute affirmative action and a less 'minimalist' approach to equal opportunity. These positions tended to reflect ideological divisions concerning the legitimacy or otherwise of intervention in the labour market and differences over whether equality should be a mainly procedural concept or involve substantive outcomes which should be the subject of targets.

Conclusion

The decade of the 1980s marked the gradual, and often acrimonious, shift towards the embedding of a bilateral approach to the issue of Northern Ireland. Although the Irish and British governments often put quite different complexions upon the process, it is instructive to compare the degree of scepticism about such a process at the beginning of the 1980s within much of the Conservative Party with the extent to which the legitimacy of the involvement of the Republic had become accepted in the early 1990s. Therefore, the 1980s can be seen as a period in which the salience of alternatives to bilateralism became increasingly marginal.

Notes

1 A. Guelke, 'The American connection to the Northern Ireland conflict', *Irish Studies in International Affairs* 11(1), 1984, p. 36. See also, P. Bew, P. Gibbon and H. Patterson, *Northern Ireland 1921–1994: Political Forces and Social Classes* (London, Serif, 1995), pp. 205–6.
2 Four MPs were not members of one of the four parties invited and Atkins undertook to accept written submissions from them and other individuals and organisations.
3 'The Government of Northern Ireland: a working paper for a conference', Cmnd 7763, 1979.
4 'The Government of Northern Ireland: proposals for further discussion', Cmnd 7950, 1980.
5 HC debates: vol. 988, cols 570–3, 9 July 1980.
6 The ideas of this group are discussed in M. Cunningham, 'Conservative dissidents and the Irish question: the "pro-integrationist" lobby 1973–94', *Irish Political Studies* 10, 1995.
7 Ten Republican hunger-strikers had died; the last in August. The SDLP did not contest the elections in which Bobby Sands and his election agent Carron were elected as anti H Block/political prisoner candidates which worsened relations with Unionists. For an account of the period see L. Clarke, *Broadening the Battlefield: the H-blocks and the Rise of Sinn Fein* (Dublin, Gill and Macmillan, 1987).
8 For Prior's formulation of the concept see HC debates: vol. 21, col. 692, 5 April 1982.
9 The Irish dimension in the White Paper had been 'watered down' because of pressure from Thatcher and Hailsham (J. Prior, *A Balance of Power* (London, Hamish Hamilton, 1986), p. 197).
10 *Fortnight* 188, October 1982; Scott HC debates: vol. 22, col. 931, 28 April 1982.
11 The SDLP received 18.8 per cent and the Workers' Party 2.7 per cent of the vote.

12 For more details see A. Greer 'The Northern Ireland assembly and account-ability of government: the statutory committees 1982–86'. *Parliamentary Affairs* 40(1), 1987 and C. O'Leary, S. Elliott and R. Wilford, *The Northern Ireland Assembly 1982–1986: a Constitutional Experiment* (London, C. Hurst, 1988).

13 'Report drawn up on behalf of the Political Affairs Committee on the situation in Northern Ireland'. Haagerup (Rapporteur), European Parliament working document 1–1526, 1983.

14 This theme is explored in J. Ruane and J. Todd, *The Dynamics of Conflict in Northern Ireland: Power, Conflict and Emancipation* (Cambridge, Cambridge University Press, 1996), ch. 10.

15 Cited in B. Girvin, 'The Anglo-Irish Agreement 1985', in B. Girvin and R. Sturm (eds), *Politics and Society in Contemporary Ireland* (Aldershot, Gower, 1986), p. 157.

16 Arthur Aughey cites Robert Blake's view that the Conservative Party can be regarded as the party of English nationalism which may help to explain the limits of Thatcher's empathy with Ulster unionism (A. Aughey, 'The party and the Union', in P. Norton (ed.), *The Conservative Party* (Hemel Hempstead, Harvester Wheatsheaf, 1996), p. 225). Garret Fitzgerald also remarks on the English nationalism of Thatcher in *All in a Life* (Dublin, Gill and Macmillan, 1991), p. 568.

17 See Bew *et al., Northern Ireland*, p. 211.

18 Both Hurd, who replaced Prior in September 1984, and Goodall had come from the Foreign Office. Unionists had long suspected the Foreign Office of pushing a pro-united Ireland agenda to curry favour with the USA.

19 Thatcher records that King, Howe and Hurd were sympathetic to the three judge idea but the Northern Ireland judiciary was opposed and she supported the latter (M. Thatcher, *The Downing Street Years* (London, HarperCollins, 1993), p. 405).

20 'Agreement between the Government of the United Kingdom of Great Britain and Northern Ireland and the Government of the Republic of Ireland', Cmnd 9657, 1985.

21 Cox argues that the position of Dublin can best be described as, 'considerably less than joint sovereignty but definitely more than "mere" consultation'. W. H. Cox, 'Managing Northern Ireland intergovernmentally: an appraisal of the Anglo-Irish Agreement', *Parliamentary Affairs* 40(1), 1987 p. 91. A useful discussion is to be found in B. O'Leary, 'The Anglo-Irish Agreement: folly or statecraft?' *West European Politics* 10(1), 1987. See also B. O'Leary, 'The Anglo-Irish Agreement: meanings, explanations, results and a defence', in P. Teague (ed.), *Beyond the Rhetoric: Politics, the Economy and Social Policy in Northern Ireland* (London, Lawrence and Wishart, 1987) and M. Connolly and J. Loughlin, 'Reflections on the Anglo-Irish Agreement', *Government and Opposition* 21(2), 1986.

22 Haughey, the Fianna Fail leader, denounced it but undertook to operate the AIA given its widespread support in the Irish Republic.

23 B. O'Leary, 'The Anglo-Irish Agreement: folly or statecraft?', pp. 15–16. Bew *et al.*, argue that retaining the support of the USA was one of Thatcher's central concerns, *Northern Ireland*, p. 213.

24 For details of Unionist opposition and politics in this period see A. Aughey, *Under Siege: Ulster Unionism and the Anglo-Irish Agreement* (London, Hurst, 1989) and F. Cochrane, *Unionist Politics and the Politics of Unionism since the Anglo-Irish Agreement* (Cork, Cork University Press, 1997).

25 For more details and a critique see P. Bew and P. Dixon, 'Labour party policy and Northern Ireland', in B. Barton and P. Roche (eds), *The Northern Ireland Question: Perspectives and Policies* (Aldershot, Avebury, 1994).

26 The most frequently discussed topics were those of security, upon which the British government tended to place emphasis, and the administration of justice in the North and public confidence in it which was a perennial concern of the Republic's representatives. Other topics which featured regularly were fair employment and anti-discrimination measures, economic co-operation and the possibility of a Bill of Rights for Northern Ireland.

27 At the 1981 Labour Party conference there were fifty-eight resolutions and amendments concerning Northern Ireland; the highest number ever.

28 'Review of the operation of the Prevention of Terrorism (Temporary Provisions) Act 1976' Cmnd 8803, HMSO, London, 1983.

29 HC debates: vol. 38, col. 573, 7 March 1983.

30 HC debates: vol. 47, col. 56, 24 October 1983.

31 See, for example, 5th Annual Report, 1979–80, HC 433 and 6th Annual Report, 1980–81, HC 143. Detention powers were allowed to lapse in 1980 but remained on the statute book.

32 'Review of the Northern Ireland (Emergency Provisions) Act 1978', Cmnd 9222, 1984.

33 Long periods of remand were often viewed as a form of 'backdoor' detention; a view with which Baker had some sympathy (Baker report, para. 174).

34 For a comparison with legal developments in the UK as a whole see J. Jackson, 'The Northern Ireland (Emergency Provisions) Act', *Northern Ireland Legal Quarterly* 39(3), 1988.

35 Additional concerns raised by the SACHR included the lack of clarification of what constituted reasonable force in the use of firearms by the security forces, the failure to restrict arrest powers to reasonable suspicion of involvement in a scheduled offence and the failure to consolidate emergency powers into one Act (13th report, 1986–87, HC 298, 1987).

36 The last of these was introduced by Powell, the Ulster Unionist MP.

37 T. Gifford, *Supergrasses: The use of Accomplice Evidence in Northern Ireland* (London, Cobden Trust, 1984), p. 10.

38 S. Greer, 'Supergrasses: a coda', *Fortnight* 249, 1987, p. 7.

39 HC debates: vol. 47, cols 3–5, 24 October 1983.

40 The SACHR recommended that all arrangements regarding immunity or financial inducements should be disclosed to the defence before the trial since these terms were material to the credibility of the evidence given (10th Report, 1983–84, HC 175).

41 S. Greer, 'Supergrasses', p. 8.

42 Stalker's own account is *Stalker* (London, Harrap, 1988). See also P. Taylor, *Stalker* (London, Faber and Faber, 1987).

43 This announcement was made by Attorney-General, Patrick Mayhew. As a result his later appointment as Secretary of State for Northern Ireland was viewed with unease by Nationalists.

44 As Secretary of State Tom King admitted (*Financial Times* 3 February 1988).

45 See Chapter 4 for the results of the Stevens report into leaks of information from RUC stations.

46 Soliciting support for proscribed organisations was already an offence under the EPA but charges were rarely brought.

47 *Guardian*, 16 December 1988.

48 HC debates: vol. 140, col. 183, 8 November 1988.

49 See P. Bew and G. Gillespie, *Northern Ireland,* pp. 221–2.

50 Although such support was based upon expected production from DeLorean in early 1981 and planned diversification at Harland and Wolff.

51 Evidence of Butler, Minister of State, to Industry and Trade Committee, 7th report, 'Government support for Trade and Industry in Northern Ireland'. HC 500, 398 (I) and (ii), 1982, para. 2.

52 Shaw, Minister of State, HC debates: vol. 952, col. 191, 1 April 1980.

53 S. Harvey and D. Rea, *The Northern Ireland Economy with Particular Reference to Industrial Development* (Newtownabbey, Polytechnic Innovation and Resource Centre, Ulster Polytechnic, 1982), p. 89.

54 The Order also merged the Department of Manpower Services with the Department of Commerce to form the Department of Economic Development.

55 IDB, 'Encouraging Enterprise: a medium term strategy for 1985–1990', Belfast, 1985.

56 Committee of Public Accounts, 'Matters relating to Northern Ireland', HC 230, 1989.

57 Job creation per annum reached just over 4,000 in 1984–85 at a cost of approximately £4,600 per job (HC debates: vol. 81, col. 417, 26 June 1985).

58 For comparison job promotions were 4,381, 4,543, 4,570 and 5,004 for the years 1985–86 to 1988–89, respectively (LEDU annual report, 1988–89).

59 Northern Ireland annual abstract of statistics (Department of Finance and Personnel), Belfast, 1986, table 10:4. HC debates: vol. 53, col. 816, 10 February 1984.

60 'An evaluation of the Enterprise Zone experiment in Northern Ireland', DOE, Belfast, 1988, p. 65.

61 *Financial Times* 1 July 1988, p. 7; *The Economist* 26 November 1988, p. 39. The degree of subsidy provoked resentment among British shipbuilders. A Ministry of Defence contract worth £160 million won by Harland and Wolff in 1986 was described as appeasement of Loyalist terrorism by Swan Hunter representatives (*Fortnight* 238, May 1986, p. 14).

62 Unemployment was approximately 10 per cent in 1979 and had reached 21. 2 per cent by 1985 ('Northern Ireland annual abstract of statistics', table 10:8, Belfast, 1986 and HC debates: vol. 74, col. 1155, 7 March 1985). Manufacturing employment fell from 145,520 in 1979 to 101,310 in 1987 (F. Gaffikin and M. Morrissey, *Northern Ireland: the Thatcher Years* (London, Zed Books, 1990), p. 55).

63 This is not intended to imply that some 'pure' neo-liberal economic revolution was instigated in the rest of the UK.

64 Cited in S. Weir, 'The Keynesians across the water', *New Society*, 9 June 1983, p. 384.

65 Ian Aitken cited in Gaffikin and Morrissey, *Northern Ireland*, p. 35.

66 Gaffikin and Morrissey, *Northern Ireland*, p. 62; see also pp. 204–5.

67 FEA 10th report, 1985–86, HC 246, 1987.

68 *Fortnight* 257, December 1987, pp. 15–16.

69 *Fortnight* 257; R. Rowthorn and N. Wayne, *Northern Ireland: the Political Economy of Conflict* (Cambridge, Polity Press, 1988), p. 130.

70 SACHR, 'Religious and political discrimination and equality of opportunity in Northern Ireland. Report on fair employment', Cmd 237, 1987.

71 *Financial Times* 6 February 1988, p. 5.

72 'Fair Employment in Northern Ireland', Cmd 380, 1988, para. 3:16.

73 R. Jay and R. Wilford, 'An end to discrimination? The Northern Ireland Fair Employment Act of 1989', *Irish Political Studies* 6, 1991, p. 27.

4

The Major administration, 1990–92

Introduction

The advent to the premiership of John Major in November 1990 seemed to herald the possibility of political progress. The failure of the Unionist attacks on the Anglo-Irish Agreement over the previous five years, the political demise of Mrs Thatcher, under whom it had been implemented and John Hume's dogged attempts to wean Sinn Fein from support for violence indicated the possibility of movement. Major himself felt that continued violence was unacceptable and, from early in his administration, made Northern Ireland one of his top priorities.[1]

Constitutional policy

The broad parameters of government policy, and that of the opposition, can be gleaned from the debate on the renewal of direct rule in early July 1990.[2] Peter Brooke emphasised that the Anglo-Irish Agreement could be replaced if something better were to be found and he outlined two reasons of principle for attempts at progress: the lack of local democracy; and the hoped for reconciliation through local political accommodation. One dissenting voice was Ian Gow, who adhered to the increasingly marginal idea of administrative devolution via regional councils which Neave had advocated in the late 1970s. The Labour opposition was broadly supportive of the government. McNamara, the chief spokesman, concurred about the democratic limitations of direct rule and that the Anglo-Irish Agreement could be transcended or supplanted.

In the debate Brooke stated that 'no agreement on any one aspect would be reached unless and until all parties were finally satisfied with the whole of what might emerge from such a dialogue'. This formulation, later reworked as 'nothing is agreed until everything is agreed', was designed to ensure that parties could not focus solely on particulars central to their concerns and frustrate parts of an envisaged settlement considered essential by ideological adversaries. By the end of 1990, the government had emphasised the other elements of its policy. In a speech on 9 November, which one commentator has described as 'one of the most significant speeches on Ireland made by any British politician since 1968 (if not long before)', Brooke emphasised the legitimacy of the Republican tradition.[3] This was to signal to Sinn Fein, in the light of the Hume–Adams discussions and recent government contacts with the IRA via intermediaries, that if violence were foresworn the party could be included in talks and that the government had no ideological predisposition towards unionism. The declaration that 'the British Government has no selfish strategic or economic interest in Northern Ireland: our role is to help, enable and encourage' served a similar purpose.[4] This claim was to be repeated in similar formulations throughout the decade in an attempt to convince Sinn Fein of Britain's neutrality (in which Hume believed) in relation to Ireland and that policy would be informed by a benign agnosticism.

It would be overly crude to reduce all governmental statements, declarations and policy documents to a simple 'balancing act' but a major objective of policy was to address adequately the concerns of both principal communities to entice them into the process of dialogue. In an effort to reassure Unionists and their representatives the government held out the possibility of the superseding of the Anglo-Irish Agreement, as noted above, with a new agreement which they could help to construct. Their position would also be bolstered by the government's commitment to the Northern majority consent principle, that is, that there would be no change to the constitutional status of Northern Ireland without the consent of the majority of its people. It should be noted in passing that unionism tended to be divided over whether or to what extent faith could be invested in governmental reassurances and what changes consistent with this principle would be acceptable.

Progress proved to be slow as the constitutional parties considered and refined their positions in relation to the 'three strands' concept. The British government argued that no settlement was likely to be stable and durable unless it addressed three strands. 'Strand one' covered relations and related structures within Northern Ireland, 'strand two' covered relations and possible structures between Northern Ireland and the Republic (or North/South structures) and 'strand three' the relations between the Irish Republic and the United Kingdom (or the east/west relationship). This formulation is important for two reasons. First, it was to form the basic framework on which subsequent initiatives of the 1990s would be built and secondly, it further reinforced the marginalisation of 'internal' or 'integrationist' prescriptions for Northern Ireland and, as such, could be read as an implicit acceptance of a Nationalist agenda.

The potential and actual areas for disagreement were numerous. They included, *inter alia*, nationalist suspicions that Unionists would wish to focus on the internal dimension and downgrade the all-Ireland one, disputes over when in the process the Irish government should be involved and the length of the period between meetings of the intergov-ernmental conference (IGC) in which talks could take place. The IGC meetings 'gap' was a concession to Unionists who had shifted from an earlier position of no talks without the abolition of structures established in 1985.

Following bilateral meetings between the NIO and the Northern Ireland parties throughout much of 1990, Brooke announced a timetable for talks to the Commons on 26 March 1991, later than had been envisaged.[5] A period of ten weeks from mid-April had been set aside in which the IGC would not meet. In the event, substantive issues such as the form and content of the three strands did not progress as procedural wrangles over the location of talks, at what stage representatives of the Irish government could join and the identity of the chair of the second strand predominated. Allied to these difficulties was the Unionist demand that Articles 2 and 3 of the Irish Constitution should be repealed as a sign of good faith prior to substantive issues, while the Irish government saw such a change as possible only within the context of an overall settlement. The first plenary session did not take place until 17 June and on 2 July the process, such as it was, was suspended. An IGC was due on 16 July and the two govern-ments refused to reschedule it and allow 'injury time' in the talks process, which the Unionists favoured as so much of the ten weeks had been taken up in procedural questions.

There was no substantial movement before the British general election of April 1992. In late 1991 and early 1992 Brooke remained 'upbeat' about the potential for progress. At the time this appeared to be the ritu-alised optimism of successive Secretaries of State; however, this period had marked the emergence of unionism from simple 'oppositionism' after the Anglo-Irish Agreement and, however tentative, the start of a process of inter-party discussion. In March 1992 Brooke reaffirmed the principal parameters of government policy including the 'nothing is agreed until everything is agreed' formulation and the inadequacies of an approach which focused only on the internal dimension. McNamara indicated the maintenance of a bipartisan approach and a commitment, in the event of a Labour victory, to 'reconvene the talks on exactly the same basis as they had been taking place before the election'.[6] Although Labour supported Irish unification as a long-term aim, a future Labour Secretary of State would not seek to impose his/her own agenda on to the talks process.

Security policy

The legislative framework of anti-terrorist activity at the beginning of the 1990s was the Northern Ireland (Emergency Provisions) Acts 1978 and 1987 and the Prevention of Terrorism (Temporary Provisions) Act 1989. In March 1990 these acts were renewed by Order for another year.

Labour opposed this renewal on the grounds that its two guiding principles in relation to 'emergency' legislation had not been respected. These
were that no power should be retained unless the case for it were clearly
established and that the Acts should be reviewed in the context of the
general body of law, both emergency and ordinary. Despite opposition,
Labour did not question the need for extraordinary legislation. Disputes
with government in the early 1990s often centred on what was perceived
as its cavalier dismissal of Labour concerns and disagreements over
particular clauses; for example internment remained on the statute book
and could be reactivated by the Secretary of State. The government
defended its retention as a reserve power whereas Labour argued for its
abolition.

Similar positions were struck over new legislation which received its
second reading in November 1990. The Northern Ireland (Emergency
Provisions) Bill was to re-enact, with amendments, the earlier versions of
the Act and incorporate Part (vi) of the PTA. This partial merger was
recommended by Viscount Colville in his report of early 1990 which
favoured a consolidation of anti-terrorist legislation for Northern Ireland,
as did the 1989–90 annual report of the SACHR. The legislation, as with
its predecessor, was to be subject to annual renewal and be of five years'
duration. Many of the provisions were simple re-enactments of sections
from preceding legislation. These included the retention of 'Diplock'
courts, the list of 'scheduled' offences to be tried in them, restrictions on
bail, detailing of police and army search powers, a list of proscribed
organisations and the penalties for membership of, support for and
providing information to these organisations.

Three new provisions were introduced. It was to become an offence to
be in possession of items intended for terrorist use, although the items
might be innocuous in themselves. The bypassing or re-opening of closed
border crossings was to become an offence; it already being one to interfere with a closed border crossing. Thirdly, security forces were given
the explicit right to look for information of possible use to terrorists.

Despite accepting the need for emergency legislation, the Labour Party
opposed the second reading. McNamara outlined seven criticisms which
informed its decision. The power of detention without trial was maintained, videotaping of suspects' interviews was rejected, the right to
silence of suspects was curtailed and 'certifying in' was rejected.[7]
Additionally, there was no ombudsman for complaints against the security
forces, the SACHR had no statutory duty to supervise such legislation
and public immunity certificates were too readily issued which prevented
examination of discriminatory practices.[8]

The fact that Viscount Colville had endorsed most of these points
bolstered Labour's position. In addition, it criticised the government for
failing to comply with the European Convention on Human Rights' posi-

tion over seven-day detention (the maximum permitted under the PTA), for maintaining the use of exclusion orders and failing to deal with controversies of deaths caused by security forces. One concern in the last of these, highlighted by the SACHR, is that manslaughter could not be brought in such cases; the alternative was usually dismissal of the case or a conviction for murder which juries might be loathe to return.

Replying for the government, Minister of State John Cope argued that detention powers should remain on the statute book since, if needed, the element of surprise would be lost if new legislation had to be introduced. Under the existing legislation and the government's proposals, the power could be activated and then approved by Parliament within forty sitting days. Videotaping was rejected on the grounds that the tapes could fall into the wrong hands and, therefore, their introduction would inhibit possible co-operation of interviewees and suspects.

A Labour amendment was defeated and the second reading given by 234 votes to 113. On 6 March 1991 the committee stage was completed and the third reading given. Building on provisions of the 1989 PTA aimed at terrorist financing, new clauses were introduced which granted investigative powers for non-police officers, for example, financial specialists, and allowed the confiscation of money and goods of 'terrorist financiers' (money launderers). Labour supported the principle and wanted it introduced into general law but Brooke argued that the provisions relied on the concept of scheduled offences and were thus restricted to Northern Ireland. A clause to introduce an Army ombudsman, in line with Colville's recommendation and endorsed by the SACHR, was accepted in principle by the government and would allow an independent element into the armed forces' procedures for handling complaints falling short of the criminal. Other minor amendments were defeated and Labour abstained on the third reading having registered its reservations at earlier stages of the bill's passage. However, five Labour members, Bob Cryer, Jeremy Corbyn, Dennis Canavan, Dave Nellist and Dennis Skinner, did oppose the legislation which came into force in late August 1991.

The PTA of 1989 was of infinite duration but still subject to annual renewal. In the 1991 Order Labour was to oppose its continuation. The two principal concerns were the powers of detention which allowed a suspect to be held for a maximum of seven days with no judicial intervention or review and the maintenance of exclusion orders. In addition to these concerns, Hattersley, the shadow Home Secretary, called for tougher provisions affecting terrorist finance, consideration of a national intelligence agency to combat terrorism and the video-recording of all interviews in custody. Barry Sheerman summarised for the Labour front bench thus, 'we shall vote against the prevention of terrorism Act not merely because it does not work and because it undermines the quality of justice in this country. . . but because it feeds terrorism and gives ammunition with which to win support at home and abroad.'[9] He concluded by claiming that Labour's offer of a complete review of terrorist legislation on a cross-party basis was rejected by the government. The motion to approve renewal was carried by 303 votes to 138.

The renewal debate of 24 February 1992, witnessed similar arguments; one of the contributors noting a feeling of *déjà vu*.[10] If the substance remained the same, the tone of the debate had become more confrontational and combative with one Conservative backbencher describing Labour policy as 'absolutely contemptible', while Clare Short accused the Conservatives of playing cheap party games. Hattersley again called for all-party discussions on the legislation and John Patten announced one reform; a tribunal to review the extension of periods of detention. In effect, the chair of the tribunal would be in an executive position since information, owing to its sensitivity, would not be disclosed to the detainees or their legal advisers. The PTA was renewed by 300 votes to 115 with Labour opposing.

The principal operational change of this period was the merging of the UDR with the Royal Irish Rangers to form the Royal Irish Regiment in July 1992. The UDR had long been seen as a sectarian force by the majority of the Nationalist community, and its reputation was further undermined by collusion with Loyalist paramilitaries. In May 1990 Brooke had told the Commons that as a result of the Stevens report ninety-four arrests had been made and fifty-nine officers charged. The report identified deficiencies in procedures for identifying and accounting for documents containing sensitive information and in the recruitment procedures of the UDR. The leaking of sensitive information to paramilitaries was officially ascribed to the misbehaviour of a few individuals and not an institutional problem.

Economic and social policy

With respect to economic policy the principal concerns of the early 1990s focused upon attempts to ensure value for money in government expenditure on forms of support for the private sector. Various, and often interrelated, themes occur in the literature. These include the problems of 'deadweight' and 'displacement' in grants to business, the need to foster competitiveness through various supply-side reforms and to ensure that a 'grants' or 'dependency' culture had not become entrenched.[11] Three policy documents of this period illustrate this trend: *Northern Ireland competing in the 1990s: the Key to Growth* (DED, 1990); *Forward Strategy 1991–93* (Industrial Development Board (IDB), 1990); and the Training and Employment Agency (TEA) strategy document of 1991.[12] All emphasise the need for competitiveness at the micro level, which could in principle be achieved in various ways including greater productivity based on greater research and development spending and better quality product. The underlying theme was not to end government support of private sector activity but to focus on the longer-term viability of a company and associated employment. Job creation was of itself no longer the main criterion, in part because of concerns that many of the jobs in figures for 'job promotions' did not materialise and that a culture of dependency had been fostered.[13]

The same broad concerns exercised the LEDU as detailed in the Northern Ireland Audit Office report of 1992.[14] The revised corporate plan of 1989–94 emphasised competitiveness as the key to employment policy and support (in the form of grants for many different activities) had to take account of the potential problems of displacement and avoid the need for subsequent payments. A problem raised by the report, and which will be returned to in Chapter 5, was the adequacy of measurement of the effectiveness of the agency's support. For example, no adequate methodology for measuring job duration or productivity, turnover, profitability and survival rates of client companies had been developed despite these being performance indicators in LEDU strategy.

Three new initiatives were introduced. The IDB's Strategic Development Planning Scheme would provide up to 40 per cent of the costs of preparing a strategic plan (and one review). The Market Development Grant Scheme was to provide up to 40 per cent grant assistance in any financial year to implement integrated marketing plans and the Company Development Programme, introduced in 1991 by the TEA, provided grant assistance towards recurrent training costs and capital costs incurred in providing in-house training facilities.

In March 1992, the Industrial Research and Technology Unit (IRTU) was founded. Its five principal objectives were to deliver promotional programmes, to increase the level of research and development expenditure, to stimulate participation and collaboration in international programmes, to provide scientific services to industry and to promote environmental management and energy conservation.[15] In essence, the broad parameters of policy, that is, the need for improved competitiveness based on supply-side reform and innovation did not differ from UK policy in general but the relatively low proportion of research and development expenditure (0.44 per cent of GDP compared with 1.09 per cent for the UK as a whole) made the question more pressing in Northern Ireland. Some commentators doubted if the industry specific problems of areas such as electronics, chemicals, office machinery and instrument engineering would be addressed adequately by a strategy of firm specific and economy-wide measures.[16]

As well as a multitude of industrial and employment support schemes directed by the IDB, LEDU and TEA, various schemes were administered by the Department of the Environment for urban and smaller community regeneration. Specific large-scale, multi-agency projects for Belfast and Derry had been on-going since the late 1980s.

The emphasis on indigenous routes to growth through increased competitiveness indicated above was introduced alongside more 'traditional' strategies. For example, despite the problems of 'branch plant syndrome'[17] the search for and subsidisation of foreign capital continued. In April 1990 a network of offices was established in New York, Los Angeles and Chicago to replace staffing previously carried out via attachment to the British consulate general network throughout the USA.

In very general terms, the economic indicators for Northern Ireland in the early 1990s were mixed. The recession was less severe than in the rest of the UK, partly because Northern Ireland had not experienced the preceding housing and credit-fuelled boom of the late 1980s. However, unemployment, although falling, remained at 13–14 per cent in 1990–92 and a much higher proportion of the unemployed were long term (over one year) than in the UK as a whole.

Within the context of this book, social policy may be broadly defined as measures taken to promote inter-communal understanding and/or those taken to address specific (often communal) grievances which cannot be categorised as constitutional, security or economic. There was little major innovation in this period though three developments will be addressed briefly. In January 1990 the Community Relations Council (CRC) was established to provide support (including financial) and recognition for local level organisations concerned with the development of community relations, awareness of cultural diversity and conflict resolution. Programmes previously funded by central government, the Arts Council and the Northern Ireland voluntary sector would become the CRC's responsibility. These themes reflected those contained in an education order of the previous year which promoted the two cross-curricular themes of 'Education for Mutual Understanding' and 'Cultural Heritage' underpinned by a pluralist and liberal agenda. Secondly, in August 1991 the Fair Employment (Amendment) (Northern Ireland) Order became law. This was simply to remedy an oversight whereby a clause of the 1976 legislation still in effect, which prevented the disclosure of an employee's religion, had meant that individuals could not bring cases of religious or political discrimination before the Fair Employment Tribunal. This oversight had rendered one of the objectives of the 1989 legislation largely inoperable.[18] Thirdly, in 1991 Brooke launched 'Targeting Social Need' through which departments were to monitor the impact of policy and, where possible to attempt to direct expenditure to the most needy. Later evidence suggests this policy was inadequately formulated and executed and this question will be addressed in later chapters.

Notes

1 J. Major, *The Autobiography* (London, HarperCollins, 1999), pp. 433–4.
2 HC debates: vol. 175, cols 1138–1224, 5 July 1990.
3 W. Harvey Cox, 'From Hillsborough to Downing Street – and After', in P. Caterall and S. McDougall (eds), *The Northern Ireland Question in British Politics* (Basingstoke, Macmillan, 1996), p. 197. See also for text of Brooke's speech.
4 Cited in Cox, 'From Hillsborough', p. 198.
5 For details see P. Arthur, 'The Brooke Initiative', *Irish Political Studies* 7, 1992, D. Bloomfield, *Political Dialogue in Northern Ireland* (Basingstoke, Macmillan, 1998) and B. O'Leary, 'Public opinion and Northern Irish futures', *Political Quarterly* 63(2), 1992, pp. 162–9.
6 HC debates: vol. 205, col. 506, 5 March 1992.
7 With 'certifying out' a series of offences in a schedule to the Act could only be tried in judge-only ('Diplock') courts. With 'certifying in', a judge would decide if an offence had terrorist connections; if not, it would be tried with a jury.
8 Many of the same criticisms are made by the SACHR (see 16th Report, 1990–91, HC 488, 1991, p. 4).
9 HC debates: vol. 187, col. 62, 4 March 1991.
10 Andrew Hunter, HC debates: vol. 204, col. 726, 24 February 1992.
11 'Deadweight' is publicly-funded investment granted to the private sector which would have been made anyway and 'displacement' the creation of jobs at the expense of existing ones, so not adding to the stock of employment. See Chapter 5 for a further discussion.
12 The TEA was established within the DED in April 1990 under the 'Next Steps' agencies' initiative and was responsible for administering all training and education support programmes. After review in 1994, its existence was extended for five years from April 1995.
13 For example, per capita industrial assistance in 1987–88 in Northern Ireland was almost five times that of other UK regions (M. Sheehan, 'Government financial assistance and manufacturing investment in Northern Ireland', *Regional Studies* 27(6) 1993, p. 528).
14 Northern Ireland Audit Office, 'Local Enterprise Development Unit: Review of Performance', HC 5, London, 1992.
15 For more details of government support for innovation see S. Roper and R. Thanki, 'Innovation 2000: an *ex ante* assessment of Northern Ireland's Research and Development strategy', *Regional Studies* 29(1) 1995, pp. 82–3.
16 'Innovation 2000', pp. 84–5.
17 See R. Harris, 'External ownership of industry and government policy: some further evidence from Northern Ireland', *Regional Studies* 25(1) 1991.
18 For more detail see the second Fair Employment Commission Report, 1990–91, HC 13, London, 1991.

5

The Conservative government, 1992–97

Introduction

The Conservative Party was returned to office in April 1992 with a much reduced majority of twenty-one. This result made the prospect of serious Unionist participation in talks more likely as they had refused to give an undertaking to engage in talks with a Labour administration. Also, the replacement of Peter Brooke, who had offended Unionists with his appearance singing on a Dublin TV programme after the killing of Protestant workmen in Northern Ireland in January, with Sir Patrick Mayhew was likely to improve Unionist–government relations. However, as the Attorney-General who had refused to bring prosecutions in the 'shoot-to-kill' cases of the early 1980s, Mayhew would have to emphasise the 'neutrality' invoked by his predecessor to win the confidence of nationalists.

Constitutional policy

Mayhew formally relaunched the talks process on 29 April; the two governments having agreed a three-month suspension of IGC meetings to facilitate Unionist co-operation. The parameters of the talks: the 'three strand' concept; 'nothing agreed until everything is agreed' were unchanged from those that had stalled under Brooke and these were to meet the same fate. Symbolically and procedurally the talks progressed beyond Brooke's attempts with all parties meeting in London for the first time in seventy years and the Ulster Unionist Party travelling to Dublin for talks.[1] By July, discussion had moved to strands two and three as the disputes that had bedevilled Brooke over the chairing and location of talks receded. However, when it came to the substance of the three strands there was still much disagreement between the Northern Ireland parties. From a Unionist perspective, the SDLP's introduction of a paper in May advocating a six-member commission (three elected in Northern Ireland and one each appointed by the EC and the British and Irish governments) to govern Northern Ireland served only to undermine the integrity of strand one. They were also concerned about a British discussion paper of September which was later withdrawn. It made mention of an 'agreed Ireland' and the presence of an NIO in Dublin and an Irish government presence in the North. The failure of the parties to agree on the scheduling of discussion of Articles 2 and 3, and the Republic's refusal to commit to definite repeal, reinforced the stalemate.

On 25 September Major and Albert Reynolds (who became Taoiseach in February) announced the final extension of IGC 'gaps' to 16 November. By 10 November the talks had stalled and the following day Mayhew addressed the Commons, accentuating the positive and calling for no recriminations among the protagonists. He reiterated the four principles informing the government position: no solution to be imposed; Britain's lack of selfish, strategic or economic interest; the necessity for majority Northern consent; and nothing agreed until everything was agreed. Labour spokesman, Kevin McNamara, offered his support arguing that it was a major breakthrough that all parties had acceded to the three strand dimension of talks. One difference in emphasis was his advocacy of increasing the sharing by the two governments of responsibility for Northern Ireland in the absence of party agreement, thus prefiguring the 'Joint Authority' proposals of the following year.[2]

The failure of the 1992 talks with the constitutional parties gave momentum to the main alternative; the construction of an inclusive policy to bring in the paramilitaries rather than to try to marginalise the 'men of violence' through the bolstering of the 'middle ground' via consociationalism. This was a policy adopted with fewer reservations by the Irish than the British government.[3] The British government had lines of communication open to the IRA (see also p. 89 below). It remained unclear if an 'unarmed strategy' was likely to emerge from Republican deliberations. However, in a major speech in Coleraine in December 1992, Mayhew emphasised both the legitimacy of the Nationalist and Republican traditions and the changes to legislation and deployment of security forces which would follow a permanent cessation of violence.[4] This was designed to emphasise that the government had no predisposition towards the Unionist cause.

1993 was characterised by what John Major termed the multi-dimensional approach whereby three potential routes forward were pursued. One was to maintain the IRA channel, the second the 'three strand' talks and the third, joint governmental initiatives with the Republic of Ireland. None of these was mutually exclusive. However, Unionist participation in the second route would be difficult to reactivate if concessions were seen to be made to militant republicanism; this was arguably to be the most difficult element of the subsequent 'peace process' to resolve.

The detail of the communications between the British government and the IRA in 1993 were subject to claim and counter-claim and, by their nature, independent adjudication on the veracity of versions is hard to obtain. Official accounts have to be treated with scepticism since until a newspaper leak of November 1993 the government maintained that it had no such contacts and then the transcript which was released by the NIO was error-strewn leading to an embarrassed Mayhew issuing corrections. It is perhaps sufficient to note that it is unlikely that the IRA stated in February 'the conflict is over, but we need your advice on how to bring it to a close' as the British government claimed. As Dillon argues, this is explained by the government wanting to justify such contacts on the grounds that the IRA had decided to embrace the unarmed struggle.[5] However, given the subsequent trajectory of events, one is inclined to believe Major's dismissal of the IRA's claim that the British government had agreed to accept a temporary ceasefire as a condition for entry into talks,[6] and it is possible that in a less bald formulation the republican movement was looking for a face-saving way out of the 'armed struggle'. At this time, the need to avoid alienating backbench Conservatives and Ulster Unionists who were bolstering Major's small majority implied the need for a long-term commitment to peace from the IRA.

The middle of the year witnessed a degree of discord between the two main British parties, although not of such significance as to mark the end of bipartisanship.[7] McNamara detected a bias against a united Ireland in an April speech by Mayhew in Liverpool and was not convinced that there had not been a move from the three strand approach towards an internal settlement and limited North–South institutions. This was denied by Michael Ancram, the minister responsible for political talks. In early July, Mayhew denounced as 'infamous' a Labour policy paper, 'Options for a Labour Government', which indicated a move towards joint authority or shared responsibility and acknowledged that this would be in breach of the majority consent principle. McNamara countered that it only had the status of a discussion document.[8] The Labour leader, John Smith, did not endorse such a policy and, as the Conservatives were well aware, Labour's official policy of 'unity by consent' was in practice non-operational and historical precedent indicated that this would be demonstrated by Labour policy in government.

The third of the options open to the British government was bilateral discussions with the Republic of Ireland. This had many attractions, particularly in the context of the failure of Brooke/Mayhew and the risks indicated above of links with paramilitaries. Any formal agreement or amicable relationship with the Republic tended to bolster the UK's position internationally and, specific to this period, neglect of the relationship was likely only to leave more space for the various discussions and drafts of Hume/Adams to be presented unchallenged to the Republic's government.[9] Over the course of 1993, Major set his face against various of the versions of Hume/Adams which he considered skewed in favour of a united Ireland. Many of the British government's concerns were addressed when, in late October, Dick Spring, deputy Prime Minister in the Republic's coalition government and Foreign Minister, set out six principles for a sustainable peace. These were:

1   the people of Ireland, North and South, should freely determine their future;
2   this could be expressed in new structures arising out of the three-stranded relationship;
3   there could be no change in Northern Ireland's status without freely-given majority consent;
4   this could be withheld;
5   the consent principle could be written into the Irish constitution; and
6   Sinn Fein could enter negotiations once the IRA had renounced violence.

This, of course, did not bind the rest of the Nationalist community and Spring's relationship with Republicans was notoriously poor. However, following intense discussions between officials and meetings between Major and Reynolds, including EU summits, a Joint Declaration (also known as the Downing Street Declaration) was issued by the two leaders on 15 December 1993.

Paul Arthur has described the Joint Declaration as 'a piece of tortuous syntax that defies textual exegesis'.[10] This is because it was trying to reconcile what still appeared to be irreconcilable formulations of self-determination and to ensure that none of the Northern Ireland actors rejected it out of hand. The most salient points are as follows: the British government reiterated the 'no selfish strategic or economic interest' clause; that the constitutional position of Northern Ireland was the decision of the majority within it; and that a united Ireland was a legitimate choice. The Taoiseach, on behalf of the Irish government, declared that, 'it would be wrong to attempt to impose a united Ireland, in the absence of the freely given consent of a majority of the people of Northern Ireland'. The government undertook to support changes to the 1937 Constitution to recognise the principle of consent in the context of an overall settlement.

Given the huge significance that decommissioning was to assume, it is worth noting that the section on violence saw both governments state that 'achievement of peace must involve a *permanent* end to the use of, or support for, paramilitary violence'. Under these circumstances, democratic parties would be invited to join discussions on the way forward.

The possibility of the evolution of structures beyond the 'internal' could be read as indicating a 'green' agenda. However, the recognition of the consent principle and close consultation in the 'run up' to the

Declaration were sufficient to gain the support of the UUP leadership if not all the parliamentary party. An attempt to provide a 'correct' reading of the Declaration is, in one sense, beside the point and parties' responses to it tended to be influenced by their degree of faith in the government's good intentions.

Major addressed the Commons on 15 December where the Declaration was welcomed by the opposition. Major stated that if there were a permanent end to violence and if Sinn Fein committed itself to the democratic process, preliminary exploratory dialogue could be entered into within three months. The term 'decommissioning' is not used and the government does not insist on a surrender of arms; however, Major stated that, 'we hope that there will be a surrender of some arms. The *sine qua non* is the absolute assurance that there is a renunciation of violence and that renunciation is shown to be carried out.'[11] It appears then that the government favoured some giving up of arms as a gesture of good faith rather than a precondition; quite what the carrying out of a renunciation involves is not clear. This formulation is important because the symbolic significance of the decommissioning issue was to remain centre stage during the subsequent discussions and the semantic formulations surrounding it important to the protagonists (see p. 93 below).

In March 1994, the government established a Select Committee for Northern Ireland. This reform could have been construed as a long overdue improvement in the scrutiny of Northern Ireland administration which had existed for all other departments since the late 1970s. However, it was an issue which revealed inter- and intra-party differences. The demand for a Select Committee had long been part of a package of measures advocated by integrationists and, in particular, by the James Molyneaux wing of the UUP. Labour opposed the measure as both symbolic of favouring one community over the other (McNamara labelled it 'triumphalist')[12] and as part of a squalid deal in which the UUP had supported the government over the ratification of the Maastricht Treaty. Major denied any deals with the Unionists; it should be noted, however, that the previous government had ruled out the measure fearing it would make Nationalist engagement in the talks process more difficult. This concern was expressed by Peter Temple-Morris, a liberal Conservative, who wished to focus on the democratic argument rather than the integrationist overtones. For Labour, the vehemence of McNamara was not matched by those MPs who felt that Labour's electoral isolationism with respect to Northern Ireland and identification with nationalism was outdated; notable among these were Frank Field, Kate Hoey and Harry Barnes. Hence, a measure ostensibly about the good governance of a part of the UK had become a site of ideological markers.

The attitude of the Labour Party towards Northern Ireland came under scrutiny as Tony Blair became leader in July 1994 following the death of

John Smith in May. As with most areas of policy, Blair was keen to stress that policy towards Northern Ireland was not determined by history or tradition and told the party conference in October that the Downing Street Declaration (DSD) had overtaken the historical positions of all the parties. An indication of Labour's (supposed) shift was the replacement of the pro-nationalist McNamara by Dr Marjorie (Mo) Mowlam as chief spokesperson in October 1994. She was cited as claiming to have, 'no ideological baggage' and a commitment to being a persuader toward a balanced political settlement rather than to a united Ireland.[13]

One has to be careful not to exaggerate the significance of such changes. There is a certain irony in the removal of McNamara in order to lay the foundation of better relations with Unionists given the depths to which their relations with Mowlam sank in the summer of 1999. More significantly, recent history had demonstrated that Labour in office did not adopt a significantly pro-Nationalist position and that its 'green' legacy did not preclude making overtures to Unionists.[14] It was also clear that before Mowlam's succession Labour had accepted that 'unity by consent', the official policy adopted in 1981, in practice had little import. In the debate on the renewal of direct rule in late June 1994, McNamara conceded that Labour would not try to impose that preference and that the party would and should support any agreement that had support of the people of Ireland. The changes and emphases of the second half of 1994 may have had symbolic importance but do not support claims of a policy sea-change.

Events moved slowly for most of 1994. Following the DSD, Sinn Fein requested clarification of concerns which the British government refused to give until May (in the form of a commentary on twenty questions submitted by Sinn Fein via the Irish government, which added very little to the original text). Most 'Provo watchers' interpreted this as delaying tactics. Sinn Fein wished neither to endorse the DSD and risk alienating Republicans who believed that its deconstruction of the consent principle and the formulation of self-determination were incompatible with Republican ideology nor to reject it and risk being marginalised in contacts with the Irish government and the SDLP. Although more complex than this, part of the Republican debate revolved around the likely result and outcome of the longer-term process to which the DSD, as blueprint, could not provide answers.[15]

Major continued to pursue the intergovernmental strand while the Republican position on the DSD was awaited and speculation about a ceasefire increased. From February Reynolds and Spring had recommitted themselves to the talks process and from May Irish and British officials were engaged in discussions which resulted in the Joint Framework Documents of February 1995 (see p. 94 below). At an EU conference in June 1994 Major failed to get a formal acceptance of the legitimacy of Northern Ireland from Reynolds and relations were further strained by the end of the year as positions on decommissioning diverged.

On 31 August the IRA called a 'complete cessation' of military activity. The British government position focused on the lack of the word 'permanent' in the formulation, which could be interpreted, as did British security assessments, that the option of renewing violence was being maintained. Therefore, the government refused immediate exploratory dialogue but on 21 October in a speech to the Northern Ireland Institute of Directors, Major said the government was prepared to make a 'working assumption' that the ceasefire was intended to be permanent and made the first reference to decommissioning.[16]

The following week the Commons debated developments. Mayhew recorded changes in responses to the ceasefire, including the lifting of the broadcasting ban on Sinn Fein and the reduction in army support for police patrols. Talks were planned for the end of the year which needed to, 'embrace the republicans' proposals for depositing and decommissioning their armaments ...'.[17] Labour were broadly supportive with Clive Soley arguing that they would not stand in the way of an agreement between the people of Northern Ireland even if this was not in line with Labour policies although he regretted the lack of a government statement on the future of emergency legislation. There was some difference of emphasis among back bench Conservatives between those advocating caution in talks and those who saw risks in moving too slowly. Michael Ancram concluded by announcing a joint working party of British and Irish officials to consider the decommissioning question and 'to draw up a strategy setting out the logistics and mechanics of a surrender of arms to underpin the peace process'.[18]

The significance of decommissioning means that a further investigation of its import and the associated convolutions will be included here in the narrative. For some actors the question became, if not an irrelevance, a secondary issue on the ground that the maintenance of the ceasefire was crucial which could be elided into the equation that the holding of arms mattered little if they were not being used. In any case, decommissioning could be followed by the acquisition of more arms if the IRA resumed the 'armed struggle'. Therefore, it was bad tactics to make decommissioning a sticking point, particularly as a rigid position on decommissioning, which would delay talks, was likely only to bolster the position of 'hard-liners'.

This reasoning was based on the premise that elements of the Republican movement were looking to move to peaceful and democratic politics. It would make it harder for this group to 'sell' such a strategy if harried over decommissioning. The contrary position is simple enough to appreciate. For the British government there was both the tactical consideration that Unionist involvement in any future process would be less likely if decommissioning were not achieved and the moral position whereby those retaining arms could not be afforded parity in discussions with constitutional parties: negotiation with 'guns under the table' was not acceptable. The simple retort to the point about possession of arms not mattering if the ceasefire held was: if republicanism supported the peace process why retain the weapons?

The thinking of republicanism is beyond the scope of this work but the arguments advanced with respect to this may be reviewed briefly. First, much has been made of the symbolism; that decommissioning would be seen as defeat and that historically, within and without Ireland, undefeated armies did not surrender arms. Secondly, the belief that the Nationalist community needed arms for self-defence with memories of 1969 looming large in the folk memory. Thirdly, there was the tactical advantage of not decommissioning; without violence or the threat of it by the IRA the imperative of keeping Sinn Fein within the talks process was diminished and it made no sense to decommission short of wringing every possible concession from unionism and the British government. Of these explanations the third has the most force and the second is residual. The activity of the IRA did not prevent attacks on Catholics by Loyalist paramilitaries, arguably the reverse, and the increased targeting of Sinn Fein activists was one factor in the reassessment of the utility of the 'long war'.

A united front over decommissioning was difficult to maintain; Major claimed the two governments did not disagree at the time of the DSD,[19] whereas by the end of 1994 the Irish government and John Hume had dropped the prior decommissioning requirement. With this issue unresolved, attention turned in early 1995 to the documents which built upon the principles of the DSD. The British government published, 'A Framework for Accountable Government in Northern Ireland' and the two governments produced 'A New Framework for Agreement' [20] commonly referred to as the Joint Framework Documents (JFD). For the British government, they were constructed around now familiar parameters: the 'three strand' concept; the UK's neutrality or agnosticism reflected in the parity of esteem accorded to the two traditions; and the need for Northern majority consent to any constitutional change. The first document deals with 'strand one' or the internal dimension. It advocated an executive comprising a collective three-member presidency (which would almost certainly ensure Nationalist and Unionist membership) which would have to operate unanimously. Its powers were to include the right to veto proposals by the new assembly and to play a role in the nomination of committee chairs. An assembly of ninety members was envisaged with a committee system based on party strengths; up to ten committees were mooted, six overseeing the work of the current Northern Ireland departments and others to cover general purposes, community relations, business and policing.

The challenge for the architects was to outline a model of checks and balances which prevented simple majoritarianism (for example, through the need for weighted majorities in the assembly and the role of the collective presidency), while not making the structure so rigid as to invite 'gridlock' between the component parts. It was hoped that 'weighted' majorities would preclude the need for artificial and fixed coalitions which had been particularly opposed by Unionists in earlier discussions.

In 'A New Framework for Agreement' the section on 'North–South Institutions' is both lengthy and vague so the main themes will be highlighted. First, there is a lack of specificity, as befits a framework document, about both the policy areas to be covered by such bodies and the extent of their powers, which could be executive, harmonising or consultative. (The precise form and responsibilities would of necessity be for discussion and agreement between the two administrations.) At least two clauses were likely to be of concern to many Unionists: paragraph 25 spoke of a 'duty of service' in such institutions by the relevant post holders in the two administrations which implied that Unionist boycotts would not be sanctioned; and paragraph 28 stated that both governments expected 'meaningful functions at executive level' to be a feature of agreement and that the British government would impose no limits on the nature and extent of functions.

The third strand, entitled 'East–West Structures' was to replace the existing Anglo-Irish Agreement but to retain many of its features. For example, a standing IGC was to be maintained which would provide a 'continuing institutional expression' (paragraph 42) of the Irish government's concern and role in relation to Northern Ireland. Two of the subsequent paragraphs acted as both carrot and stick to the Unionists. Paragraph 45 outlined the limitations of the competence of the ICG in areas covered by the new institutions within Northern Ireland; thus participation in the devolved assembly would potentially limit the scope of the 'third strand' which Unionists had largely opposed. In paragraph 47 the British government undertook to maintain the North–South bodies created in the event of devolution in Northern Ireland failing so non-participation in the latter by Unionists would not put in jeopardy the operation of the other two strands.

The JFD outlined and gave examples of the form institutions might take building on the principles of the DSD. As a framework there was much detail to be negotiated allowing protagonists to make different assumptions and readings about the final shape of any settlement.[21] What was clear, however, was that all the Unionist parties felt the documents to be too 'green' and that the supposed special relationship between the UUP and the Conservatives had been exposed and Molyneaux's minimalist Westminster-based strategy found wanting. Major later claimed that the documents were too long and dense and so facilitated selective quotation and that the build-up to the 1994 ceasefire had distracted attention from them.[22] However, it is unlikely that drafting amendments would have made fundamental differences. It is arguable that brevity and specificity in such documents would alienate particular parties and groupings on reading them, while length and discursiveness (texts littered with 'envisageds') allows multiple readings which serves to confirm fears. Therefore, the process is fraught in whatever way formulated.

The government's position was made more difficult by a 'leak' in *The Times* in late January which claimed that joint authority was a likely option and that a united Ireland was closer than at any time since the 1920s. Having produced documents the language of which was 'green' the government then proceeded on a damage limitation exercise to reassure Unionists. In responding to the 'leak' on 1 February, Mayhew emphasised that the need for consent from the Northern majority ruled out joint authority. Unionists also had the safeguards of the 'triple lock', by which any agreement had to have the support of Westminster, the people of Northern Ireland via a referendum and the Northern Ireland parties. The last of these was a somewhat ambiguous point since, in a response to Ian Paisley, Mayhew seemed to imply that all-party support would be needed, whereas majority support within each of two main communities was deemed sufficient in the referendum of 1998. The provisional nature of the documents was also stressed; they were to be offered as discussion papers not blueprints to be imposed.

Major's statement to the Commons on 22 February at the time of the documents' publication emphasised similar themes in offering reassurance to Unionists. In particular he tried to play down the significance of a North–South body stating that it would probably have 'primarily an advisory role' and that any further powers devolved to a North–South body would be determined by the Northern Ireland Assembly.[23] Although the evidence is not conclusive, both at this time and at the time of the Good Friday Agreement the British government seemed to favour a more minimalist interpretation of the likely powers and remit of cross-border institutions.

The precise relationship between strand one and two institutions would remain an academic point if there were no meaningful inter-party talks to resolve it. The topic which was to dominate the rest of 1995 was decommissioning; issues included whether if the British government softened its position any decommissioning would be forthcoming, and if there were no decommissioning whether any Unionists would enter talks. Theoretically, the government could try to move the process forward without Sinn Fein in the absence of decommissioning but both the SDLP and the Irish government saw their involvement as central to a lasting settlement.

On 7 March 1995 in Washington Mayhew outlined the government position, which became known as 'Washington 3' and ran as follows:

> A willingness in principle to disarm progressively; a common practical understanding of the modalities, that is to say, what decommissioning would actually entail; in order to test the practical arrangements and to demonstrate good faith, the actual decommissioning of some arms as a tangible confidence-building measure and to signal the start of a process.[24]

Major described this formulation as 'an inherently reasonable proposition' and felt, if anything, that the government had softened its position.[25] The move from decommissioning *in toto* to 'some arms' bears this out and Unionists and some Conservative backbenchers expressed concern. In the debate on the renewal of the PTA the following day, Mayhew denied any slippage and attempted to clarify the government's position by stating 'before inclusive political talks about future structures in Northern Ireland can take place, substantial progress must be made on the decommissioning of arms'.[26]

It is no surprise that David Trimble (UUP) accused the government of confusion since this did not clarify the position; did 'progress' mean actual giving up of weapons or a firm commitment as to when and how (the modalities) this would be done? This was left unresolved; towards the end of April the NIO announced that exploratory dialogue would take place between ministers and Sinn Fein, and twice in May Ancram met with Sinn Fein representatives. Immediately after the second meeting Ancram offered this formulation to the Commons, 'we have made it clear that to move from exploratory dialogue to substantive bilateral dialogue will require a tangible beginning to the process of decommissioning and that to move to inclusive talks around the table will require substantial decommissioning.'[27] This 'clarity' raised more questions than it answered; what did tangible mean – one gun or piece of semtex – similarly what constituted 'substantial'.

In June 1995 at Cannes Major and John Bruton, the Fine Gael Taoiseach, discussed the possibility of establishing an international commission to consider the question in an attempt to overcome the impasse. One may deduce from this that the British government was concerned about being marginalised. The parties and government of the Irish Republic, Northern Nationalists and elements of the security forces, including the RUC, were disposed to focus more on the gains of the ceasefire than risk gains over decommissioning. Relations became more strained between the two governments over the summer with the release of Private Clegg, a soldier convicted of murdering a 'joy rider', and the violence surrounding the Drumcree Orange march and a September summit of the two prime ministers was called off because of decommissioning differences.

Towards the end of October Ancram informed the Commons that the government was still committed to Washington 3 and that the two governments were considering the setting up of an international body to consider decommissioning. A NIO document, 'Building Blocks' released on 3 November advocated what became known as the 'twin-track' approach, whereby all-party preparatory talks would run parallel to the decommissioning body's deliberations and a joint communique of 28 November issued by Major and Bruton marked the formal launch of the strategy. Such a move by the British government could be seen as an intelligent tactical compromise, in that the de-coupling of the talks process and decommissioning by 'internationalising' the latter might influence Republican thinking or, alternatively, as a climb-down. Some back bench Conservatives and Unionists saw the drift of events in 1995 as one-sided concessions, with changes to sentencing remission (see p. 107 below) and military deployment occurring against a backdrop of punishment beatings and the maintenance of paramilitary structures. On 29 November Major tried to reassure them by stating that the international body did not have in its remit to question the government position of Washington 3 and that the partial decommissioning of arms was sought before the start of all-party talks. However, the judgement must be that the government's stance had weakened since the period before the ceasefire of August 1994.

The international commission, chaired by former US senator, George Mitchell, issued its report on 24 January 1996. It concluded that there was no chance of decommissioning before substantive talks and advocated decommissioning during negotiations, splitting the difference between British demands for prior decommissioning and Sinn Fein's argument that it should follow an overall settlement. In addition the Mitchell report contained six principles relating to commitments to non-violence and democracy and, in what some saw as a throwaway line, mentioned the possibility of an elective process as a confidence-building measure.[28] Major seized on this as Trimble, leader of the UUP since September 1995, argued that new elections from which to choose parties' negotiating teams would give Sinn Fein a mandate allowing him to talk to them without decommissioning.

In early February 1996 the IRA ended its ceasefire. This, and Sinn Fein's rejection of the Forum for Peace and Reconciliation's report which accepted the legitimacy of Northern majority consent, confirmed the duplicity of the Republican movement in the view of the right and the futility of what it saw as the concessions, if not appeasement, of 1995. A simple equation was raised. Either Adams knew about the end of the ceasefire, was not committed to non-violence and therefore should not be negotiated with or else he did not know and this lack of influence on or insight into the thinking of the IRA meant it was not worth making concessions to keep him and Sinn Fein in the process.

However, the bulk of Nationalist opinion, including the Irish government, blamed the British government for prevarication. It was eight months after the ceasefire before ministers had met with Sinn Fein and, just as rigidity over decommissioning was being relaxed, elections to a forum were introduced to further delay the process and without prior discussion. At best Nationalists saw elections as an irrelevance since parties already had negotiating teams and mandates derived from electoral support and at worst as an attempt to revive 'strand one' institutions in isolation from the previously agreed integrated package.

On 28 February, Major laid out the forthcoming agenda. It had been agreed at an Anglo-Irish summit that the two governments would consult intensively with the parties until mid-March. This would be followed by legislation for the elective process and all-party negotiations were to be convened on 10 June. At the beginning of negotiations, all participants would have to make clear their commitment to non-violence as laid out in Mitchell and address the report's proposals on decommissioning. In late March Major announced 30 May as the date for elections; elected representatives would provide negotiating teams and, in addition, meet as a Forum to promote dialogue and mutual understanding. The Forum's existence was limited to an initial twelve months, renewable for up to a further twelve months.

It was also announced that the Forum would have 110 members: five elected in each of the eighteen Westminster constituencies by the list system and two additional seats would go to the ten parties with most support across the province. This departure from the established STV system has been called 'truly Byzantine'[29] and its adoption was never fully explained by government. As indicated above, the Nationalist parties did not want an election and there was no consensus on the system to be used. One motivation of the 'top up' section was to increase the likelihood of representation of the small Loyalist parties attached to the paramilitaries which had a crucial role in maintaining the ceasefire.

During March various discussion papers relating to the election system were produced by the government and there was debate concerning which parties would be recognised to contest the election – parties having no formal legal status in the UK. On 18 April the Northern Ireland (Entry to Negotiations etc.) Bill was presented for second reading and was to provide the detail of the election, the forum and possible subsequent referendums. Two main themes emerge from the second reading debate. First, that there is broad agreement between the two main parties with Labour supportive of the establishment of the Forum and the parallel process recommended by Mitchell. Secondly, is the concern by some Conservative backbenchers that the government position on decommissioning had weakened – David Wilshire being the most vocal proponent of this view. In response to his probing, neither Mayhew nor Mowlam were prepared to employ the term 'permanent' but favoured 'unequivocal' as the form of ceasefire which would allow Sinn Fein to re-enter talks. Soley, a Labour member, thought any stronger formulation would run the risk of jeopardising progress: 'we did not go further forward with the wording precisely because both Governments and both major political parties in the House want negotiations to proceed'.[30]

Similar positions were struck in committee stage of the legislation. Mayhew was conscious that Unionists feared that decommissioning was being postponed almost out of sight, while Nationalists feared the Forum would become a proto-Stormont. Implicitly, the government was trying to steer a middle course between these two concerns. The Conservative MPs Wilshire, who moved an amendment requiring a 'permanent' renunciation of violence, Tony Marlow, John Wilkinson and Nicholas Winterton expressed concerns over the government position. In an attempt at reassurance, Mayhew emphasised the three preconditions for admission to negotiations; the restoration of the ceasefire; 'total and absolute' commitment to the Mitchell principles; and the requirement that at the beginning of negotiations, decommissioning proposals would be 'addressed' as part of the parallel process. Given that one could logically address decommissioning proposals without any decommissioning being effected, this did not convince Conservative back bench critics.

Front bench comments included the admission that the electoral system was a compromise as no system had satisfied all parties, and that the primary function of the Forum was to conduct hearings of public submissions from civil society with a view to promoting a more positive climate for the talks themselves. Forum meetings could not precede the start of all-party negotiations which had primacy. After a lengthy committee stage the bill received a third reading on 23 April with no division. In the short run at least, the government's 'twin track' strategy appeared successful. At Westminster, back bench concern over the weakening of decommissioning conditions had been vocal but limited to a small grouping and Labour had supported the elective process despite the criticisms of Nationalists.[31] Paralleling Conservative concerns, only a few 'greener' Labour MPs, such as Canavan and McNamara, opposed the election. Within Northern Ireland, both the SDLP and Sinn Fein were to contest seats in the Forum election as the former had rejected the latter's idea of a joint boycott. Elements within unionism had been placated by the election process and government adherence to Major's commitment of October 1994 that any agreement in all-party negotiations would have to be approved by the people of Northern Ireland in a referendum. However, substantive progress was likely to prove difficult. Semantic convolutions by government, which in June 1996 conceded that it had shifted its position[32] and occasionally placatory statements by Sinn Fein could not resolve the basic question. Without IRA decommissioning it was unlikely that a substantial grouping within unionism would enter government with Sinn Fein and without the latter it was unlikely that the process as a whole would work, especially if the SDLP were not prepared to enter an administration which excluded Sinn Fein. Therefore, decommissioning remained the key.

The election to the Forum was held on 30 May. Four parties, including the two Loyalist ones associated with paramilitary organisations, won no constituency seats but received two seats through the regional 'top up' system, thus vindicating the hybrid system adopted. The other most significant result was the 15.5 per cent of votes gained by Sinn Fein, which suggested that the Nationalist electorate did not blame it for the collapse of the ceasefire and may have been consciously blaming Major for his perceived procrastination.

On 6 June details for the talks process were published. Mitchell was to chair plenary sessions and a decommissioning sub-committee, Mayhew would chair the strand one element and John de Chastelain, a member of the Mitchell Commission, would take charge of discussions over strand two structures. Talks began on 10 June, although procedural matters were still to be resolved and Unionists were concerned about the 'internationalising' of the chairing of the talks, and the Forum had its first meeting on 14 June.

The slim prospects for progress became worse following riots associated with the Drumcree parade of July; Anglo-Irish relations worsened and the SDLP withdrew from the Forum leaving it with no Nationalist representation. By the end of 1996 there had been no renewal of the ceasefire, no decommissioning and Sinn Fein had not signed up to the Mitchell principles. In this context, the introduction of the Northern Ireland Arms Decommissioning Bill in December seemed optimistic rather than prudent. This was enabling legislation which would give effect to the decommissioning of weapons in line with the principles contained in the Mitchell report. These demanded that the process should suggest neither victory nor defeat, it should take place to the satisfaction of the independent commission, it would result in the complete destruction of firearms, it would be fully verifiable, it would not expose individuals to prosecution and it would be mutual.

The main provision of the bill was to provide an amnesty for those who would be committing an offence were they not acting in accordance with a decommissioning scheme; for example, to prevent a charge of possession being brought. Weapons handed over could not be used as evidence and information derived from any scheme would not be admissible in a prosecution. Interventions in the debate struck familiar positions with MPs disposed towards nationalism criticising the government for delays and imposing new conditions for Sinn Fein entry into talks. From the other end of the political spectrum, Wilshire introduced a new clause (later withdrawn) which would require a period of one year between an end to violence and entry to talks to ascertain that a second ceasefire was real and not a tactical move.

John Wheeler summarised the government position; the bill built on the Entry to Negotiations Act 1996 and reflected the most recent statement by Major on 28 November that, if a ceasefire were announced, the government would need to be assured that it was genuine and unequivocal. This could be demonstrated by the ending of terrorist violence, the end of punishment beatings and the standing down of the means to participate in terrorism. If these conditions were met, Wilshire's amendment would delay the decommissioning process. Two other minor clauses were withdrawn and the bill received an unopposed third reading on 16 January 1997.

The lack of progress was highlighted by the approval of the Northern Ireland (Entry to Negotiations, etc) Act (Cessation of Section 3) Order in March 1997. On 5 March Mitchell stated that no basis had emerged for reaching agreement on decommissioning and the Order suspended the forum until 3 June as there was no prospect of movement before the general election. However, both Labour and the Conservatives were committed to reactivate the Forum if in government after the election.

Security policy

As indicated above, the decommissioning issue *de facto* merged security and constitutional questions; therefore, the emphasis in this section will be the party positions and concerns relating to anti-terrorist legislation between 1992 and 1997. The PTA was subject to annual renewal by Order and in 1993 Labour maintained its opposition to the Act. Tony Blair, shadow Home Secretary, reiterated Labour's two principal concerns: the use of exclusion orders; and the lack of a judicial element in extended detention. The Home Secretary, Kenneth Clarke, rejected changes. He argued that surveillance would be a costly and ineffective alternative to exclusion and that judicial intervention in detention would make little material difference since it would, in effect, be the carrying out of an executive rather than legal judgment and safeguards had been improved by the introduction of an independent commissioner for police holding centres in December 1992.[33] Apart from Labour's specific reservations, two general points emerge from this debate. First, differing methodologies for evaluating the effectiveness of the Act remained. Opponents had for years pointed to the low number of charges brought relative to arrests made as an indication that the Act was principally used for generalised information 'trawling' and/or harassment. Clarke responded to Hattersley's concerns by arguing that, as the Act existed to assist the prevention and investigation of terrorism, the number of charges brought was not a measure of success. Secondly, Labour's tone appeared to be softening as opposition focused on what was seen as government resistance to a full-scale review rather than the need for anti-terrorist legislation *per se*.

Renewal in March 1994 saw the positions maintained. Blair repeated the two substantive concerns which the government rejected, although Michael Howard, the Home Secretary, emphasised that the number of exclusion orders in place was the lowest since 1975 (eighty at the end of 1993). Blair and Howard both accused the other of playing party politics over the issue; Blair claiming that he wished to see the House uniting but this would need a full independent review since there had not been one since 1987. This position was supported by Unionists and the SDLP. Blair's more emollient tone gives credence to the observation of Graham Riddick, a Conservative MP, who believed that Blair wanted to move towards supporting the PTA but the pro-Republican left-wing of the party made this difficult.[34]

The following year's debate[35] took place against the backdrop of the first ceasefire and minor security reforms. However, as paramilitary structures remained intact and the PTA's remit also covered non-Irish terrorism the government deemed renewal necessary. The absence of a general and comprehensive review of the legislation was again attacked by Labour and Jack Straw, shadow Home Secretary (replacing Tony Blair who became Labour Party leader in July 1994 after the death of John Smith), argued that a division on the motion was the only way to register Labour's concerns given the 'take it or leave it' nature of Orders. He accused the government of blocking consensus and argued that Labour wanted a bipartisan approach to the issue. Howard in return claimed that Labour's position was determined by backbenchers who would never accept such legislation.

Howard's predictive powers were shown to be lacking as on 14 March 1996 Labour abstained on the continuance order. This was the first time since 1982 that Labour had not opposed the legislation. In January, a full review of the legislation had been announced and this decision laid the foundations for bipartisan agreement. Straw maintained this could have been achieved earlier had not Smith and Blair's private discussions with the government in 1994 been leaked and if Howard's attitude had been less intransigent. Straw argued that the increased proportion of those detained being charged had reduced some of the concerns about the injustice of the Act and hoped that the review would address other Labour reservations. While the review may have been the immediate cause of Labour's change of position, there had been a longer-term movement to change policy and insulate the party from accusations of being 'soft' on terrorism and Straw was not overly concerned with maintaining the party's supposed liberal credentials. This change of position prompted twenty-five Labour MPs, including McNamara and Roger Stott, to ignore the party line and vote against renewal but they escaped being disciplined as Straw took a conciliatory approach and spoke of respecting the rebels' views.[36]

These Labour tensions surfaced again the following month as the government pushed through in one day the stages of the Prevention of Terrorism (Additional Powers) Bill which clarified and strengthened miscellaneous police powers. These included the stopping and searching of pedestrians, the searching of non-residential premises, the searching of unaccompanied freight at ports and the cordoning off of areas. Labour's formal position was to abstain although Straw indicated his broad support and Howard commended the 'reasonable speeches' of Labour's front bench. However, twenty-one Labour MPs supported a motion by McNamara to deny the bill a second reading and eighteen and thirteen Labour MPs voted against the second and third readings, respectively.

The final renewal order of the PTA under the Conservative government took place on 5 March 1997.[37] Changes in legislation were likely following the Lloyd report (see below) but the government had not reached firm conclusions. Decision had been delayed in part because the Lloyd report's remit was to consider legislation against terrorism in the context of a cessation of violence 'leading to a lasting peace' and since the start of the inquiry the IRA ceasefire had ended. Straw wanted cross-party discussion on the basis of Lloyd with a view to the possible drafting of legislation flexible enough for conditions both of peace or a renewed emergency and repeated Labour concerns about exclusion orders and extended detention. Howard rejected changes and, with an eye to the forthcoming election, concluded the debate with an attack on Blair claiming that as he had never voted for the PTA he was unfit to become Prime Minister. Labour abstained with thirteen MPs voting against renewal.

The Lloyd report, 'Inquiry into Legislation against Terrorism' was published in October 1996.[38] Its main recommendation was for permanent anti-terrorist legislation for the whole of the UK which would cover both international and domestic terrorism. This marked a further development away from the temporary and *ad hoc* nature of the original legislation of the 1970s and vindicates the concerns voiced by critics since the mid-1970s that a drift to permanence was likely. The tenor of the report was generally conservative in its rather uncritical acceptance that terrorism was a major threat in the UK. With respect to the specifics of the current legislation, enacted in 1989 and 1996, the report endorsed the powers to stop and search vehicles and pedestrians, powers to examine people at ports, proscription of terrorist organisations, the offence of belonging to a terrorist organisation and the seizure of terrorist funds.

The main reforms recommended were as follows: detention should be initially limited to forty-eight hours with extension of up to another forty-eight hours subject to judicial authorisation which would bring the legislation into line with the Police and Criminal Evidence Act 1984. The provisions regarding forfeiture of terrorist funds should be extended and a statutory reduction of sentence be introduced for a terrorist who provides evidence against another. Exclusion and internment clauses should be removed and 'Diplock' courts should be ended in the context of a lasting peace. The annual review of legislation, carried out by a senior legal figure, should no longer be necessary. These recommendations indicate the process of 'normalisation' of the so-called emergency legislation and the consolidation of its scope beyond Northern Ireland.

The other principal piece of anti-terrorist legislation was the Northern Ireland (Emergency and Prevention of Terrorism Provisions) Act 1991. Labour opposed its renewal in 1992 principally because of the retention of the internment clause, although it had not been used since 1975. In the 1993 debate,[39] the government outlined recent reforms to the operation of the emergency legislation. In July 1992 a scheme had been introduced to reduce the maximum time permitted for remand to one year and an independent commissioner had been appointed at the end of 1992 to monitor conditions and procedures in holding centres. McNamara, the Labour spokesman, outlined four concerns. Two related to the legislation itself; provisions relating to terrorist finances in the two Acts should be consolidated into one permanent Act and the internment provision should be repealed. The other two concerns related to the operation of the EPA. Neither the video nor audiotaping of interviews of suspects had been introduced, despite being recommended in the annual review of the Act and defendants were too frequently denied speedy access to lawyers. Internment remained Labour's main concern, although Stott referred to the general erosion of civil liberties in justifying Labour's vote against renewal. These positions were adopted again in 1994. Mayhew rejected the taping in either form of interviews because of fears expressed by the Chief Constable that they might 'fall into the wrong hands' making suspect co-operation less likely. This was criticised by McNamara who repeated that internment was the main reason for Labour's continued opposition, since the party accepted the need for some emergency powers.

Evidence of Labour's shift to a more conciliatory position in discussions over the PTA (see p. 103 above) is mirrored in the renewal debate of June 1995.[40] Mowlam conceded that Labour had been split over the EPA with some MPs opposed in principle and other wishing to retain certain provisions. Both Mowlam and her deputy, Tony Worthington, expressed a desire for bipartisan co-operation in any forthcoming discussions over legislation to succeed the PTA and EPA and hoped for a fundamental and independent review. Labour also favoured the replacement of 'certifying out' with 'certifying in' as an immediate reform and a transition to jury trials with the phasing out of 'Diplock' courts.

The EPA had to be re-enacted by 1996 and, in May 1994, Mayhew had announced a review to precede this. The Rowe review was published in 1995[41] and recommended the retention of the vast majority of the provisions of the 1991 Act including the concept of 'scheduled' offences and the retention of 'certifying out'. As Lloyd was to recommend the following year, Rowe advocated the consolidation of anti-terrorist measures into one statute but, unlike Lloyd, he favoured three years' duration for the legislation and the maintenance of annual renewal.

In January 1996 Mayhew introduced the second reading of the new Emergency Provisions Bill. The Lloyd review had been established so it was likely that the EP provisions would soon be superseded. Therefore, the bill was to be of two years' duration and be subject to annual renewal without amendment. There were only minor changes proposed to the existing legislation including the removal of provisions relating to terrorist financing which were to be replaced by measures covering all crime and dealt with in a separate order and a new offence of failing to stop and be searched if requested by the police or army.

Labour attacked the government for delay in undertaking a thorough review to which Labour had offered support the previous year which necessitated the use of more temporary legislation. Specifically, Mowlam detailed five concerns: the failure to remove the internment provision; failure to tape-record interviews; the lack of provision for full-time legal advice at holding centres; the lack of a 'certifying in' provision; and the lack of scope for annual amendment. Mowlam also argued that some of the powers could be kept in reserve which would act as a signal about wanting to keep the peace process moving.

Labour adopted a compromise position on the legislation; an amendment was moved and the second reading was opposed to signal the disquiet indicated above but it pledged not to oppose a third reading. While individual MPs, such as McNamara and Canavan, the latter believing bipartisanship to be an insult, opposed the legislation *in toto* the Labour front bench clearly accepted the need for emergency measures.[42] The report stage and third reading were taken on 19 February; most of the debate focused on the way forward and the form of confidence building measures needed as the IRA ceasefire had recently ended. A new clause was introduced to allow for the silent video recording of interviews which offered safeguards to both suspects and to the RUC in the case of false claims of abuse. This was a compromise between the previous Conservative rejection and Labour's desire for both audio and video recordings to be made. Labour indicated its concern that the review requested was not established until after the second reading but, as pledged, did not oppose the third reading.

As a whole, the period 1992 to 1997 saw no great shifts in emergency legislation, with caution informing government policy. As indicated above, Labour was gradually moving towards an overt acceptance of the need for emergency provisions which prompted protests from some of its own backbenchers who interpreted this development as a sign of growing illiberalism in the party which was part of the search for electoral rehabilitation.

The outstanding piece of legislation not covered by the discussion of emergency legislation or decommissioning above is the Northern Ireland (Remission of Sentences) Act 1995. In August 1995 Mayhew had proposed that the remission on sentences for scheduled offences should be increased to 50 per cent, as it had been between 1976 and 1989 when it was reduced to one-third. Introducing the second reading at the end of October, he argued that it was 'a positive, but proportionate and prudent, response to the continuance of the ceasefires ...'.[43] A released prisoner was subject to recall up to two-thirds into sentence if he/she were likely to commit further offences or be a risk to others. The power to revoke a licence would be held by the Secretary of State. In restoring the *status quo ante* the bill could be seen as non-contentious; however, it provided examples of different perceptions of the 'peace process'. Among Conservatives, Andrew Hunter supported the bill as it reflected changed circumstances and was likely to promote further peace and political agreement. David Wilshire, in contrast, spoke of his deep reservations at the August announcement and of how the process had been marked by one-sided concessions. Seamus Mallon of the SDLP contrasted the Conservative contributions with Howard's jingoism at the party conference and stressed the centrality of prisoners to the peace process. Harry Barnes, one of the leading opponents within the party of Labour's 'green tendency', supported the bill as a response to changed circumstances but argued that it should not be used as a vehicle to nudge the process forward. Mayhew concluded by emphasising that the measure did not indicate the acceptance of the concept of the political prisoner and did not mark the move to further concessions. The question of prisoner releases and the divergent range of attitudes related to them was a subject that would recur during the next administration.

Economic policy

As noted in Chapter 4, at the beginning of the 1990s the strategy for employment moved from job creation *per se* to an emphasis on supply-side factors to ensure the longer-term viability of jobs. The institutional structures of industrial support (the IDB, LEDU, TEA) remained unchanged so this section will focus upon some of the reports on their activities and some of the economic indicators for Northern Ireland.

A reading of some of the official reviews of the operation of the support agencies reveals two consistent concerns; one is the problem of developing a suitable methodology to measure the efficiency of various forms of financial support, and the other is the accuracy of measurement of jobs created. For example, the IDB had three formal criteria for providing selective financial assistance (SFA). These were: additionality, which referred to the amount of assistance needed to bring about benefits associated with the project and should be kept to a minimum; viability, which meant that a company should be able to operate after receiving SFA on a 'once and for all' basis; and efficiency, which was concerned with net economic benefits of a project and the question of displacement.

However, a Committee of Public Accounts report of 1993 on SFA noted the following concerns.[44] The efficiency of companies was not tested after the receipt of assistance, which was considered 'a serious shortcoming',[45] and a high proportion of companies had not achieved the projected turnover after three years, although viability might have been achieved at a lower turnover. Of jobs promised only 50 per cent were in place after three years and the committee urged the IDB to get better value for money in job promotions. There was also evidence of 'deadweight' in the disparity between employment figures at the time of the offer of SFA and the benchmark against which additional employment was measured. Finally, there was no proper investigation or assessment of alternative offers of support, for example, from the Irish Republic, so there was a risk of the 'bidding up' of support.

Some similar concerns are to be found in the report of the Northern Ireland Select Committee on employment creation.[46] It argued that the evidence taken from the DED and IDB did not address sufficiently the extent to which jobs promoted were converted into actual jobs. Figures were compiled on the basis of promotions despite estimates of promotions becoming actual jobs varying between 40 per cent and 60 per cent. Measures of effectiveness of client companies by the DED were lacking and estimates of 'deadweight' (that is, jobs which would have been created without the support of government agencies) had been put at between 40 per cent and 62 per cent.[47] These concerns were echoed by one of the witnesses to the committee, the chairman of the Northern Ireland Economic Council, who criticised the methodological shortcomings of the development agencies and the lack of clarity and transparency in their performance and accountability.

The small business support agency, LEDU, had also shifted its focus from jobs to the encouragement of competitiveness as the key to ensure the viability of jobs created and similar concerns were expressed that the measurement of job creation was opaque. The Public Accounts Committee in 1993 believed that the cost-per-job figures were artificially low since they did not allow for displacement and deadweight. In the

1980s, at least, there was no other way to assess the effectiveness of the LEDU since no other performance indicators were collected of companies in receipt of support. A Northern Ireland Audit Office (NIAO) report of 1998 indicates that these concerns persist until the end of the period. It records that the Northern Ireland Economic Council was calling for a more coherent and consistent approach to performance measurements from the IDB, and the NIAO itself noted that limited lessons had been learned from closures and abandoned projects and that all such cases should be formally reviewed. There was also no clear measurement of the effectiveness of the overseas programme of the IDB which had representatives in Germany, the USA and the Far East to try to attract inward investment.[48]

To the methodological layperson, it appears that the question of performance measures, and the deadweight and displacement concerns in particular, persist because of counterfactual problems. It is difficult to see how an accurate prediction of how many jobs would be created in the absence of publicly-funded investment can be made, especially if estimates rely on projections of the firm bidding for support. Similarly the estimation of existing jobs displaced by the support of new ventures by the development agencies would seem to be largely educated guesswork. The tenor of the Audit Office and committee monitoring of the development bodies outlined above suggests that none of them challenged the need for government intervention *per se*, and that the switch in emphasis to the promotion of competition and supply-side strategies was broadly endorsed.

The provision of grants and loans to encourage private sector investment was the responsibility of the LEDU and IDB. An extensive series of schemes for improving skills and competencies within companies and for their workforces and training schemes for the unemployed was managed by the TEA (see Chapter 4). An example of some of its initiatives will give a flavour of its scope; in 1996–97 it spent approximately £23 million on projects aimed at improving skills within companies. These included the Company Development Programme, which had replaced the Manpower Training Scheme, management development schemes and the promotion of enterprise. Just under £144 million was devoted to training for work and career guidance which included the ACE scheme, Enterprise Ulster, Training Centre networks and various open and flexible learning initiatives. Two recent additions in this area had been the Community Work Programme (CWP) and Jobskills. The CWP was established in April 1995 on a pilot basis with the TEA partnering community-based firms and organisations to provide jobs for the long-term unemployed. Jobskills was introduced at the same time and replaced the Youth Training and Job Training Programmes which had been criticised for the poor level of skills provided.[49]

The other main employment scheme (ACE) was under review during this administration. From a peak in the early 1990s of providing over 10,000 places, its target for occupancy had been reduced to 7,200 by 1996–97.[50] In February 1997, Minister of State, John Wheeler, justified reductions in support for training and employment schemes in public expenditure priorities to the Northern Ireland Grand Committee on the grounds that unemployment was falling and on job market changes and Ancram made a similar point in the Commons.[51] Approximately 60 per cent of those placed on the scheme returned to unemployment after leaving which indicated that the training element was insufficient and had influenced the government's decision.

Overall, the period 1992 to 1997 saw little institutional innovation in the field of industrial support, with the government resisting demands for a merging of the development agencies. The choice of indicators would influence a judgement on the condition of the Northern Ireland economy but it was generally faring better than during the 1980s. Unemployment rates for the period are as follows: June 1992, 14.3 per cent; December 1993, 13.6 per cent; January 1995, 12.2 per cent; May 1996, 11.1 per cent; and February 1997, 9.2 per cent. As official figures they should be treated with some caution; however, they probably indicate broad trends. Two particular features of unemployment set Northern Ireland apart from the UK; the much higher proportion of unemployment which was long term and demographic trends which meant large numbers were entering the job market. Government policy did try to influence the location of investment; for example, higher rates of SFA were offered for firms locating in deprived areas. However, some evidence suggests that this had little impact on companies' location decisions.[52]

Social policy

The most important policy initiative in the period in question was the attempt to deal the issue of contentious parades (see p. 111 below). Prior to a discussion of this some more general observations about social policy trends will be made. In the area of fair employment, new legislation had been introduced in 1989 (see Chapter 3). Whether the direct result of this or not, the problem of Catholic disadvantage and under-representation in the workforce seemed to be declining. The SACHR report of 1997 indicated four areas that had shown improvements in the 1990s: equal opportunity policy; the working environment (for example fewer flags and emblems associated with one community on display); more formal recruitment policies; and more objective and systematic recruitment and selection policies.[53] The Commission concluded that there 'was no evidence that either community is experiencing systematic discrimination at the point of selection'[54] and that the increase in Catholic employment since 1990 was strongest in 'white collar' occupations. The Commission recommended that affirmative action be permissible for the long-term unemployed irrespective of religion.

Although a class dimension had never been absent from patterns of disadvantage, and that earlier Catholic disadvantage had a class element to it, there is some evidence that the government was focusing, at least formally, on disadvantage more generally. This was institutionalised by Policy Appraisal and Fair Treatment (PAFT) which was launched in January 1994 after guidelines had been drawn up by the Central Community Relations Unit (CCRU). PAFT was intended to integrate 'conditions of equality into policy formulation and the administration of government at every level'[55] and had five principal objectives. These were to promote positive and proactive approaches to equality of opportunity and equality of treatment, to ensure there was no unlawful discrimination or unjustifiable inequality in any aspect of public administration, to incorporate fair treatment dimension into all policy making and consideration of new provision of services, to take account of fair treatment aspects when reviewing existing policies and provision of services and to monitor the impact of government policies.

By the end of the Conservative administration, the evidence suggested that PAFT had had a limited impact. The guidelines had no statutory force and some departments and agencies had ignored them or else there was little evidence of how or whether they monitored the effect of their policies on equality of various forms. The SACHR was particularly critical of the Department of Finance and Personnel which, given its role in the funding and administration of other departments, could have prosecuted the policy more rigorously and of the CCRU which was content to devolve responsibility to individual departments. Therefore, the SACHR recommended that PAFT have statutory force and be integrated more fully into the NIO administration.[56] If one were to accept that the government was committed to equality at least as a broad principle two problems occurred in implementation. One is that of bureaucratic inertia and fragmentation and the other is the potential conflict between the social good of equality and the government construction of efficiency in economic terms; for example, where competitive tendering informed by the latter conflicted with or led to the marginalisation of PAFT guidelines.

By 1995 the CCRU had a budget of £4.64 million, much of which was devoted to the promotion of good community relations and was administered by district councils. One area that threatened to undermine any progress was that of marches and parades. The confrontations at Drumcree and the Garvaghy Road and the associated disorder in 1995 and 1996 led to the establishment of a review of the issues surrounding marches and parades in August 1996.[57] It was chaired by Peter North of

Oxford University and the other two members were clergymen. At the risk of over-simplifying the complex of issues surrounding marches two are worth highlighting here. One is the broad issue of perception; the two communities often held such different positions over the meaning of certain marches that it might prove beyond the wit of a report suffused with tolerance and liberal concerns to resolve the question. Secondly, there was the practical concern for policy-makers that the role of the police in allowing, re-routing, etc. marches served only to politicise (or perhaps further politicise) their position in Northern Ireland society.

The preliminary part of the review considered both these questions, included much survey material of Northern Ireland opinion on marches and, having reviewed the Human Rights framework, concluded that there was no absolute right to march or to counter-demonstrate. It then outlined four criteria for new proposals. First, any new arrangements should assist the search for accommodation and reinforce the rule of law. Secondly, they should ensure that the competing rights of marchers, residents and the wider community could be accommodated. Thirdly, roles and responsibilities should be clarified with greater transparency in the process and, fourthly, any new arrangements should lead to greater consistency in decision making and seek to achieve accommodation for specific parades over a longer timeframe.

From these criteria two main points emerged. These were the need for statutory criteria which took clearer account of the underlying rights and responsibilities of those involved and the need to remove from the police decisions over contentious parades, particularly as they decide both on conditions attached to parades and then enforce the conditions.[58]

The main recommendation was for the creation of an independent body, the 'Commission'. Its remit should be fivefold: education in community understanding; promotion of mediation and local accommodation; imposition of conditions on specific parades if mediation failed; reviewing Codes of Conduct which were to be introduced; and arranging for contentious parades and protests to be monitored. The review placed considerable emphasis on local mediation and the role the Commission could play in supporting it. Successful resolution of conflicting views through this mechanism would preclude the necessity of further intervention, and many parades and marches would not be considered by the Commission since they were non-contentious. It was envisaged that they could come within the Commission's jurisdiction in one of three ways: through referral by the police; by the Commission's own initiative; or by public representation. In the last case, the government should consider the level of public representation necessary to trigger action by the Commission.

Additional recommendations included the following. The report rejected the 'classification' of parades, as favoured by the Loyal Orders, by which some would be given a higher status and be exempt from or subject to less regulation. The Commission should have full decision-making powers, rather than be an advisory body, and the 1987 Order currently in force should be amended to allow consideration of the wider impact of a parade on community relations when making decisions on banning or re-routing. The period of notice concerning a march given to police should be a minimum of twenty-one days, rather than seven days under the 1987 Order.

In summary, the major institutional change would be the creation of the Commission and the major themes of the report were the emphasis on mediation and promotion of dialogue and the need for transparency so that the grounds on which any parade would be subject to regulation and the responsibilities of organisers, stewards and participants would be made manifest and printed as Codes of Conduct. The government's response to the report's publication in January 1997 was cautious. Mayhew summarised the recommendations to the Commons and announced that the government was to seek the views of interested parties by the end of March. Seemingly because of the controversial nature of the issue and the opposition of the Loyal orders and much of unionism, the government opted for changes that did not require legislation.[59] An independent body with five members would be granted education, mediation and conciliation roles on a non-statutory basis and the following reforms would be introduced: a code of conduct for parades and protests; a registration scheme for bands; notice given by organisers would be extended to twenty-one days; and controls on alcohol would be introduced for those travelling to parades. In March, the Public Order (Amendment) (Northern Ireland) Order 1997 gave effect to the extension of notice and the controls on alcohol; the areas not subject to the consultation process. Labour criticised the response as inadequate and called for the full implementation of the North report.[60]

Conclusion

Three themes in government policy stand out in the period 1992 to 1997. First, the 'three strand' approach which had its genesis in Brooke/Mayhew becomes more firmly entrenched and attempts at giving it institutional expression are advanced. Such is its dominance as orthodoxy that it feeds into the second theme, the large degree of agreement between the two principal British parties over Northern Ireland constitutional policy. Third, is the time and effort at domestic and intergovernmental level devoted to trying to resolve the decommissioning impasse which had become the dominant issue of inter-party discourse.

Notes

1 See P. Arthur, 'The Mayhew Talks 1992', *Irish Political Studies* 8, 1993 for details of the process.
2 HC debates: vol. 213, cols 877–893, 11 November 1992.
3 P. Bew, H. Patterson and P. Teague, *Between War and Peace: the Political Future of Northern Ireland* (London, Lawrence and Wishart, 1997), p. 203.
4 For more details of the speech see W. Harvey Cox 'From Hillsborough ...' pp. 198–200.
5 Cited in W. Harvey Cox, 'From Hillsborough ...', p. 200.
6 J. Major, *The Autobiography*, p. 446. See also P. Arthur, 'Dialogue between Sinn Fein and the British Government', *Irish Political Studies* 10, 1995.
7 See P. Dixon '"A House divided cannot stand": Britain, bipartisanship and Northern Ireland', *Contemporary Record* 9(1) 1995, pp. 176–8.
8 HC debates: vol. 227, cols 476–80, 24 June 1993, cols 1090–5, 1 July 1993.
9 A discussion of the numerous drafts of Hume/Adams and the confusion surrounding them is beyond the scope of this work: see E. Mallie and D. McKittrick, *The Fight for Peace: the Secret Story Behind the Irish Peace Process* (London, Heinemann, 1996).
10 P. Arthur, 'The Anglo-Irish Joint Declaration: towards a lasting peace?', *Government and Opposition* 29(2) 1994, p. 219.
11 HC debates: vol. 234, col. 1090, 15 December 1993.
12 HC debates: vol. 239, col. 350, 9 March 1994.
13 *New Statesman and Society*, 17 March 1995. See also M. J. Hickman, 'Northern Ireland, the Union and New Labour', in S. Hall, D. Massey and M. Rustin (eds), *Sounding Special: the Next Ten Years* (London, Macmillan, 1997).
14 See the work of P. Dixon, '"The usual English Doubletalk": the British Political Parties and the Ulster Unionists 1974–94', *Irish Political Studies* 9, 1994 and 'Labouring under an illusion?', *Fortnight,* 303 and 304, February and March 1992.
15 Differing interpretations of Republican intentions are summarised in J. Dingley, 'Peace processes and Northern Ireland: squaring circles?' *Terrorism and Political Violence* 11(3) 1999.
16 *Independent*, 9 March 1995, p. 2.
17 HC debates: vol. 248, col. 1024, 27 October 1994.
18 HC debates: vol. 248, col. 1102, 27 October 1994.
19 J. Major, *The Autobiography*, p. 470.
20 For more details see B. O'Leary, 'Afterword: What is framed in the Framework Documents?', *Ethnic and Racial Studies* 18(4) 1995 on which the following draws.
21 B. O' Leary uses the metaphor of the Trinity to illustrate the different ways the North/South institutions might develop ('Afterword', p. 869).
22 J. Major, *The Autobiography*, pp. 468–9. According to Major, Molyneaux refused to see the text of the JFD for fear of being implicated in the proposals and was not reassured by Major's triple-lock safeguard (p. 466).
23 HC debates: vol. 255, cols 357, 370, 22 February 1995.
24 *Independent*, 8 March 1995, p. 3.
25 Major, *The Autobiography*, p. 474.
26 HC debates: vol. 256, col. 382, 8 March 1995.
27 HC debates: vol. 260, col. 923, 25 May 1995.
28 D. McKittrick, *The Nervous Peace* (Belfast, Blackstaff, 1996), p. 164.
29 G. Evans and B. O'Leary, 'Northern Irish voters and the British–Irish

Agreement: Foundations of a stable consociational settlement?', *Political Quarterly* 71(1), 2000 p. 99, n. 3. See this note for a more technical explanation of the system. See also P. Mitchell and G. Gillespie, 'The Electoral Systems', in P. Mitchell and R. Wilford (eds), *Politics in Northern Ireland* (Boudler, Co., Westview, 1999), pp. 80–2. For more detail on background to the election and the results see S. Elliott, 'The Northern Ireland Forum/Entry to Negotiations election 1996', *Irish Political Studies* 12, 1997 and G. Evans and B. O'Leary, 'Frameworked futures: Intransigence and flexibility in the Northern Ireland elections of 30 May 1996', *Irish Political Studies* 12, 1997.

30 HC debates: vol. 275, col. 864, 18 April 1996.

31 Major expressed his gratitude for Labour's public and private bipartisan support (HC debates: vol. 270, col. 357, 24 January 1996).

32 See Mayhew, HC debates: vol. 279, col. 970, 19 June 1996.

33 HC debates: vol. 220, cols 959–69, 10 March 1993.

34 HC debates: vol. 239, col. 328, 9 March 1994.

35 HC debates: vol. 256, cols 348–97, 8 March 1995.

36 *Independent*, 13 March 1996, p. 9.

37 HC debates: vol. 291, cols 917–59, 5 March 1997.

38 Cmd. 3420, London, 1996, for details of provisions of emergency legislation.

39 HC debates: vol. 226, cols 149–98, 8 June 1993.

40 HC debates: vol. 261, cols 501–47, 12 June 1995.

41 'Review of the Northern Ireland (Emergency Provisions) Act 1991' (J. J. Rowe), Cmd 2706, London, 1995.

42 Alex Carlile, a Liberal Democrat, spoke of the gap between the ideas and thinking of Mowlam and McNamara (HC debates: vol. 269, col. 65, 9 January 1996).

43 HC debates: vol. 265, col. 26, 30 October 1995.

44 'Northern Ireland Industrial Development Board: selective financial assistance criteria', Committee of Public Accounts (51st Report), HC 544, session 1992–93, London, 1993.

45 Committee of Public Accounts, p. vi.

46 'Employment Creation in Northern Ireland', Northern Ireland Affairs Committee 1st Report, HC 37, 1995. This report contains useful summaries of the condition of the Northern Ireland economy at this time.

47 Northern Ireland Affairs Committee, p. xxxvi. The government's anodyne response to this report is 'Government observations on the First Report from the Northern Ireland Affairs Committee, session 1994–5, "Employment Creation in Northern Ireland HC 37–1"', HC 642, London, 1995.

48 'Inward Investment', Report by the Comptroller and Auditor General for Northern Ireland, Northern Ireland Audit Office, HC 1096, London, 1998.

49 See the CBI reference in Select Committee report, p. xxviii. For a critical view of TEA activity see SACHR, 'Employment equality: Building for the future', Cmd 3684, 1997, p. 50 and for details of the TEA's structure see Northern Ireland Audit Office, 'The Training and Employment Agency: evaluation and performance,' HC 475, London, 1998, p. 3.

50 HC, vol. 288, col. 659, 22 January 1997 (written answer). For eligibility criteria for this scheme see HC, vol. 219, col. 532, 23 February 1993 (written answer).

51 Northern Ireland Grand Committee, 'Public Expenditure', 18 February 1997; Ancram, HC, vol. 291, col. 411, 27 February 1997.

52 Chief Executive of the IDB; minutes of evidence to Committee of Public Accounts, p. 7, 8 March 1993.

53 SACHR 'Employment equality: Building for the future', Cmd 3684, 1997, p. 9.
54 SACHR, 'Employment ...', p. 11.
55 SACHR, 'Employment ...', p. 68.
56 For more details see C. McCrudden, 'Equality and the Good Friday Agreement', in J. Ruane and J. Todd (eds), *After the Good Friday Agreement: Analysing Political Change in Northern Ireland* (Dublin, University College Dublin Press, 1999). Reforms will be discussed in Chapter 6.
57 Published as 'Independent Review of Parades and Marches' (North Report), Belfast, 1997. For more on the significance of marching see N. Jarman, 'Regulating rights and managing public disorder: Parade disputes and the peace process, 1995–1998', *Fordham International Law Journal* 22(4), 1999.
58 North Report, p. 135.
59 Legislation was enacted in 1998 by the Labour government; see Chapter 6.
60 HC debates: vol. 292, cols 1030–46, 19 March 1997.

6

The Labour government, 1997–

On 1 May 1997 the Labour Party won the general election with an overall majority of 165 seats. Marjorie (Mo) Mowlam became Secretary of State for Northern Ireland, Adam Ingram and Paul Murphy were appointed Ministers of State and Tony Worthington and Lord Dubs appointed Under-Secretaries. In the period preceding the election there had been much speculation about how different policy would be under a new administration. Predictions included a rightward shift in Conservatism if defeated and an end to bipartisanship[1] and a greater urgency by Labour to try to restart the 'peace process'.

Constitutional policy and the political process[2]

As indicated in Chapter 5, Blair had already stated that developments since 1993 had overtaken previously adopted positions. This was endorsed by the 1997 manifesto which argued that neither a united Ireland nor the existing status of Northern Ireland commanded the support of both communities. Labour was 'therefore committed to reconciliation between the two traditions and to a new political settlement which can command the support of both.'[3]

The practical implication of such a policy meant attempts to reassure both communities. Before the election Mowlam had indicated that an IRA ceasefire three months before the scheduled renewal of talks in June would allow Sinn Fein entry and that Labour was keen to inject a sense of urgency to the process.[4] Arguably, it was a sense of dynamism, rather than significant policy shifts which differentiated the parties in this as in other areas. On his first visit to Northern Ireland as premier on 16 May, Blair's emphasis was on reassuring Unionists as he spoke of valuing the Union (though stressing that domination by either tradition was unacceptable). He believed that a united Ireland in the lifetime of his audience was unlikely as the consent principle had become widely accepted.[5]

On 2 June an Order in the Commons, under the terms of the Northern Ireland (Entry to Negotiations etc.) Act 1996, was laid to revive the Northern Ireland Forum. Introducing the Order, Mowlam stated that the government endorsed the Mitchell principles and on 25 June Blair expanded on the government position. An aide-memoire had been sent to Sinn Fein following a second meeting with British officials. If, in Mowlam's judgement, 'words and deeds ... consistent with a genuine and unequivocal ceasefire' were in evidence Sinn Fein would be invited to join the plenary session of talks after six weeks.[6] The British and Irish governments proposed to establish an independent commission for decommissioning (which was established in September) which would monitor its implementation and a sub-committee of the plenary session would be established to consider these issues. It was hoped that substantive talks would start by early September at the latest and be completed by May 1998 when the legislative basis for the process expired.

Some of the pre-election predictions mentioned above were proven wrong as bipartisanship was endorsed by William Hague, leader of the opposition, who accepted the six-week provision for entry to talks on condition of adherence to the ceasefire formula cited. Therefore, both major parties advocated the 'twin track' process and the stipulation of 'permanence', as under the Major administration, was sidelined. The bipartisan emphasis was again evident at the end of June when Andrew MacKay, the Conservative shadow spokesman, described Labour's proposals as a 'logical extension' of the process initiated by Major.[7]

On 19 July the IRA announced its second ceasefire with a 'complete cessation of military operations' from the following day. This would allow Sinn Fein into talks and, hindsight indicates, that as prior decommissioning was off the agenda Republicans hoped to prolong the whole process of the 'twin track' and avoid any early decommissioning.

Sinn Fein signed the Mitchell principles on 9 September and the talks were formally launched the following week. Blair emphasised that an IRA breach of the principles would mean Sinn Fein's exclusion from the talks process to which the consistent Republican response was to hold that they were separate organisations (which no other party to events believed) and therefore the linkage was unacceptable. Progress over succeeding months was slow, punctuated by 'fringe' paramilitary violence. Decommissioning was effectively sidelined and the two governments concentrated on developing constitutional policy.

The broad outline for a settlement was published in a position paper, 'Propositions on Heads of Agreement', on 12 January 1998. It contained general propositions by the two governments, and adhered to the 'three strand' process, advocated a Northern Ireland Assembly, a new British–Irish agreement to replace the Anglo–Irish one of 1985 and a North–South ministerial council. Within the last of these, the Northern contingent would take decisions 'within the mandate of, and accountable to, the Northern Ireland Assembly'. The paper seemed to play down the scope and autonomy of cross-border bodies and emphasise the British dimension in strand three by including representatives of devolved institutions in Britain on a future intergovernmental council. This implied movement towards a Unionist agenda compared with the 'greener' JFD of 1995.[8] Additionally, both governments undertook to make constitutional changes as part of an overall settlement; the British were to repeal section 75 of the Government of Ireland Act 1920 and the Irish government to alter Articles 2 and 3 of the 1937 Constitution.

After another three months of talks, proposals and counter-proposals agreement was reached on 10 April 1998. This was achieved against a background of pessimism in the previous week as Unionists rejected a draft prepared by Mitchell on 7 April as being too 'green'.[9] Blair personally supervised the last three days of talks; his intervention being widely interpreted as a snub to Mowlam, whose relationship with Unionists was poor, and principally intended to reassure Trimble whose support was fundamental to the success of any agreement (for more on these reassurances, see p. 122 below).[10]

In gaining the support of all the major Northern Ireland parties except the DUP and United Kingdom Unionists (UKU), and the support of the two governments and the USA, the Good Friday Agreement was potentially the best opportunity for a settlement in the current round of 'troubles'.[11] Therefore, the following section will consider it in some detail and subsequently offer more general reflections.[12]

The opening section on constitutional issues emphasised that the new institutions were interlocking and interdependent and that the principles of consent and the formulation of self-determination were as set out in the DSD of 1993. Whichever government had sovereignty over Northern Ireland, it was pledged that such jurisdiction would be exercised with rigorous impartiality. The agreement then dealt with the detail of the three strands that had underpinned constitutional blueprints throughout the 1990s.

The assembly was to have 108 members elected by STV from existing Westminster constituencies and exercise legislative and executive competence. Various mechanisms would ensure safeguards for minorities and prevent discriminatory practices. No legislation would be valid if in breach of the European Convention on Human Rights (ECHR) or any future bill of rights in Northern Ireland. Specified key decisions, and others which could be designated so through a petition of a minimum of thirty assembly members, would require one of two procedures to be valid. Either parallel consent, a majority of these present and voting including a majority of Nationalists and Unionists present and voting[13] or a weighted majority of 60 per cent of those voting with at least 40 per cent each of Unionist and Nationalist designations. 'Non-key' decisions would be taken on simple majority voting. Committees would be drawn from the assembly to both scrutinise the executive and aid it in policy development. The committees, the chairs and deputy chairs would be allocated in proportion to party strengths. The executive would comprise the First and Deputy Minister, jointly elected on cross-community basis, and up to ten ministers. It would not require collective responsibility and the holding of an executive position necessitated a formal pledge to democratic and non-violent methods. These positions would be allocated in proportion to party strengths in the assembly. Subsequent sections set out the limits to the assembly's legislative powers, for example, the necessity of conforming to human rights legislation and the roles of the secretary of state and the Westminster Parliament.

Strand two was named the 'North/South Ministerial Council' and was to bring together those with executive responsibilities, North and South, to develop 'consultation, co-operation and action within the island of Ireland'[14] which implied that it might (would?) not have executive powers. Participation was an essential responsibility of those holding executive posts which would reassure Nationalists concerned that Unionists would try to emphasise strand one structures and marginalise strand two. The same motivation informed the later statement in this section that the two strands were interdependent and one could not function without the other. To act as a balance, the Northern Ireland representatives were to remain accountable to the assembly, thus emphasising that the North–South body would not develop the autonomy that nationalists would tend to favour. Paragraph 12 of this section stated that any further development of North–South arrangements would need the *specific* endorsement of the Northern Ireland Assembly (emphasis added).

The areas of responsibility had yet to be decided. The agreement suggested twelve possible ones and members of the transitional assembly and the Irish government were charged to try to agree the areas of co-operation by the end of October 1998.[15] There was also provision, though optional, for the establishment of a joint parliamentary forum to supplement the discussions of the North–South body.

Strand three provides for a British–Irish Council (BIC) which will comprise representatives of devolved administrations within the UK, the Irish Republic and those of the Isle of Man and the Channel Islands. As with strand two, it was envisaged that co-operation on matters of mutual interest would be undertaken; however, there would be no obligation to participate and it appeared that the structure would have a residual or marginal role to play. More significantly, a new British–Irish Agreement was to be effected. It would establish a British–Irish Intergovernmental Conference, subsuming the structures established under the AIA of 1985. The conference will 'bring together the British and Irish Governments to promote bilateral co-operation at all levels on all matters of mutual interest within the competence of both Governments.'[16] The Irish government would have the right to put forward views on non-devolved matters and the conference was to address, 'in particular, the areas of rights, justice, prisons and policing in Northern Ireland.'[17] In an echo of the AIA, it was stated that there was no derogation from the sovereignty of either government and that determined efforts would be made to overcome any disagreements between them.

The sections on institutional and constitutional structures, which comprise just over half the agreement, are informed by two broad ideas. First, is the well-established one that some form of power sharing or consociationalism is necessary for a stable settlement. Where the agreement goes further than previous documents is the extent to which it makes possible, if does not necessarily require, the development of confederal structures whereby powers may be delegated to new bodies by the existing jurisdictions. Also, in the context of devolution in other parts of the UK, it is worth noting that devolution for Northern Ireland is arguably of a different order. As O'Leary argues, the UK's relationship to Northern Ireland '*at least in international law*, is explicitly federal because the Westminster parliament and executive cannot, except through breaking treaty obligations, and except through denying Irish national self-determination, exercise power in any manner in Northern Ireland that is inconsistent with the Agreement' (original emphasis).[18]

In addition to the detailed and complex recommendations for constitutional change the agreement outlined reforms to promote and defend human rights and equality of opportunity and a review of policing and the criminal justice system.[19] The whole agreement is imbued with a holistic approach; every significant area of public life and civil society is subject to review and possible reform. Therefore, although elements of the agreement can be traced backed to the Sunningdale Agreement of 1973 and it builds upon the framework documents, the scope and ambition of the agreement is much greater.

The remaining two sections of the agreement will be considered here since, as detailed below, they were fundamental to the disputes which followed. The section on decommissioning ran to only five paragraphs; the most significant of which stated:

> All participants ... reaffirm their commitment to the total disarmament of all paramilitary organisations. They also confirm their intention to continue to work constructively and in good faith with the Independent Commission, and to use any influence they may have, to achieve the decommissioning of all paramilitary arms within two years following endorsement in referendums North and South of the agreement and in the context of the implementation of the overall settlement.[20]

In subsequent discussions Sinn Fein was to hold to the letter of the agreement and argue that they were honouring it as they themselves had no weapons. Furthermore, as decommissioning did not have to take place until 22 May 2000, and even then only in the context of an 'overall settlement', there was no obligation for decommissioning prior to or parallel with the establishment of all the three-strand institutions.

Sinn Fein was able to exploit the situation whereby, in trying to facilitate agreement, last minute concessions and re-drafting had occurred and inconsistencies arose. It might be churlish to blame Blair for this since without 'fudges' and ambiguities the agreement would probably have foundered. In an attempt to keep Sinn Fein involved in talks, the time limit on prisoner releases was reduced from three to two years and the decommissioning requirements weakened.[21] To try to ensure Trimble's support, strand two bodies were not, explicitly at least, to be granted executive functions and the BIC was included. Separately from the agreement, Blair gave Trimble reassurances over decommissioning in a letter part of which stated: 'I confirm that in our view the effect of the decommissioning section of the Agreement, with decommissioning schemes coming into effect from June, is that the process of decommissioning should begin straight away'.[22] This conflicts with the agreement's text and was thus exploited by Sinn Fein. It was to cause some embarrassment to the government since it consistently argued in the agreement's defence that one could not 'cherry pick' from it, while it had made assurances separate from it and in contradiction with it.

The other major area of contention in the months following the agreement was the release of prisoners. The date by which this would occur would be fixed through later legislation. The most significant point, taken with the discussion above, is that prisoner release was not tied to decommissioning. Therefore, the former could (and was to) take place without the latter.[23] This was a problematic issue for the government; it believed that prisoner release was crucial to maintaining Sinn Fein and the smaller Loyalist parties' support for the process yet it appreciated that this would cause offence to many within Northern Ireland. It also implicitly recognised the political nature of the offences which had been denied in official discourse during the course of the 'troubles'.[24]

It may be instructive here to consider a little more the intentions of government in constructing the agreement and why it thought that it would find support within Northern Ireland. By including the commitment to review and reform institutions and structures beyond the narrowly political, the government signalled an intent to recast Northern Ireland society. While a large minority of the Unionist community had misgivings and voted against the agreement, commentators have noted that the various safeguards for minorities built in to the political structures and the commitment to 'parity of esteem' for different traditions would benefit the Unionist community if demographic changes were to render it the minority.[25] The commitment to equal treatment (for example, in material terms or in terms of recognition of communal or national identity) of citizens whatever the constitutional future of

Northern Ireland, a commitment endorsed by the Irish Republic, meant that the agreement could be portrayed as a 'positive sum' game.[26]

It is not the principal concern here to chart Unionist and Nationalist responses. Suffice to say, it is clear that the agreement could be (and was) read as both bolstering and betraying unionism and republicanism, if not nationalism.[27] A judgement on this would depend upon what, if anything, is considered essential to the respective ideologies or their political projects. For example, for Unionists who set great store by recognition of the principle of Unionist consent by the Irish government the agreement was likely to be acceptable; for those opposed to consociational structures that included Republicans in government the agreement would be rejected. If the strategy underpinning government policy was that the carefully constructed and comprehensive agreement could be 'sold' as a positive sum initiative, the tactical manoeuvring in the final few days was aimed at securing support from the two constituencies most important to its likelihood of success. These were the Trimble wing of the UUP and Sinn Fein. It was this imperative that determined the fudging and contradictions around the question of prisoner releases and decommissioning.

There were two elements to the government's agenda after the agreement: to enact the necessary legislation to give effect to the provisions; and to rally support for the agreement before the referendum on 22 May. On 20 April Mowlam addressed the Commons, paid tribute to her Conservative predecessors and spoke of a 'broad political consensus'.[28] Opposition spokesman MacKay stated that the agreement marked the best way forward for Northern Ireland but expressed concerns that paramilitary splinter group activity was continuing and no decommissioning was taking place. He argued that no assembly member should become a minister until paramilitary associates had disarmed and that there should be no prisoner releases until decommissioning was well established.

In the period between the agreement and Mowlam's statement both Hague and MacKay had been conspicuous by their silence on the issue.[29] This seems to have a tactical response to party divisions. Major had paid a fulsome tribute to Blair and Michael Ancram and Lord Cranborne among senior Conservatives had welcomed the agreement. Others, particularly David Wilshire and Andrew Hunter, who had chaired the Conservative Northern Ireland Committee from 1992 to 1997, had serious reservations and doubted it would bring peace.[30] The Conservative tensions over the agreement and their difficulty in formulating a coherent and united response would be manifest in subsequent debates.

The Northern Ireland (Elections) Bill, which was to provide the legislative basis for assembly elections, was introduced on 22 April and was to go through all stages within seven hours with the use of the guillotine. It also provided for the establishment of a shadow executive committee to meet with Irish ministers in the shadow North–South ministerial council to identify approximately six areas for future co-operation. The Conservatives supported the bill but expressed concerns over the decommissioning question and the question of Blair's guarantee to Trimble was raised. Five members (Douglas Hogg, Laurence Robertson, Andrew Hunter, Anne and Nicholas Winterton) supported an amendment opposing the 'rushing through' of the bill and four (those above excluding Hogg) opposed the third reading together with six Unionists. On the same day, the Northern Ireland Negotiations (Referendum) Order 1998 was approved which provided for a referendum and the Forum was wound up under the Northern Ireland (Entry to Negotiations, etc.) Act 1996 (Cessation of Section 3) Order 1998.

Within Northern Ireland, developments favoured government policy. In April 72 per cent of the Ulster Unionist Council supported Trimble over the agreement and, in May, 96 per cent of delegates at a Sinn Fein *ardfheis* voted to change the party constitution to allow members to sit in a Northern Ireland assembly. On 14 May, Blair tried to reassure Unionists by stating that complete and unequivocal ceasefires must include the ending of beatings and the acquisition of weapons and the progressive dismantling of paramilitary structures.[31] Without this there would be no executive places for parties associated with paramilitaries or accelerated release of prisoners.

This was one of three visits made by Blair during the referendum campaign. It is difficult to judge what part these reassurances played especially as the government also tried to bolster acceptance through the announcement of a 'Minister for victims' and additional public expenditure.[32] The 'Yes' campaign triumphed and did better than most of the polls predicted. To the question 'Do you support the agreement reached at the multi-party talks on Northern Ireland and set out in Command Paper 3883?' there was 71.12 per cent vote in support and 28.88 per cent against on a turn out of 81.1 per cent.[33]

Importantly, there was a majority, albeit small, within the Unionist community although the majority of the UUP parliamentary party was opposed. Following the referendum, Mowlam set out the future timetable: the assembly was to meet in shadow form in July when a Presiding Officer, First and Deputy Minister would be elected and other ministerial posts decided and by the end of October areas for North–South co-operation would be identified.

The next piece of legislation introduced was the Northern Ireland (Sentences) Bill which was to give effect to prisoner releases as outlined in the agreement. The second reading was held on 10 June 1998. Prisoners would have to be serving five years or more of a scheduled offence and must have served one-third of their sentence before they could be released on licence. The scheme would apply only to prisoners who supported groups not engaged in violence and the secretary of state would have the authority to judge the condition of the ceasefire. Mowlam stated that criteria would include punishment beatings and the instigation of paramilitary activity. The principal concern for the Conservatives was that there was no clear legislative link between decommissioning and the accelerated release programme and they were to table an amendment insisting on the linkage. MacKay claimed that Blair agreed to this in a Commons statement on 6 May. In fact, his phrasing seems ambiguous and it is worth citing the relevant sections. In reply to a question from Hague, Blair quoted Major with whom he wholeheartedly agreed: 'When sensitive matters such as prisoner release on licence are discussed ... the independent Commission, and the Secretary of State, are bound to have regard as to whether decommissioning has taken place'. He then added, 'it is essential that organisations that want to benefit from the early release of prisoners should give up violence. Decommissioning is part of that, of course, but it goes further. It is not just a question of decommissioning, but a question of making sure, as the agreement says, that there is a complete and unequivocal ceasefire.'[34] These statements do imply some linkage though presumably the secretary of state could 'have regard' but choose to ignore any lack of decommissioning.

Such linguistic convolutions strained party relations as Hunter made the point, as did others, that many Unionists had voted 'yes' in the referendum believing that the prime minister had made a direct link between decommissioning and both Sinn Fein being allowed into the executive and the early release scheme. As the bill stood, it marked the triumph of terror and the 'peace process' had become one of appeasement.[35] Another concern was that although 'full co-operation' with the decommissioning commission was required, logically, this could occur without decommissioning.

The government was keen to try to maintain a bipartisan approach. This is evidenced by their consultation with the opposition over the drafting of the bill, and the Conservatives supported the second reading but were to move amendments in committee.[36] On 15 June an amendment supporting the linking of decommissioning to the early release scheme was defeated. The Conservatives argued that the 'co-operation' formula was weak and insufficient, and on 17 June Malcolm Moss asked what he deemed a simple question: was it possible that at the end of two years all prisoners could be released without any decommissioning having taken place? It was a simple question to which Ingram could not provide an unambiguous answer. A second amendment which would allow early release only if the organisation represented by the prisoners had 'already decommissioned a substantial proportion of its illegally held firearms' was defeated by 260 votes to twelve with five Conservatives opposing.[37]

The Conservatives opposed the third reading because of the lack of linkage. However, their wish to avoid a serious rift with government was shown by the failure of nine members of the shadow cabinet, including Hague, to vote and the imposition of only a two-line whip.[38] MacKay stated that he wanted to continue the bipartisan policy wherever possible despite what he believed to be a breach of trust. A more charitable interpretation of Blair's breach of trust would be that he was engaging in realpolitik. The government was frequently to claim that the agreement had to be observed and was not subject to selective interpretation. This often seemed to be related to Republican concerns so his statements at the time of the referendum and before the sentences bill were aimed at reassuring Unionists in a form of 'balancing'. Thus arose the 'complete ambiguity' concerning decommissioning, prisoner release and entry into the executive upon which commentators remarked.[39] The Conservatives could not easily exploit this since they formally supported the agreement and had no alternative policy yet senior figures, including John Redwood and Michael Howard, were opposed to the release of prisoners.

The assembly election was held on 25 June 1998. There were 108 seats with six candidates elected by STV in each of the eighteen Westminster constituencies. Nationalists won forty-two seats, of which twenty-four went to the SDLP and eighteen to Sinn Fein. The most significant outcome in respect of the prospects for a workable assembly was going to be the division of support between pro- and anti-agreement unionists. Pro-agreement Unionists won thirty seats (twenty-eight for the UUP, two for the Progressive Unionist Party (PUP) and anti-agreement Unionists won twenty-eight (twenty DUP, five UKU and three others). The remaining eight seats were won by the Alliance Party and the Women's Coalition which supported the agreement.[40] Therefore, eighty of the members were pro-agreement. The Unionist division was roughly of the same proportion as at the recent referendum and was encouraging for the government as pro-agreement Unionists had a narrow majority, although the lack of stability in the UUP meant this could not be safely predicted in the longer term. Despite the split in unionism, the election was not marked by a recasting of electoral cleavages as there was very little transfer of preferences from Nationalist to pro-agreement Unionist candidates or vice versa.[41] The lack of decommissioning had not affected Sinn Fein's support which increased to 17.7 per cent of first preference votes and constituted approximately 45 per cent of the Nationalist vote.

The electoral arithmetic and the decisive referendum vote appeared to augur well for political progress. The first meeting of the assembly was held on I July when Trimble was elected First Minister and Mallon, of the SDLP, the Deputy First Minister. The legislative basis for the implementation of the Belfast Agreement was completed with the passage of the Northern Ireland Bill which was the third part of the 'triple lock' safeguard which Major had introduced. During the second reading on 20 July, members were informed that devolution would take place once the Secretary of State had judged 'sufficient' progress had been made in the carrying out of shadow functions, that is, decisions on ministries in the assembly and the form and competence of the North/South Council and BIC. Decisions on exclusion from the assembly for not supporting the principles of non-violence would be the responsibility of the assembly. The Conservatives supported the bill despite concerns over prisoner releases and representatives in government of those linked to paramilitaries. In a defeated amendment, tabled by Bottomley, a Conservative and Hoey, a Labour member, there was an attempt to tie the taking up of ministerial positions to the end of punishment beatings and full compliance with the decommissioning commission which would mean all guns and explosives handed in within two years.

Most of the amendments and changes at report and committee stage concerned the detail of procedures, and safeguards around the legislation introduced, in the assembly. The bill received its third reading on 31 July, the day after the appointment of the commissioners charged with determining on individual prisoner releases under the Northern Ireland (Sentences) Act 1998.

With the legislative framework for the agreement in place and the 'triple lock' criteria fulfilled, implementation depended on resolving the question of decommissioning and disputes over the structures of the new institutions. Although Sinn Fein appointed a representative to the commission in September, there had been no movement by the end of 1998. This effectively precluded Unionist participation in the assembly unless the SDLP were prepared to enter government without Sinn Fein members in the executive. With respect to the new bodies, the UUP favoured fewer departments in the new assembly since this was more likely to give them a disproportionate number of portfolios relative to their electoral strength[42] and also favoured a minimalist interpretation of the scope of the North–South bodies. It was not until December that the UUP and the SDLP agreed that there should ten departments in the assembly and six North–South implementation bodies should be established, which was the minimum requirement of the Good Friday Agreement.[43]

The frustration at the stalemate felt by the opposition was made clear when the Conservatives used an Opposition Day in December to introduce a motion which stated that no further early prisoner releases should occur until 'substantial and verifiable decommissioning' had taken place. There was, argued MacKay, an imbalance in the process in that in the seven months since the agreement more than 200 prisoners had been released and no decommissioning had taken place. He also argued that there was no incentive for paramilitaries to decommission if all their prisoners were released so tactically the current policy made little sense. The problem for the government was that, according to the letter, the issues were not linked in the agreement and despite uneven progress Mowlam argued that the opposition were too quick to call for a halt to one dimension of the agreement.[44]

Much of this disagreement, as before and subsequently, related to whether one believed the IRA intended to decommission at all and on one's definition of a ceasefire and the renunciation of violence. The Conservatives were inconsistent on the latter questions and the emphasis varied from member to member. MacKay accepted that the ceasefire was holding, which was Mowlam's 'touchstone', but the absence of decommissioning meant that there had been no renunciation of violence and, therefore, there was no basis for the release of prisoners. Among Conservative members, Hunter was particularly scathing claiming that, 'what was intended to be a peace process, long ago turned into a shameful process of appeasement'.[45]

The rejection of decommissioning by the IRA two days later further strained bipartisan relations[46] and in January 1999, MacKay moved a motion that prisoner releases should stop until punishment beatings ended as this breached the agreement. As with his equation over decommissioning, he argued that punishment beatings were more likely to stop if prisoners were not released so the government could use this as a bargaining ploy.[47] MacKay also argued that punishment beatings meant that sections of the 1998 Act were being breached. However, Mowlam responded by arguing that the ceasefire was intact, as MacKay had acknowledged in the December debate, and therefore if releases were halted it would amount to a unilateral change to the agreement and harm the process. To avoid breaching the agreement and by way of a compromise, Harry Barnes, a Labour member more sympathetic to unionism than most, tabled an early-day motion advocating a 'slow down' in releases. In summary, Moss, Conservative deputy spokesman, stated that prisoner release without decommissioning was unacceptable to the opposition, while Ingram argued that there was no guarantee that stopping releases would stop punishment beatings and thus rejected the opposition's punitive approach.

Before a consideration of the detail, it might be worth considering briefly the government's position at the beginning of 1999. If decommissioning were not forthcoming, it had to decide whether to exclude Sinn Fein from the process. The evidence would indicate that the government concurred with the judgement of the Irish government that a stable settlement could not be constructed on such grounds. Therefore, many of the twists and turns, formulations and convolutions of 1999 can be explained by and largely reduced to trying to find a way to establish an executive in the absence of decommissioning.

In January the government announced that it hoped to see the transfer of powers on 10 March, although Mowlam later had to revise this to early April. The following month the Northern Ireland Arms Decommissioning Act 1997 (Amnesty Period) Order 1999 was introduced. This provided for a one-year extension to a limited amnesty which would prohibit any forensic and evidential tests on decommissioned items. This was uncontroversial and supported by the Conservatives since without the Order there would be no prospect of decommissioning. The debate again provided illustrations of differing views of the relationship between the issues. Mowlam argued that it was up to the parties to decide on the ordering of decommissioning and executive formation; Barnes thought it reasonable to see some movement towards decommissioning first. Wilshire, the Conservative backbencher, believed that there was no intention by the IRA ever to disarm and both he and Hunter spoke of 'appeasement'.[48]

In early March the North/South Co-operation (Implementation Bodies) (NI) Order 1999 was approved which gave statutory basis to the six agreed bodies (see note 43, p. 149 above) and covered areas like grants, staffing, financing and the provision of annual reports. At the same time the British and Irish governments signed a series of treaties concerning the 'strand two' and 'strand three' bodies, thus completing the formal underpinning of the agreement.

The 10 March deadline, like others before and since, came and went with no devolution and, therefore, no other institutions established. On 1 April, after three days of discussion, Blair and Bertie Ahern (who became Taoiseach in June 1997) produced the Hillsborough Declaration. It proposed the nomination of ministers and, within one month, 'some arms to be put beyond use on a voluntary basis'. This would allow the triggering of devolution. Along with the putting of arms beyond use, there would be a 'collective act of reconciliation' which would include ceremonies of remembrance for victims and a reduction in the British security presence.

This attempt at a compromise, underpinned by what the framers presumably saw as a liberal package which offered something to everyone, failed. The UUP was split over the proposal but agreed to it as a basis for negotiation; however, on 13 April Sinn Fein rejected it. This was on the now familiar grounds that Sinn Fein's right to inclusion in an executive derived from its electoral mandate and that the Hillsborough Declaration was inconsistent with and an attempt to rewrite the agreement which only required decommissioning by May 2000. (The chronology of attempts at a 'breakthrough' will be revisited after a consideration of the victims' remains legislation of May.)

On 10 May the Northern Ireland (Location of Victims' Remains) Bill was given its second reading. On 29 March the IRA had stated that it knew of the whereabouts of nine of its victims who had not previously been found. The bill contained three main provisions. First, information and evidence leading to the discovery of remains would be inadmissible in criminal proceedings and the forensic testing of remains would be restricted. Secondly, it made provision for a commission which had been set up on 27 April to receive information concerning remains, and thirdly, it allowed for the entry and search of premises where remains were likely to be found.[49] These provisions would make it easier to locate the remains of victims and allow funerals to take place.

Given the support of the families for the bill and the solace it might bring, the Conservatives did not oppose it, although they would have found it more palatable if an executive had been established and decommissioning were under way. Andrew Hunter, one of nine Conservatives who opposed the second reading, described the bill as 'odious' and a means through which executive wishes were undermining the judicial process and the law was undermined by political expediency. An amendment to 'time limit' the bill was withdrawn in committee and the third reading passed with only five votes against. For the government, Ingram accepted the distasteful aspects of the bill but felt there was no choice but to introduce it.

In mid-May Blair had set 30 June as another deadline for the conclusion of talks as devolution was due the following day for Scotland and Wales. When no agreement was reached, the two governments engaged in intensive discussions to produce a joint statement: 'The Way Forward'. At the beginning of July, the mood of Blair was very optimistic with talk of 'historic and seismic shifts in the political landscape' in reference to the belief that Sinn Fein was to recommend full decommissioning to the IRA within a year.[50]

On 2 July he outlined the process thus: 'Devolution will begin. Shortly afterwards, within days, the process of decommissioning begins, both notification and authorisation that it should happen. Within weeks of that, actual decommissioning, continuing right through until complete decommissioning of all paramilitary weapons within Northern Ireland by May 2000.'[51]

Blair addressed the Commons on 5 July. On 15 July Northern Ireland ministers were to be nominated and de Chastelain, who had submitted his decommissioning report on 2 July, expected decommissioning within a 'couple of days'. This seemed to be in the form of a statement of intent and, if this did not happen, the executive would be unwound. Following a statement of intent, the commission would then set a further time limit within which there would have to be a start to actual decommissioning. In trying to reassure Unionists, Blair argued that it was a better deal than that of Hillsborough in April as the present scheme required full rather than token decommissioning, did not require reciprocal steps by the two governments and had the fail-safe of executive suspension.[52] Also, it was the paramilitaries themselves and not the parties that had to make the statement within days. There followed days of uncertainty about whether Unionists would accept the proposals and reassurances, since it meant executive establishment before any actual decommissioning. An additional concern was that if Sinn Fein were suspended in the absence of decommissioning whether the SDLP would participate in any subsequent executive without them.

The bill to give effect to the proposals was taken in one day on 13 July, with devolution intended for 18 July and the commission to sort out the modalities for decommissioning for May 2000. If requirements were not met, the bill provided for the suspension of the executive and a process of review. The Conservatives offered support if the fail-safes were legally binding and specified three that were missing and would be pushed for through amendments. These were the need for a transparent and specific timetable, the suspension of Sinn Fein if the IRA did not decommission since suspension of the assembly would punish all parties and the sanction of the end to prisoner releases was needed against those groups which had no interest in the assembly or executive. The prospects for success appeared poor as Trimble attacked Mowlam's handling of the process, noted the complete absence of any 'seismic shift' and stated that he understood Blair's assurances to mean decommissioning should have begun in June 1998. Unionists and ten Conservatives, mainly from the right of the party, opposed the second reading.[53]

In committee, MacKay introduced a clause to halt prisoner releases if there was no decommissioning and the Conservatives supported various amendments tabled by Wilshire and Trimble to provide a precise timetable. For the government, Murphy countered that deadlines for various stages or completion of decommissioning should be left to the Commission which was more likely to be trusted than government and the opposition was accused of 'cherry-picking' the agreement by bringing in the question of prisoner releases. The amendments were defeated; on the third reading the Conservatives abstained with sixteen voting against the bill.

In a last effort to sway Trimble and the UUP, Blair announced the following day that three amendments would be tabled in the Lords to include the publication of a specific timetable by de Chastelain and that if the IRA defaulted, Sinn Fein would be named as the defaulting party under the legislation.[54] These concessions failed to make a difference and on the 15 July the UUP, the DUP and the Alliance Party failed to nominate candidates for the executive. In farcical scenes, an all-Nationalist executive was nominated and promptly dissolved since it failed to meet the cross-community requirements of the 1998 agreement and Mallon resigned as deputy First Minister.

The official government line was not to engage in recrimination since it would make any revival of the process more difficult. However, individual Labour MPs, such as Soley and McNamara, accused the Conservatives of encouraging Unionist 'rejectionism', while MacKay pointed the finger firmly at the terrorists for the stalemate. While the Conservatives had not formally repudiated the agreement, bipartisanship was strained as there was more of a disposition among Labour to blame Unionist intransigence and to stress the indivisibility of the agreement while Conservatives increasingly saw the process as one of concessions to republicanism with no reciprocity.[55]

The government announced that the implementation of the agreement, though not the agreement itself, would be reviewed. This would begin in early September under the chairmanship of Senator George Mitchell. In the interim, elements of the agreement under the control of government would continue to be implemented. Before the *de facto* summer recess Republicans made increasingly 'hard line' statements about decommissioning and the prospects of progress.[56]

Inter-party relations were still strained on the eve of the review to which neither the UUP nor Sinn Fein had pledged themselves. Both Blair and Mowlam were critical of elements in the Conservative Party and relations had been worsened by Mowlam's judgement on 26 August that the ceasefire was holding. This was despite the continuation of punishment beatings, the killing of an IRA informer and the capture of arms being smuggled from Florida for the IRA in July.[57] This meant that the policy of prisoner releases would not be suspended.

On 12 October Mowlam was replaced by Peter Mandelson as Secretary of State. Relations between Mowlam and Unionists had been poor since the early summer and made worse by her judgement concerning the ceasefire. This had been interpreted as one more example of her over eagerness to placate Republicans and it had been widely predicted that she would be removed in a summer 'reshuffle', but had convinced Blair to allow her to remain.[58] Thus, it was hoped that Mandelson's appointment would improve the chances of Unionist co-operation in the review since, as a New Labour exemplar, he was not perceived to have any pro-Nationalist leanings commonly associated with the Labour Party.

This policy appeared to work as, after intense negotiations, agreement was reached whereby the UUP agreed to take up places in an executive before the actual decommissioning of arms.[59] This was facilitated by an IRA statement that it was prepared to appoint an interlocutor to de Chastelain's Commission, although it offered no timetable or acceptance of the obligation to disarm. On 22 November, Mandelson informed the Commons that the Mitchell review had concluded on 18 November. Interlocutors would take up their roles on the day that devolution occurred which, in Mandelson's formulation, meant that the process of decommissioning would effectively start at the beginning of devolution. If there was default on either devolution or decommissioning then the institutions would be suspended. On 30 November the Northern Ireland Act 1998 (Appointed Day) Order 1999 was approved which provided for devolution. This occurred on 2 December and the parallel strand two and three institutions were established. The Irish government repealed the old Articles 2 and 3 which laid claim to Northern Ireland and the IRA appointed an interlocutor to the de Chastelain's commission.

At this stage, at least two potential problems remained. First, if Sinn Fein stuck to the letter of the agreement, it would argue that decommissioning need not occur until May. Trimble had agreed with the Ulster Unionist Council (UUC) to review the situation in February 2000 and, if no decommissioning had taken place by that date, Mandelson had undertaken to suspend devolution. Secondly, Trimble's position within the UUP was not unassailable. It was only late in the process that his deputy John Taylor, often seen as a 'weathervane' of UUP opinion, was persuaded to support the deal via personal correspondence from Mandelson.

The decommissioning commission's report of 10 December stated that it believed that decommissioning would occur although none had so far and no timetable had been agreed. On 3 February Mandelson announced that a second report of 31 January revealed that no decommissioning had taken place. These reports were not published, on the ostensible grounds that this was not in the provenance of the British government as they were jointly owned with the Irish government. However, this fuelled the sceptics' belief that the IRA had no intention of decommissioning which was a reality that the government was reluctant to acknowledge. On 8 February provision for the suspension of the institutions of the Good Friday Agreement was made by the Northern Ireland Act. The legislation was supported by the Conservatives with nine Labour MPs supporting Nationalists who opposed suspension on the second reading and eight on the third reading.

Suspension took place on 11 February. Nationalists were angered and also felt that this reduced the likelihood of progress on decommissioning but Mandelson had little room for manoeuvre. Given assurances made to Trimble and the government's need to defend his position within the UUP, it had little alternative but to suspend and hope that future talks could resuscitate the process.

A major breakthrough occurred on 6 May when an IRA statement committed the organisation to a 'process that will completely and verifiably put arms beyond use' and to resume contact with the decommissioning commission. The IRA stated that it was prepared to allow independent inspectors to examine arms dumps, a role which was to be filled by Cyril Ramaphosa, former Secretary General of the ANC and Martti Ahtisaari, a former president of Finland. In a Commons statement on 8 May, Mandelson announced that new legislation would not be needed as the Northern Ireland Decommissioning Act of 1997 was sufficiently flexible to allow for this process.[60] He emphasised, in an effort to reassure Unionists, that it was important to distinguish between initial measures to make arms safe and the necessary, subsequent process of decommissioning. This was emphasised later in the month by Blair as the restoration of devolution crucially depended on the response of the UUC. On 27 May it voted narrowly to support a return to the assembly and on 31 May devolution was re-established.

Security policy

This section will cover two main areas: the legislative framework of security policy; and the review of policing in Northern Ireland. In October 1997, Jack Straw, the Home Secretary, announced that he proposed to replace the PTA and EPA with permanent UK-wide counter-terrorist legislation as recommended in the Lloyd report (see Chapter 5), and in the interim both pieces of legislation would be extended. On 18 November the Northern Ireland (Emergency Provisions) Bill was presented for second reading. This was to provide amendments to existing provisions and to extend the 1996 Act which was due to expire in August 1998.[61] The Act would be extended to August 2000, subject to annual renewal, and there were to be three main changes. First, additional scheduled offences could be 'certified out', for example riot and some firearms offences, as 'Diplock' courts were to be retained. Secondly, provision for internment was to be dropped from the statute and, thirdly, the audio-recording of suspect interviews was to be introduced.

The first of these marked a change from opposition where Labour had supported the concept of 'certifying in'. Ingram argued that difficulties could arise if the judicial system had to be involved in judgements about which cases should be subject to a jury trial which failed to convince McNamara given that the criterion used – whether terrorism was involved or not – was the same whether certifying in or out. Worthington, for the government, responded that with the former system the Attorney-General was put in the invidious position of deciding who was to be denied a jury trial while with the latter it is parliament that denies certain categories of defendant jury trial.

The Conservatives supported the legislation although MacKay did not miss the opportunity to barrack Labour over its changed position on emergency legislation and to oppose the first two of the proposed changes. The first smacked of 'tokenism' and the second was motivated by political rather than security concerns.[62]

At the report stage, two amendments tabled by Trimble over the renewal date of the legislation and increased 'certifying out' were withdrawn, leaving a Conservative one supporting the retention of internment. A division over this prompted Ingram to argue that it could be seen as a breakdown in bipartisanship, though this was denied by MacKay. The amendment was defeated and the third reading of the bill was unopposed.

The second of the long-established pieces of emergency legislation, the PTA, was renewed in March of the following three years. The only changes of note were the ending of exclusion orders in 1998 and an amendment brought about by the passage of the Criminal Justice (Terrorism and Conspiracy) Bill 1998.

This bill was presented to the Commons on 2 September 1998, which had been recalled in the wake of the Omagh bombing of 15 August. All stages of the bill were to be completed in one day with the government allowing a maximum of six hours' discussion after the second reading which induced protests from MPs of all parties. Straw invoked precedent in his defence; both the original PTA of 1974 and amendments in April 1996 had been 'rushed through' the House.

The bill had four major provisions. First, in relation to trying to prove membership of a proscribed organisation the opinion of a police officer of the rank of superintendent or above would be admissible, though conviction could not be secured on this evidence alone.[63] This was to have the effect of rendering admissible in evidence assessments of intelligence material which would otherwise have been dismissed as hearsay. Secondly, and also to facilitate conviction, the court would be permitted to draw inferences from the failure of a suspect to answer relevant questions in respect of a membership offence. Thirdly, the bill provided for the forfeiture of property following conviction of membership of or support for a proscribed organisation. Fourthly, conspiracy to commit terrorist acts abroad would be an offence, if that act were also an offence in the UK.

Labour backbenchers, including Chris Mullin, Tony Benn and McNamara expressed various concerns, including the right to confiscation and the question of the compatibility of the legislation with the European Convention on Human Rights and the International Convention on Civil and Political Rights.[64] Additionally, the clause on conspiracy did not differentiate between democracies and dictatorships or take account of regimes' human rights records. The bill, therefore, had the implication of criminalising opposition such as that of the ANC to apartheid South Africa. McNamara's motion to deny a second reading was defeated by 391 votes to seventeen with the Conservatives supporting the government and the third reading was unopposed. The Act would be subject to annual review.

The group responsible for the Omagh bombing was later to declare a ceasefire, so it is questionable whether such legislation was necessary, although the government could not, of course, foresee this development. Previous legislation relating to proscription and membership of terrorist organisations had made little impact, so there remains the suspicion that legislation at speed was a response to the need to be 'seen to be doing something' rather than a considered strategy.

Following the Lloyd report and earlier pledges (see p. 104 above), a new terrorism bill was introduced and given a second reading on 14 December 1999 and a third reading in March 2000, and was to replace the EPA and PTA. The legislation was to be permanent, UK-wide and cover both domestic and international terrorism. Terrorism was defined as such activity which 'involves the threat or use of serious violence for political, religious or ideological ends'. This formulation was broader than that used in 'emergency' legislation and indicated the further relegation of the protection of civil liberties on Labour's agenda.

The structure and role of the police service in Northern Ireland was a subject which elicited a high degree of polarisation of community attitudes. In late 1997 the Police (Northern Ireland) Bill had introduced reforms in the complaints system by the introduction of an ombudsman and required more openness and community consultation by the Police Authority. However, a much more thoroughgoing review of policing was part of the Good Friday Agreement which stated that, 'an independent Commission will be established to make recommendations for future policing arrangements in Northern Ireland including means of encouraging widespread community support for these arrangements ...'.[65] In June 1998 Chris Patten, a junior minister in Northern Ireland between 1983 and 1985 and former Governor of Hong Kong, was appointed to chair the commission which submitted its report in September 1999.[66]

There are three recurring themes in the report: those of police relations with the community they serve; the question of accountability; and the transparency of the objectives of the police service. In these areas the system was in need of reform. In the introduction, the report noted that the existing Police Authority, in the absence of local government, had operated as a 'surrogate for an accountability mechanism' and that a Select Committee report of 1998 had argued that the Police Authority had taken a very restricted view of its statutory duties.[67] In the section on accountability the report details two interconnected problems. One is the lack of democratic input into policing as the Police Authority is appointed by the Secretary of State who, in turn, is not elected by the people of Northern Ireland. The other is the lack of 'explanatory and co-operative' accountability; that is, people not knowing what the police are doing and why.

In light of these failings, the report recommended a new Policing Board to replace the Police Authority. It would be the responsibility of the Secretary of State, or his/her equivalent in a devolved government, to set long-term government objectives for policing and the Policing Board to set medium-term (three to five year) objectives and priorities. It would have a supervisory role over the police service but should also consider the wider issues of policing and the role of other agencies in respect of public safety. Its chief statutory role would be to hold the Chief Constable and the police service publicly to account and be responsible for appointing all chief officers.

In relation to composition, nineteen members were recommended. Ten would be members of the assembly from parties which comprised the executive, although not executive members. The remaining nine members would be drawn from corporate groups such as business, trades unions, the legal profession and the voluntary sector. They would be appointed by the Secretary of State or, in the event of devolution, the First and Deputy Ministers.[68]

The report had expressed concern about the perceived balance of influence within the tripartite Chief Constable/Secretary of State/Police Authority relationship with the last of these lacking influence. It would, therefore, be necessary to ensure that the Policing Board would not be seen as government-controlled, especially after devolution as this would risk a return to the pre-1969 position. To stress independence, section 39 of the Police Act 1998 allowing the Secretary of State 'guidance' to the police should be repealed and the Chief Constable should have operational 'responsibility' rather than 'independence'.

The second major reform advocated the replacement of the 'elitist' Community and Police Liaison Committees by District Policing Partnership Bodies (DPPB), which would be committees of district councils. There would be one for each council area with the majority of members elected and the rest independently selected by district councils with Policing Board agreement. The function of the DPPB would be advisory, explanatory and consultative as well as to facilitate public consultation about annual policing plans.

To encourage transparency, all general principles about policing should be in the public domain unless it was in the public (but not police) interest to withhold them. The role of the new police ombudsman, created by the Police (Northern Ireland) Act 1998, should be proactive and not limited to specific complaints received.

The other principal recommendations of the report covered the structure of the force, size, composition, culture, ethos and symbols and human rights. The number of sub-divisions should be reduced and there should be one district command for each district council area. This would make local government, policing and DPPB boundaries coterminous and facilitate police–community linkages, which was the report's central theme.[69] The special branch should be reformed and integrated into normal policing structures to address the perception that it was 'a force within a force'. The size of the RUC should be reduced from nearly 13,000 (including 1,300 part-time reservists) to 7,500 if the peace process were to hold.

Composition was a vital area because of the overwhelmingly Protestant complexion of the RUC. At the end of 1998, 88.3 per cent of regulars were Protestant, 8.3 per cent Catholic and 3.4% 'other'.[70] The report set targets of a recruitment profile over the following ten years of 50:50 and a doubling of Catholic officers in four years and a quadrupling in ten years to between 29 per cent and 33 per cent. To facilitate these targets, all leaders in the Nationalist community should encourage people to join.

Partly because of the security situation, RUC culture was overly hierarchical and militaristic and a culture of openness, public consultation, customer service and human rights were all underdeveloped. More controversially, the report suggested four changes to make the service more acceptable to the Nationalist community. The force would be renamed the Northern Ireland Police Service, a new badge and symbols associated with neither the British nor Irish states would be adopted, the Union flag would no longer be flown from police buildings and a NIPS flag would be flown when one was required. Finally, it was recommended that an oath be taken to uphold human rights and a new code of ethics developed which integrated the ECHR into police practice.

The Patten report, which placed much emphasis on consultation and community, followed its own brief and over 10,000 people attended public meetings on the future of the RUC. However, this did not produce consensus. While much of the report was non-contentious, Conservatives supported Unionists in opposition to the name and badge change and the disbanding of the special branch.[71] Mandelson was acutely aware of Unionist sensibilities and a period of consultation on the report until the end of November was announced. In late November, and just before the vote by the UUC on the proposals for entering the assembly, it was announced that the RUC was to be awarded the George Cross; a move that was widely seen as an emollient. On 19 January 2000, Mandelson announced the government's response to the report. It accepted all the main recommendations and that the name would be the Police Service of Northern Ireland (PSNI). Mandelson stated that in an ideal world the title RUC would be kept but without a fresh start the police service would not gain the support of both the communities. MacKay indicated that he preferred the compromise RUC–PSNI and some Conservatives interpreted changes as another step on the road to appeasement.[72]

In early April the Conservatives supported a UUP opposition day motion which condemned the removal of the RUC title and demanded that other changes await a confirmed improvement in the security situation. Many of Mandelson's statements marked a retreat from Patten in an attempt to deal with Unionist concerns. For example, he revealed that the new oath would not be taken by existing officers but only by new recruits, that the new title would not be adopted until autumn 2001, that DPPBs would initially be purely consultative and measures would be taken to exclude anyone convicted of a terrorist offence from serving on DPPBs as an independent member. Additionally, various structural changes such as phasing out the full-time reserve and amalgamating the special branch and CID would depend on the Chief Constable's assessment of the level of terrorist threat. For the Conservatives, MacKay argued that any changes to the police force related to security should be the subject of separate legislation and not be introduced by affirmative order within the scope of the main bill.

The second reading of the Police (Northern Ireland) Bill was presented on 6 June.[73] Mandelson conceded that much detail had to be dealt with in committee and it appeared that concessions would have to be made to Nationalists given the recent 'drift'. Evidence of susceptibility to Unionist concerns and those of the security establishment include provision in the bill for an RUC George Cross foundation to keep the RUC name alive and the bill would also include a 'legal description' incorporating the RUC to make it clear that it was not being disbanded. Both the government reserve power to limit police board inquiries and its opposition to an executive or expenditure role for DPPBs were a minimalist reading of Patten and seemed likely to reduce democratic accountability and transparency of operation.

The opposition moved an amendment to decline a second reading on the grounds that the bill failed to preserve the name and insignia of the RUC, it allowed political representatives of paramilitaries to sit on DPPBs and the police board without the start of decommissioning, there were inadequate safeguards against those convicted of scheduled offences sitting on bodies and the bill threatened to politicise policing in Northern Ireland. However, the Conservatives would abstain on second reading if the amendment were defeated given they supported many of the changes and MacKay advocated a 'dual' naming for the service.

Labour backbenchers including Norman Godman and John McDonnell argued that the bill was a retreat from Patten and downgraded the role of the police board and the DPPBs and McNamara detected the influence of the NIO and the security services in the process of emasculation. Brian Mawhinney, a former Conservative Northern Ireland minister, argued that Mandelson's position was one of 'innate conservatism' and that he had been over-sensitive to Unionist concerns.[74] The second reading was passed with six Conservative MPs voting against the proposals.[75] It seemed likely that Mandelson's hints at strengthening the power of the police board and a greater commitment to equalising recruitment would be necessary in committee stage to satisfy Nationalist concerns.

With the reform of emergency legislation and the police service, the third strand of policy relating to security to be addressed was the criminal justice system. There was a commitment to review in the Good Friday Agreement. The main points to be addressed were arrangements for appointments to the judiciary and magistracy, arrangements for organisation of the prosecution process, the scope for co-operation between the criminal justice agencies in both parts of Ireland and consideration of which aspects of criminal justice functions might be devolved to the assembly. A period of consultation with interested parties started in August 1998 and was to be completed by the following summer; however, this process was still on-going in July 2000.

Economic policy

The advent of a Labour administration in Northern Ireland resulted in no major shifts in either the general parameters of economic policy or the institutional structures for economic support and regeneration. This can be explained in part by New Labour's embracing of enterprise, its commitment to inherited public expenditure targets and the fact that, under the Conservatives, Northern Ireland had tended to experience more *dirigisme* than the rest of the UK. A flavour of contemporary government thinking and review of the Northern Ireland economy can be found in the report of the DED Strategy Review Steering Group, 'Strategy 2010' published in March 1999.[76] In his evidence to the Northern Ireland Grand Committee, Ingram emphasised the importance of business and the government's favourable view of the private sector. However, the strategy review attempted to go beyond a narrow focus of industrial policy to include factors such as education, infrastructure and the cultural context.[77] The steering group identified the following strengths and weaknesses of the Northern Ireland economy. Strengths included the telecommunications infrastructure, demography (a young population), a competitive investment location and a flexible labour force. Weaknesses included high long-term unemployment and benefit dependency, too much manufacturing in low-growth sectors, too little research and development expenditure, over-dependence on grants for project finance, deficient technical training and high energy costs. Specific recommendations included the need to focus on information and communication technologies, to increase innovation and research and development and to promote business collaboration and networking. A shift from investment grants for existing businesses to support for equity finance and more extensive tax incentives were advocated and the establishment of a single economic development agency.

The evidence of IDB executives to the Northern Ireland Select Committee gives a 'snapshot' of the operation of industrial support policy.[78] The need to develop hi-tech industries is indicated by its targeted sectors for 1998–2001: software, network services, telecommunications, health technologies, electronics and automotive components. There was also a social aspect to IDB operation as one of its five key objectives for 1998–2001 was to locate 75 per cent of all first-time inward investment in or adjacent to Targeting Social Need (TSN) areas. Capital grants of up to 50 per cent were available for such areas compared with 30 per cent elsewhere in the province.[79] It was revealed in the evidence given that the conversion rate of jobs promoted to those delivered was 70 per cent and the average duration of a promoted job was eight years. As earlier government reports had indicated, it was difficult to devise methodologies to measure the effectiveness of agencies involved in industrial support; however, in terms of investment attracted relative to the rest of the UK pro rata their performance appeared good.[80]

To deal with the problem of long-term unemployment two new schemes were introduced. As in the UK as a whole, 'New Deal' was introduced in April 1998 with a five-year budget of £140 million. Those aged between eighteen and twenty-four who had been unemployed for more than six months and those over twenty-five unemployed for more than two years (eighteen months in a pilot scheme introduced in November) were guaranteed training and threatened with benefit cuts if it was not undertaken. In August 1999, 'Worktrack' was introduced to replace the ACE scheme, which had been reduced in scale towards the end of the previous administration. It was targeted at the long-term unemployed who were not eligible for the 'New Deal'. For 1990/2000 1,050 places which offered 'high quality temporary employment with training' were allocated. In 1995, according to government figures, there had been 49,885 long-term unemployed, a figure which had dropped to 33,138 by July 1997 and 29,000 by June 1999.[81] The trend is clear; what is more difficult to judge is how much of this reduction is a result of government schemes and how much is due to a more general economic revival.

To conclude, the government laid much emphasis on 'supply-side' improvements as the way both to increase the competitiveness of Northern Ireland business, including the intention of fostering an entrepreneurial culture, and to cut unemployment. This, however, did not imply solely a market-led approach since public support for investment was maintained and the social element indicated through differential rates for TSN areas.

Social policy

In the period from 1997 to date (2000), two major areas dominated the social policy agenda. One was the issue of fair employment and its relationship with other areas of equality, and the other was the establishment of a new human rights commission to replace the SACHR. The second of these was an express commitment in the Good Friday Agreement whereas consideration for changes in the first area predated this.

In November 1994 the Secretary of State had asked the SACHR to take over the review of the effectiveness of fair employment legislation from the Central Community Relations Unit within the NIO. The SACHR report was published in 1997 and much of it contained criticisms of governmental agencies or guidelines intended to address social exclusion or to ensure equality of treatment. The Training and Employment Agency (TEA) was accused of complacency and failing to place sufficient numbers in work and the Department of Finance and Personnel was upbraided for a failure to promote and plan strategically for the implementation of TSN.[82] Information by which the impact of TSN could be adequately gauged was often lacking. There was also the wider question of whether departmental concepts of parity in expenditure limited the scope for manoeuvre and whether the ideology of the government (Conservative up to this point) and declining public expenditure were compatible with effective TSN which implied a proactive and interventionist government. To strengthen TSN, the SACHR recommended that the Secretary of State be personally responsible for its political direction and implementation.

The Commission was similarly critical of the implementation of PAFT. PAFT was intended to 'integrate considerations of equality into policy formulation and the administration at every level'.[83] However, the SACHR found that implementation was very patchy and some government agencies took little or no notice of the guidelines (which had no statutory basis) and some believed them to be in conflict with the commercial criteria regarding competitive tendering. When PAFT was adhered to procedurally, it was unclear that there was effective monitoring or assessment of its substantive impact. There was no central lead provided for implementation from either the CCRU or the Department of Finance and Personnel whose role was deemed 'particularly unsatisfactory' given its relation to other departments.[84] In light of these deficiencies, the SACHR recommended that there be a stronger political commitment to the policy, the guidelines be given legislative form and enforcement be the responsibility of an internal NIO unit, such as a strengthened CCRU.

In respect of legislation (the existing Act being introduced in 1989) the SACHR recommended the following. The legislation should be extended to cover the provision of goods, services and facilities. Recruitment of long-term unemployed or those from a specific geographic area, if there was a clear and persistent imbalance in the workforce, should not be deemed discriminatory. The Fair Employment Tribunals (FET) should be able to award compensation in all cases of indirect discrimination and legal aid should be available for all court and tribunal proceedings. The operation of the legislation should be kept under review by the Fair Employment Commission and its funding kept under review by the government.

The government's response to the SACHR report was published as a White Paper in March 1998.[85] The criticisms of TSN were endorsed (a position made easier as the report covered the period of a Conservative administration). TSN was to be 'revamped' and prosecuted with greater vigour. The administrative direction was to be shared by two bodies: a Social Steering Group composed of senior officials of the NIO and Northern Ireland departments to promote and co-ordinate TSN; and a strengthened CCRU which would provide operational training and advice and monitor and evaluate initiatives. In July 1998 'new' TSN was launched after all Northern Ireland departments and the NIO had been reviewed by external consultants to identify how TSN objectives could be pursued more effectively. 'New' TSN had three complementary elements: a particular focus on tackling the problems of unemployment and enhancing employability; action to tackle key inequalities in areas such as health, housing and education; and the promotion of social inclusion through cross-departmental strategies.[86]

In respect of PAFT, the government favoured guidelines having statutory force and the possibility of public bodies being required to adopt schemes to show how statutory obligations featured in their day to day work but cautioned against excessive expectations. This may be read as an implicit recognition that the government's commitment to the free market (as endorsed in the White Paper) and public expenditure rectitude might sit uneasily with the prosecution of policies implicit in TSN and PAFT.

The White Paper recommended the merging of the four existing agencies promoting equality, that is, the Equal Opportunities Commission, the Fair Employment Commission, the Commission for Racial Equality (Northern Ireland) and the Northern Ireland Disability Council into one new Equality Commission. This proposal was included in the Good Friday Agreement, although the SACHR report had not been in favour but had suggested that the question of merger be kept under review.[87]

The legislative response to the SACHR report occurred in December 1998 with the introduction in the House of Lords of the Fair Employment and Treatment (Northern Ireland) Order.[88] The order consolidated the 1976 and 1989 legislation and added amendments. The principal changes were as follows. The existing Acts covered discrimination in employment and henceforth were extended to cover provision of goods, facilities, services and the management and disposal of premises, including land. The scope of affirmative action was broadened. This permitted employers to train non-employees of one religion where that religion is under-represented in the workforce without it being deemed discrimination and the long-term unemployed could be recruited on the same principle. The monitoring of the workforce composition was extended to part-time workers and job applicants and larger employers had to monitor leavers. Compensation was to be extended to cover unintentional discrimination and an appeals procedure was to be introduced for those whose claims of discrimination were not investigated because the Secretary of State had issued a certificate on national security grounds. Finally, the new Equality Commission (see below) was to have a duty to review the operation of the Order.

These changes were all in accord with the SACHR's recommendations. However, the government rejected others including the use of 'contract compliance' to promote equality, designating the targeting of specific geographic areas as non-discriminatory, the provision of legal aid in FET hearings and the extension of the Northern Ireland Constitution Act 1973 to cover indirect discrimination by government departments and ministers.

Two additional points should be noted about the legislation. First, it was enacted by Order rather than by primary legislation which was criticised by both the opposition and the Northern Ireland Affairs Committee.[89] The government did not provide an explanation for this; it may have been the pressures of the Commons' timetable. Secondly, the legislation was contemporaneous with the final passage of the Northern Ireland Act which would establish the new Equality Commission. This timing seemed strange since the agency responsible for the new legislation, which might reasonably be expected to have an input into draft legislation would not be constituted until after it had become law.

The Northern Ireland Bill received its third reading in the Commons at the end of July 1998. Over 400 amendments were then considered in the Lords, many of a technical nature relating to devolution and a new assembly and the necessity for consultation. The bill returned to the Commons on 18 November, the day after its third reading in the Lords.[90] The Act established the Equality Commission to be overseen by the Secretary of State as a reserved matter. A statutory obligation was placed on public authorities to have due regard to the need to promote equality of opportunity and to submit equality schemes to the Equality Commission. This would apply not only to Northern Ireland authorities but also to the NIO and any UK-wide authority operating in Northern Ireland. These schemes were subject to five-yearly review to assess their impact. An amendment had provided for the establishment of a tribunal to which an individual could appeal if the Secretary of State issued a national security, public safety or public order certificate which nullified any equality provision.[91] An independent chair was to be appointed to co-ordinate the merging of the four commissions into the one new commission. Establishment of the commission had been scheduled for

March but it was finally appointed on 2 August 1999 and took over the functions of the former agencies on 1 October 1999.

To conclude, it is too early to make a judgement about the effectiveness of the new Equality Commission. What is clear is that at a procedural level the government has gone beyond the activity of its predecessors in 'mainstreaming' equality within public policy formulation. Whether this will translate into substantive improvements in the position of under-represented or marginalised groups might depend on resources devoted to implementing such policies and overcoming some bureaucratic resistance to equality 'mainstreaming'. The government appear not to countenance that there might be tensions or contradictions between an increasingly uncritical attitude towards markets and their outcomes and the demands and implications of an equality programme.[92] Pressure on public expenditure is another potential barrier to substantive reform which could build upon the legislative framework.

The 'politics' of the equality agenda is beyond the scope of this work but a few brief observations will be offered. First, an agenda of equality of opportunity was broadly endorsed by the majority of Northern Ireland parties but the concept and practice of equality does not exist in an ideological vacuum. The most obvious example of this is the suspicion that some in the Unionist community held for the FEC, seeing it as a Catholic employment agency and the general agenda of equality was often seen as being closer to Nationalist than to Unionist concerns.[93]

The agreement of April 1998 contained a commitment to introduce a Human Rights Commission (HRC) with an 'extended and advanced role beyond that currently exercised by the Standing Advisory Commission on Human Rights'.[94] It was established by the Northern Ireland Act. During the Commons passage of the bill, provisions were strengthened so that all assembly bills would be considered by the HRC and it would have an advisory role with respect to the assembly as well as to the Secretary of State. Further amendments were accepted over the summer of 1998 during its consideration in the Lords. These required the HRC to review the adequacy of its powers within two years of establishment and it was granted the power to carry out investigations with which the government was obliged to co-operate subject to national security and public safety provisos. However, it was to have no authority to oblige people to attend or give evidence to inquiries or to enforce the discovery of documents. Paul Murphy, the government minister, argued that during the consultation period there had been insufficient consensus to allow for compulsory witness attendance or the power of discovery of documents.[95]

The HRC was established in March 1999 with a full-time chief commissioner and ten part-time commissioners and replaced the SACHR. Its five principal duties are: to keep Northern Ireland law, policy and practice relating to the protection of human rights under review; to advise the Secretary of State and the assembly about measures which ought to be taken to protect human rights; to advise the assembly whether a bill is compatible with human rights; to consult and advise government on a draft bill of rights for Northern Ireland; and to conduct investigations into human rights concerns.[96] In relation to the fourth point, the HRC started a process of consultation in March 2000 to run until December 2000 about the contents for a bill of rights.

A third area in which legislation took place was that of the regulation of parades. The Parades Commission had been established as a non-statutory body in March 1997 and, in opposition, Labour had pledged to give legislative effect to the North report proposals (see Chapter 5). The Public Processions etc. (Northern Ireland) Act was introduced in the Lords and received its second reading there in October 1997.[97] Its Commons second reading took place in December; the title now omitted the 'etc.' since the government had withdrawn plans to allow the Commission to consider examples of cultural expression other than parades. Following changes in the Lords, the Conservatives undertook to give the bill an unopposed second reading and their two spokesmen, MacKay and Moss, voted with the government. At committee stage, the two principal changes were the requirement that those organising protests against parades had to provide fourteen days' notice and that the Commission was to facilitate mediation in disputes over parades rather than be directly involved in mediation. During the consultation period, many submissions had argued that direct involvement might lead to a conflict of interest as the Commission was responsible for determining conditions attached to parades or their banning.[98]

The Act came into effect from February 1998. It laid upon the Commission the duty to promote greater understanding among the general public of issues concerning public processions and to promote and facilitate mediation. Where mediation failed to resolve disputes, the Commission had the power to issue determinations.[99] These determinations, which could involve banning or re-routing parades or marches, could be reviewed by the Secretary of State on application of the Chief Constable of the RUC. The Secretary of State could revoke, amend or confirm a determination. The police were empowered to decide on the day whether a parade could go ahead on the grounds of public order.

Additionally, the Commission had a statutory duty to produce three documents. 'Guidelines' provided clarification of the factors taken into account when reaching decisions on whether to impose conditions, 'Procedural rules' outlined the way in which the Commission performed the function of making determinations and a 'Code of Conduct' advised those organising parades and laid down standards of behaviour for participants.[100] The Commission was also given the duty of keeping under review the operation of the legislation.

Conclusion[101]

One is struck by the sheer scope of Labour's reforming zeal within Northern Ireland. A feature of the administration is that virtually all areas of public administration and policy making are subject to review or reform. This marked the embedding of the government's view that a holistic approach was required. A lasting settlement in Northern Ireland required the establishment of equality between the two traditions both in material and substantive terms and in terms of the legitimacy of national aspiration. Perhaps more than in any other administration political, security, economic and social policy were seen as mutually supporting and reinforcing. Much of this was explicit in the Good Friday Agreement and this allowed important sections of it to be implemented irrespective of progress in political talks and the establishment of the assembly.

Another notable feature of the period is the dominance of the agreement within government discourse to the extent that the notion of an alternative policy disappeared from the agenda. This *de facto* unanimity hamstrung the Conservative opposition. Despite reservations about the 'peace process' and frequent strains between the parties, bipartisanship was never seriously threatened since there was no coherent alternative policy articulated by the Conservatives. This is despite the fact that Labour often, especially in the second half of 1999, went to great lengths not to exclude Republicans from the process despite the complete absence of substantive movement on decommissioning. This indicates that Labour believed that republicanism was committed to the ending of the 'armed struggle'; otherwise the tactical shifts and the granting of the 'benefit of the doubt' to republicanism would have been illogical courses of action.

Notes

1 *Guardian*, 24 January 1997; *Fortnight* 361, May 1997, p. 5.
2 As in the previous administration, it is increasingly difficult to de-couple constitutional issues from those which may be seen as security questions. When the two are closely interrelated they will be discussed in this section and the security section below will deal principally with emergency legislation and policing reform.
3 'New Labour: because Britain deserves better' (Labour general election manifesto, London, 1997), p. 35.
4 *Fortnight* 362, June 1997, p. 7.
5 See M. Hickman, 'Northern Ireland, the Union and New Labour', p. 39 and P. Bew and G. Gillespie, *Northern Ireland: a Chronology of the Troubles 1968–1999* (Dublin, Gill and Macmillan, 1999), p. 341.
6 HC debates: vol. 296, col. 848, 25 June 1997.
7 HC debates: vol. 297, col. 58, 30 June 1997.
8 J. Ruane and J.Todd, 'The Belfast Agreement: context, content, consequences', in J. Ruane and J. Todd (eds), *After the Good Friday Agreement: Analysing Political Change in Northern Ireland* (Dublin, University College

Dublin Press, 1999), p. 11.

9 *Guardian* 8 April 1998, p. 1.

10 *Guardian* 11 April 1998, p. 2.

11 The title of the document is, *The Agreement: Agreement Reached in the Multi-party Negotiations*. It is also referred to variously as *The Good Friday Agreement, The Belfast Agreement* and *The British–Irish Agreement*. For further commentary and interpretation see J. Ruane and J. Todd, 'The Belfast Agreement'; B. O'Leary, 'The Nature of the British–Irish Agreement', *New Left Review* 233, 1999 and R. Wilford, 'Epilogue', in P. Mitchell and R. Wilford (eds), *Politics in Northern* Ireland (Boulder, Co., Westview Press, 1999).

12 The following is taken from the NIO website version (http://www.nio.gov.uk/agreement.htm) and page references refer to this version.

13 All assembly members had to self-designate as 'Unionist', 'Nationalist' or 'other'.

14 *The Agreement*, p. 15.

15 The twelve suggested areas are listed on p. 18 of the agreement.

16 *The Agreement*, p. 20.

17 *The Agreement*, p. 21.

18 O'Leary, 'The Nature of the British–Irish Agreement', p. 84. For a further discussion of the confederal and federal elements see pp. 79–86.

19 See security and social policy sections on pp. 136–46 for more details.

20 *The Agreement*, p. 27.

21 Bew and Gillespie, *Northern Ireland: a Chronology,* p. 358.

22 Bew and Gillespie, *Northern Ireland: a Chronology,* p. 358. See also G. Fitzgerald, 'What happened to Good Friday?', *London Review of Books,* 2 September 1999, pp. 9–10.

23 For more on the significance of the prisoner issue, see K. McEvoy, 'Prisoners, the Agreement, and the political character of the Northern Ireland conflict', *Fordham International Law Journal* 22(4) 1999, *Fortnight* 375, December 1998/January 1999 and *Guardian* 19 May 1998, p. 15.

24 According to McEvoy, 'Prisoners ...' (p. 1555), on the day of the Agreement Powell, Blair's Chief of Staff, sent a note to Ken Maginnis of the UUP pointing out that large numbers of prisoners would have been released anyway under existing remission arrangements. This was an attempt to reassure the UUP over the issue.

25 See O'Leary, 'The British–Irish Agreement', p. 92. See also J. Ruane and J. Todd, 'The Belfast Agreement', pp. 16–23 for what the Agreement provides to the two communities.

26 Change in Northern Ireland has often been portrayed as a 'zero sum' game.

27 For survey data on attitudes to the Agreement see G. Evans and B. O'Leary, 'Northern Irish voters and the British–Irish Agreement: foundations of a stable consociational settlement?', *Political Quarterly* 71(1), 2000.

28 HC debates: vol. 310, col. 481, 20 April 1998.

29 *Guardian* 20 April 1998, p. 15.

30 See, for example, Hunter's letter to the *Daily Telegraph* on 17 April 1998 and the editorial criticising the Conservative response to the Agreement.

31 Bew and Gillespie, *Northern Ireland: a Chronology,* p. 364.

32 On 12 May, a £315 million package was announced which included allocations for increased capital subsidies for small- and medium-sized firms, road improvements and upgrading employee skills.

33 For more details see S. Elliott, 'The referendum and assembly elections in

Northern Ireland', *Irish Political Studies* 14, 1999 and M. O'Neill,
'"Appointment with history": the referenda on the Stormont Peace
Agreement, May 1998', *West European Politics* 22(1), 1999.
34 HC debates: vol. 311, col. 711, 6 May 1998.
35 HC debates: vol. 313, cols 1116–17, 10 June 1998.
36 Three Conservatives (N. Winterton, Flight and Robertson) voted against the
second reading.
37 Brady, Hunter, Swayne, Robathan and Robertson.
38 *Guardian* 19 June 1998. One Conservative, Douglas Hogg, supported the
government. The question of Blair's phrasing became more contentious as
accusations were made of tampering with *Hansard* to expunge his commitment to the decommissioning link. The Speaker announced an investigation
which rejected such a charge (*Guardian*, 19 June and 23 June 1998).
39 See *Fortnight* 372, July/August 1998, p. 8.
40 For a breakdown of results by constituency see *Irish Political Studies* 14,
1999, p. 207 and for commentary see S. Elliott, 'The referendum and assembly elections in Northern Ireland', *Irish Political Studies* 14, 1999.
41 S. Elliott, 'The referendum. . .', pp. 148–9.
42 B. O'Leary, 'The Nature of the British-Irish Agreement', p. 72.
43 These were to cover the relatively non-contentious areas of inland waterways,
food safety, trade and business development, special EU programmes, the
Irish and Ulster Scots languages and aquaculture and marine matters. This
can thus be seen as closer to a Unionist than a Nationalist agenda.
44 HC debates: vol. 322, col. 335, 9 December 1998.
45 HC debates: vol. 322, col. 366, 9 December 1998.
46 *Guardian*, 12 December 1998, p. 3.
47 Punishment beatings were primarily carried out to reinforce paramilitary
influence over communities.
48 HC debates: vol. 326, col. 148, 22 February 1999.
49 As some remains were located there, parallel legislation was to be introduced
in the Irish Republic.
50 *Independent* 2 July 1999, p. 1. See also p. 2 and *Independent*, 3 July 1999
for a very optimistic reading of the likelihood of Republican shifts by David
McKittrick.
51 Cited, in *Independent*, 3 July 1999, p. 1.
52 HC debates: vol. 334, col. 640, 5 July 1999.
53 The Conservatives were Body, Cash, Gill, Hunter, Maclean, Robertson,
Swayne, Wilkinson, Wilshire and N. Winterton.
54 *Independent*, 15 July 1999, p. 1.
55 The view of the *Independent* that the bipartisanship approach was 'in sham-
bles' is overstating the case (16 July 1999).
56 *Guardian* 23 July 1999, *Independent*, 23 July 1999. However, the former
makes the point that IRA statements are often deliberately vague and open to
differing interpretations (p. 8).
57 A legal challenge to this judgement, supported by Trimble, was not upheld as
the legislation made the decision a political one taken by the Secretary of
State. Between 1 January and 18 June there were casualties resulting from
forty-three shootings and eighty-one assaults in 'punishment beatings'
(written answer, HC, vol. 334, col. 179, 30 June 1999). For Mowlam's criticism of the Conservatives see *New Statesman*, 27 September 1999, p. 18.
58 *New Statesman*, 27 September 1999. It was also claimed that Mowlam's lack
of attention to detail and nuance had led to Blair taking a central role in the

summer negotiations (*Guardian*, 12 October 1999, p. 20 and 3 December 1999 p. 4).

59 The Ulster Unionist Council approved this position by 480 votes to 329 on 27 November. For party positions at the end of the review see *Guardian*, 17 November 1999, p. 6.

60 In May 2000, this Act was extended by Order for another year.

61 Two small paramilitaries, the Loyalist Volunteer Force and the Continuity Army Council, were proscribed in June 1997 under an amendment to the 1996 Act.

62 HC debates: vol. 301, cols 181–3, 18 November 1997.

63 The Irish Republic already had legislation providing for this.

64 For further consideration and critique see 24th report of the SACHR (1998–89), HC, 265, Belfast, 1999, Annex F(1) and C. Walker, 'The bombs in Omagh and their aftermath: The Criminal Justice (Terrorism and Conspiracy) Act 1998', *Modern Law Review* 62(6), 1999.

65 *The Agreement*, p. 28.

66 'A New Beginning: Policing in Northern Ireland', the Report of the Independent Commission on Policing for Northern Ireland, 1999 (the Patten Report). For communal attitudes towards the RUC see L. Moore, 'Policing and change in Northern Ireland: the centrality of Human Rights', *Fordham International Law Journal* 22(4), 1999 and for an earlier review, C. Walker, 'Police and community in Northern Ireland', *Northern Ireland Legal Quarterly* 41, 1990.

67 'A New Beginning', pp. 7–8.

68 'A New Beginning', p. 30.

69 'A New Beginning', p. 71.

70 'A New Beginning', p. 82.

71 *Guardian*, 8 October 1999. However, their position becomes more conciliatory as MacKay suggests RUC NIPS as a compromise name (HC debates: vol. 339, col. 606, 24 November 1999).

72 HC debates: vol. 342, cols 845–64, 19 January 2000.

73 HC debates: vol. 351, cols 177–262, 6 June 2000.

74 HC debates: vol. 351, col. 217, 6 June 2000.

75 Hogg, Howard, Hunter, Robertson, Swayne and N. Winterton.

76 The summary document provides an example of the prevailing ideas: 'The days of an economy cushioned by public expenditure are over. What we want to spend, we have to earn through our own enterprise and self help. We must take responsibility for our own future'. (no page number).

77 Northern Ireland Grand Committee, 'Economic Development Strategy Review' (25 March 1999), p. 3.

78 Northern Ireland Affairs Committee, 'Public Expenditure – inward investment in Northern Ireland', Minutes of Evidence, 16 June 1999. (HC 551i, session 1998/9, 1999).

79 See, 'Public Expenditure – inward investment in Northern Ireland', for IDB job creations and expenditure for 1993–99.

80 See Northern Ireland Audit Office: Report by the Comptroller and Auditor General. IDB for Northern Ireland, 'Inward investment' (HC 1096, London, 1998), p. 17.

81 HC vol. 297, col. 512, 9 July 1997, wa; vol. 334, col. 180, 30 June 1999, wa. In early 1999, unemployment was 6.7 per cent ('Economic Development Strategy Review', p. 2).

82 TSN had been introduced in 1991 by the then Secretary of State, Peter Brooke.

83 For more details of PAFT see 'Employment Equality', p. 68, 24th Report of
   SACHR 1998/89 (HC, 265, Belfast, 1999) Annex G(ii) and C. McCrudden,
   'Mainstreaming equality in the governance of Northern Ireland', *Fordham
   International Law Journal* 22(4), 1999, pp. 1710–21. See also C.
   McCrudden, 'Equality and the Good Friday Agreement', in J. Ruane and J.
   Todd (eds), *After the Good Friday Agreement*, for the claim that the main
   objective of PAFT was to deal with anti-Catholic disadvantage and it was
   framed in more general language about fairness and rights to make it more
   generally acceptable.
84 'Employment Equality', p. 72.
85 'Partnership for Equality: the Government's proposals for future legislation
   and policies on Employment Equality in Northern Ireland'. (Cmd 3890,
   London, 1998).
86 Northern Ireland 'Expenditure plans and priorities: the Government's expenditure plans 1999–2000 to 2001–2002' (Cmd 4217, Department of Finance
   and Personnel/HM Treasury, 1999), p. 3.
87 The government stated that, 'the main purpose of amalgamation would be to
   enable their [the Commission's] work to be greatly extended into a new area,
   a positive engagement with the public sector to promote equality of opportunity in a broad sense' ('Partnership for Equality', p. 28). For reservations see
   24th report of SACHR, annex I.
88 HL, vol. 595, cols 755–73, 7 December 1998.
89 Cope, HL, vol. 595, col. 766, 7 December 1998; 4th Report of Northern
   Ireland Affairs Committee, 'The operation of the Fair Employment (Northern
   Ireland) Act 1989: ten years on' (HC 95–I, 1998/9), p. xi.
90 Detail of the passage of the bill is to be found in 'Mainstreaming Equality',
   pp. 1741–55.
91 See 'Mainstreaming Equality', pp. 1755–67.
92 In relation to public policy generally, New Labour claims that market
   outcomes and an enterprise culture are compatible with fairness and social
   justice.
93 See the concerns over the January 1998, 'Heads of Agreement' paper. Much
   of the input into the equality agenda came from NGOs and groups like the
   Women's Coalition which were or sought to be outside the 'traditional'
   communal divide. Parity of treatment for the Irish language, also contained in
   the Good Friday Agreement, was included in the Education (Northern
   Ireland) Order 1998. The Department of Education had a statutory duty to
   facilitate and encourage the development of Irish-medium education.
94 *The Agreement* pp. 23–4. The SACHR had, in various reports, expressed
   dissatisfaction with its lack of influence on government policy, particularly in
   the area of emergency legislation. For a review of the SACHR see S.
   Livingstone, 'The Northern Ireland Human Rights Commission', *Fordham
   International Law Journal* 27(4), 1999. For the views of its future chief
   commissioner see B. Dickson, 'Creating an effective Human Rights
   Commission for Northern Ireland' (Annex H, 24th SACHR report, HC, 265,
   1999).
95 HC debates: vol. 319, col. 1065, 18 November 1998.
96 From HRC advertisement, *Fortnight* 384, April 2000. See this edition for
   essays on Human Rights issues.
97 For a summary of the bill's clauses see HL debates: vol. 582, cols 982–8, 28
   October 1997.
98 Much of the committee stage was taken up with failed unionist amendments.
99 Parade organisers had to give twenty-eight days' notice (the North report had

recommended twenty-one days) to the RUC which then passed the relevant request to the Commission.

100 More detail of the Commission's operation can be found in 'Parades Commission for Northern Ireland', 1st Annual Report, 1998/9, HC 406, 1999.

101 These themes will be explored further in Chapter 7.

7

Aspects of British policy: concluding remarks

The preceding chapters of this work have outlined the main areas of British policy within Northern Ireland; the purpose of this chapter is to explore in more detail some aspects of policy formulation and execution. In places this will take the form of a tentative raising of issues since the contemporary nature of the question precludes access to official material which would illuminate the discussion of policy making.

The question of consistency and continuity

As Brendan O'Leary has indicated in relation to the Conservative administrations of 1979 to 1997, it is clear that government policy in Northern Ireland has involved various contradictory elements.[1] Examples he cites include the claim that government would not talk to terrorists followed by admissions that it does, protestations of British sovereignty over Northern Ireland while engaging in bilateral attempts to manage the problem and contradictory statements concerning commitment to the Union. However, O'Leary argues that behind these twists and turns a more consistent policy can be discerned.

This is a convincing claim. I have argued elsewhere that there is a strategic continuity to British policy which is maintained despite tactical shifts. Over the period of direct rule from 1972 to date (2000) it is banal to point out that policy will not be reproduced in exactly the same way. However, for virtually all of this period successive governments have been committed to the establishment of some form of devolved assembly, informed by the belief that Northern Ireland is 'different' and thus needs different political structures. The 'difference' of Northern Ireland – the conception that it is unlike the other constituent parts of the United Kingdom – has informed the second feature of policy, the bipartisan approach which has prevailed for the majority of the period; the exception being the late 1970s. This formulation is close to the one propounded by O'Leary in 1987 when he outlined the internal and external track approach of the Northern Ireland Office, which indicated a consistency of policy.[2] Thirteen years later this remains a fruitful way to conceive of British policy.

In arguing for this fundamental continuity of policy, it is contended that two other broad approaches to understanding British policy in Northern Ireland are misconceived. First, what may be termed the 'anti-imperialist' approach which does, or did, ascribe a continuity to British policy based on imperial interests so necessitating support for unionism and the suppression of republicanism. With the decline of familial establishment linkages between Britain and Ireland over the course of the last century, the end of the Cold War and the economic marginality of Northern Ireland it is difficult to discern any compelling reason why Britain would wish to remain involved in Northern Ireland. Additionally, it is difficult to read the recent trajectory of events, for example, through the 1990s, as bolstering the position of unionism within Northern Ireland.

A recent chapter by Tomlinson may be used an example of the strengths and weaknesses of such an approach. Entitled 'Walking backwards into the sunset: British policy and the insecurity of Northern Ireland'[3] the work focuses largely on the illegal activities and killings carried out by the British security forces. This focus is entirely legitimate in that it draws attention to the repressive element of British activity which much work ignores; the question is how to read such activity. This focus does not take one very far in explaining what, fundamentally, drives British policy. As Tonge has pointed out, the objectives of British rule are not adequately analysed.[4] Tomlinson himself recognises that British policy is not one of simply repressing republicanism and shifts in Sinn Fein indicate that a reappraisal of British intentions has taken place. By the nature of such activity it is difficult to tell at what level the sanctioning of security force collusion with Loyalist paramilitaries occurred or the endorsing of other illegal activity. It does not seem inconsistent to deplore such activity and explain it through state repression of anti-state violence and a reluctance or inability of the government to control adequately intelligence and security force activity while arguing that this does not demonstrate a consistent anti-Republican or 'imperialist' set of policies pursued by the British government. To put it simply, there is too much empirical evidence indicating that the British government does not take a consistently pro-Unionist position.[5]

A second, and diffuse, approach to British policy is one that sees it as inconsistent, contradictory and little more than 'crisis management'. This claim has been made by Garret FitzGerald, the former Taoiseach, and is found in the work of Padraig O'Malley.[6] The brief outline above of what I take to be the broad consistencies in British policy indicates that this conceptualisation is flawed. Ill-considered or over hasty reactions to particular incidents undoubtedly took place; the point is that these do not demonstrate a lack of policy or the dominance of crisis management.

Rather they co-exist with a broader strategic consistency and focusing on twists and turns obscures the larger picture. FitzGerald's criticisms are partly related to a different conceptualisation of the root causes of the problem between the British and Irish governments. In the period around the signing of the AIA in 1985, it is clear that the Irish government had an agenda for reform in Northern Ireland which was unacceptable to important actors within the British government and the Northern Irish judiciary. It seems plausible that FitzGerald's different understanding of what was necessary, and also what reforms had been agreed, influenced him to claim that Britain had no Northern Ireland policy.[7] To conclude, a consistency and continuity in British policy is discernible constructed around the notion of Northern Ireland's 'difference' and a sensitivity to international opinion.

The question of policy makers

The purpose of this section is to address some of the issues about government policy making in Northern Ireland and to try to identify some of the key actors in the creation of policy. An initial observation is that the British government has a large degree of autonomy in policy formulation in relation to domestic politics. Unlike the nineteenth century, there is no evidence of elite groupings, for example, landowning, commercial or religious, which have concerns about Northern Irish policy. Similarly, there is no wider pluralistic or popular pressure within Britain that impinges on Northern Ireland policy making. Northern Ireland is an issue of low electoral salience. The series of comprehensive election studies by David Butler and Dennis Kavanagh reveal a consistent story over the period 1974 to 1997.[8] Northern Ireland is rarely mentioned in campaign speeches and it is rarely raised by constituents with candidates. In the rankings of issues by their prominence in news coverage, Northern Ireland was eighth equal in 1983, tenth in 1987 and eleventh in 1992 and 1997.[9] One may fairly assume that there is some rough correlation between the amount of news coverage an issue receives and the media's assessment of its importance to the public, although Northern Ireland perhaps gets more coverage than would be warranted by reference to the British electorate's interest. One possible reason why Northern Ireland has remained relatively unimportant is that the number of British military casualties, partly related to the 'Ulsterisation' policy, did not reach levels which would have precipitated a widespread withdrawal campaign within Britain.

Put simply, there is no evidence of groupings, interests or networks within Britain which, in a traditional pluralist or elite model of politics, determine or even influence British policy. This would suggest that British policy is either 'state-centred'; that is, it is driven by governmental actors (for more see p. 157 below) and developed in isolation from social groupings or that non-British pressure groups or interests have a large input into policy making. If one tries to extend a pluralist analysis to within Northern Ireland itself and to the international sphere there are examples of policy whereby government appears to be trying to 'balance' the concerns of different groups and interests. Indeed, one could argue that the strategy of consociationism, and particularly in its recent form, is premised on trying to balance the concerns of Nationalist and Unionist blocs and reacting to the relative pressure that they are able to exert in any given period. The lengthy discussions over issues such as reform of the RUC and changes to fair employment legislation in the late 1980s and the contemporary period, and the problems surrounding the detail of implementation are good examples of areas where the strength of conflicting interests makes government policy hard to effect. In the first example, there is an alliance of international and domestic interests convinced that wholesale change in line with the Patten report was both necessary and a commitment of the Good Friday Agreement. This includes President Clinton, who likened the present situation to having an all-white police service in the southern United States, the Irish government, the Northern Nationalist community and civil liberties groups. Ranged against at least some of the Patten proposals was much of the Unionist community, including representatives who wanted to link the question of RUC reform to the re-entering of the assembly in 2000 and the Conservative party. In the second example, pressures for changes to fair employment provisions in the late 1980s witnessed alliances between external actors, such as the USA and the Irish government, and Northern Irish pressure groups which argued that the narrowing of employment differentials was important to help reconcile Nationalists to the administration of direct rule. Concerns about the proposals came from Unionist representatives who tended to see fair employment as having an implicit anti-Protestant bias and from employers concerned that the autonomy and efficiency of private sector concerns would be eroded by 'red tape'. More recently, New Labour has argued that there is no inherent tension between the promotion of market inspired notions of efficiency and the tackling of material deprivation and social injustice though it remains to be seen if both can be delivered.

This form of pluralist approach provides certain insights. It seems clear that at certain times over certain issues coalitions of interest groups can be identified and 'winners' can be identified.[10] However, cruder forms of pluralist analysis suggest that government is reactive, acting like a 'weathervane' in response to societal pressures. It is important to note that the government has a degree of autonomy in the construction of Northern Ireland policy both because of its lack of salience in British politics (see p. 155 above) and because, typically, bipartisanship and the 'democratic deficit' allows it a degree of insulation from groupings and politicians within Northern Ireland.[11] It is implausible to argue that the British government does not have interests of its own which shape policy and which provide limits to the influence of pluralist mobilisation.

This contention, however, raises more questions. The focus of this work has been on government policy and party differences (or otherwise) but this is not to claim that the state is a unified actor. Since the introduction of direct rule in 1972, various actors within the governmental process can be easily identified. These would include the politicians, in particular the Prime Minister, the Secretary of State and the Home Secretary, who is responsible for the Prevention of Terrorism Act, and members of the cabinet committee. The permanent administration includes the Northern Ireland Office which is split between London-based officials and those in Northern Ireland, the Northern Ireland civil service and the Foreign Office; reflecting the fact that Northern Ireland is uniquely neither a domestic or foreign policy issue. The third important agency is the security forces, which can be sub-divided into the army and RUC. Additionally, there is the role of covert forces and intelligence branches whose influence can only be guessed at.

The situation is somewhat confused by the definition of what might constitute part of government or be deemed to be a government agency. For example, there has been an increased use of executive agencies which execute government policy but are not subject to parliamentary scrutiny and Northern Ireland has over one hundred non-departmental public bodies.[12]

As indicated above, it is easy to identify actors in the policy process and to find some evidence of 'bureaucratic segmentation' and tensions between agencies; what is difficult is to allocate a weighting to the relative influence of the different interests. Examples of the tensions are provided by the memoirs of Richard Needham who served as a Northern Ireland minister from 1985 to 1992.[13] His account records a lack of liaison between the security forces, the NIO and other departments, inter-ministerial tensions, tensions between the IDB and its controlling minister and a general lack of co-ordination of security policy with other policy areas. In fact, in places the book reads like a case study demonstrating a theory of bureaucratic fragmentation within government.

Another example of an analysis which emphasises the lack of unity within government is that of Bew, Patterson and Teague in their review of the evolution of the AIA.[14] In this period, the views of the Foreign and Commonwealth Office and the Cabinet Office tended to prevail over the NIO; the latter favouring a more cautious approach given the likely degree of Unionist opposition.

These accounts raise the question of whether evidence of tensions and bureaucratic fragmentation is compatible with a *broad* strategic continuity in government policy as indicated above, and I would claim that it is. Secondly, this continuity is maintained by the permanent administration and thus successive Secretaries of State inherit an established policy. The general model of incrementalism in policy making claims that policy is not developed from first principles by successive policy implementers and this appears to fit Northern Ireland. Many accounts, particularly biographical and journalistic ones, emphasise the style and character of Secretaries of State (for example, Mason's 'gung ho' approach, Rees's indecisiveness, Atkins' lack of knowledge of Northern Ireland, Brooke's sharpness concealed beneath a Wodehousean exterior, Mowlam's informal approach and Mandelson's forensic grasp of detail). Without endorsing a structural determinism, a good deal of scepticism should be accorded to accounts which emphasise the role of personalities. Since the inception of direct rule there is no evidence that a new Secretary of State has engaged in a fundamental re-thinking let alone implementation of Northern Ireland policy. Also, the strength or otherwise of the relationship between successive Prime Ministers and Taoiseach has frequently been the subject of discussion. Yet whoever the holder of either position there has been a maintenance and deepening of the bilateral approach to Northern Ireland since 1980. However, as a note of caution, this does not mean that at crucial junctures the question of personnel is unimportant. For example, it seems that once Mowlam had lost the confidence of Trimble and the pro-Agreement Unionists it was necessary to replace her in order to salvage movement in the peace process.

The question of bipartisanship

A recurring theme in the preceding chapters has been the extent to which bipartisanship has marked British policy. In 1995 Dixon offered this definition of the term: 'a general agreement between the two main political parties on the principles of their *constitutional* approach towards the conflict in Northern Ireland' (original emphasis).[15] This approach has endorsed the necessity for the consent of a majority in Northern Ireland for any change in its status. Bipartisanship has been constructed on two main foundations. One is the shared belief that Northern Ireland is 'different' and thus different political and administrative arrangements are necessary and legitimate; the other is that inter-party disputes could be exploited by extremists and the 'men of violence'.[16] These foundations were erected before the introduction of direct rule and have persisted since. All major constitutional initiatives by government have been endorsed by the opposition and the period of greatest strain was the late 1970s when the Conservatives moved towards a more 'integrationist' position (see Chapter 2 for more details).

It is perhaps worth emphasising that bipartisanship does not imply an exact coincidence of outlook or of policy prescription. For example, if one reviews the 1990s there is much evidence of party disagreement; in some cases this is because of genuine reservations about aspects of the opponent's policy and in others more because an adversarial system makes unreserved support for the opposing party tactically injudicious and contrary to political instinct. However, *Hansard* reveals that all the principal politicians, including Blair, Mowlam, Hague, Major, McNamara, Straw, Mayhew, Moss, Mandelson and Ancram have endorsed bipartisanship and supported its maintenance even when disputes have occurred.

If one widens the concept to include other aspects of policy, the early to mid-1990s witnessed a consolidation of bipartisanship. Blair's declaration that the DSD of 1993 overtook existing party positions effectively downgraded Labour's commitment to 'unity by consent' and in 1996, for the first time since 1982, Labour did not oppose the renewal of the PTA. Despite the somewhat ritualistic attacks from some Conservatives, it became increasingly implausible to label Labour as 'soft on terrorism' as Straw presided over its illiberal shift. In the area of economic policy, the trajectory of New Labour with respect to an embracing of markets and supply-side reforms to improve efficiency tended to reduce the ground on which Conservatives could mount an attack.

With the accession of a Labour government, relations between the parties became more strained. However, this did not result in an end to bipartisanship. The period following the agreement of 1998 proved difficult for the Conservatives because they had serious reservations about aspects of policy including legislation for prisoner release before decommissioning (which they voted against), Mowlam's judgement that the ceasefire was intact in the summer of 1999 and proposed reform of the RUC. Despite these concerns, there was adherence to the agreement and no development of an alternative policy. In this period Conservative tactics often consisted of 'keeping a low profile', as though this would deflect attention from the contradictions or at least tensions of supporting the process yet opposing much that flowed from it.[17]

In conclusion, bipartisanship has been a feature of the entire period of direct rule. Despite tensions, it has probably become more firmly entrenched as the plausibility of alternatives to the prevailing government policy recedes. For example, the 'integrationist' strategy promoted by some back bench Conservatives in the late 1970s and early 1980s and the 'green' tendency within Labour promoting a united Ireland have become increasingly marginal as the bilateral management of Northern Ireland has become the orthodoxy.

The evolution or otherwise of policy

The purpose of this section is to address whether and in what ways British policy has evolved over the period of direct rule. Consistent with the argument concerning continuity above, one can find echoes of contemporary policy back in the early period of direct rule in the early 1970s. Examples include the commitment to devolution, the acceptance of the legitimacy of a role for the Republic of Ireland (both reflecting the 'otherness' of Northern Ireland) and the belief, though somewhat ill-theorised, that social and economic conditions impact upon the prospects for political progress or resolution (see p. 161 below for more on this).

However, this does not mean that policy is static. There are features of policy in the 1990s that are different from the previous two decades, though the process of change has been largely incremental.[18] The most obvious and profound development is that from 1992 the government moved from trying to marginalise 'extremists' by bolstering the 'moderates' to trying to incorporate the 'extremists' within a settlement. For this policy to be adopted two changes had to have taken or be taking place. One was that the British government believed that there was a constituency within the paramilitaries which considered that violence was providing limited returns and that this constituency could be cultivated and encouraged. The other was that to shun and condemn the 'men of violence' and to act as if terrorism were a simple evil divorced from political and social contexts did not help to provide a long-term solution and a degree of re-thinking had to engaged in.[19]

A second development in the 1990s was the evolution and embedding of the 'three-strand' approach. In outline, this had an affinity with the Sunningdale proposals of 1973. Two differences in the 1990s are the deepening and widening of the process and also the extent to which it becomes the 'received wisdom'. From the period of the Brooke/Mayhew talks through to the agreement of 1998 it is striking the degree of consensus among policy makers, or potential policy makers, that this is the only viable approach and that there is no realistic alternative.

A third notable feature of the 1990s is the extent to which the management of the 'problem' has been internationalised. The most obvious examples are the role of Mitchell, de Chastelain and Holkeri in the considerations on decommissioning, the use of international inspectors of paramilitary arms dumps and the personal intervention of President Clinton at crucial times to try to bolster the 'peace process'.[20] The complex detail of this intervention will not be addressed here; however, it is worth noting that it is indicative of two developments in British policy making. First, the narrow conception of national sovereignty which up to approximately the early 1970s denied the legitimacy of a role for external actors has been further eroded. Not only is the Irish Republic embedded in the process but other non-British actors are engaged. Secondly, this development is related to the strategy of inclusion discussed above to the extent that it was felt that the 'internationalising' of particular problems would reassure those who were suspicious of the good intentions of the British government. It seems that this process is evidence of both a reconsideration and evolution of notions of sovereignty and also involves a pragmatic use of international actors to deal with specific issues.

A feature of the agreement of 1998 was its holistic approach. It remains to be seen if policy implementation will match ambition and intention, but the agreement signaled that the government believed that all areas of policy and civil society needed scrutiny and reform. For example, the recognition of two national identities, the need for changes to the legal and security apparatus, a greater emphasis on equality within public administration, 'parity of esteem' for cultural traditions and the material dimension to deprivation are all explicit or implicit within the agreement. The question may be asked: To what extent is this emphasis on different dimensions a novel approach and a possible example of O'Leary's point about learning in the policy process?

This ties in with a question that is simple to posit and harder to answer; namely, what policies have successive governments deemed necessary to deal with Northern Ireland. Statements by Secretaries of State, junior ministers and sections in White Papers can be traced back to Callaghan's opinion of 1969, when Home Secretary, that issues of law and order and social and economic policies had to considered as a whole.[21] At least at a rhetorical level, government spokespersons have argued that political progress, aspects of social reform, the defeat of terrorism and economic progress are mutually reinforcing and advances (or regressions) in one area can have a 'knock on' effect in others.[22]

However, there is little evidence that this went beyond the level of assertion given the methodological problems in demonstrating causal links and whether there was a reciprocal relationship. For example, many commentators have claimed that political stability would aid economic regeneration; conversely would economic regeneration influence political attitudes in such a way as to make political accommodation more likely?

Three points can be made here. First, it is clear that the idea that reform should be integrated across different policy areas is not new in Northern Ireland policy making. Secondly, there is little evidence that ministers could demonstrate quite how these linkages might work. Thirdly, there is little evidence that there was an institutional and departmental strategy aimed at trying to implement this. The memoirs of Needham suggest this is the case, though as one source it should be treated with caution. In language reminiscent of earlier Conservative Ministers, Atkins and Prior, he stated: 'our policy is built on three interlocking strategies: economic and social regeneration, political devolution and the eradication of terrorism.'[23] He then claims that there was no machinery for co-ordinating or delivering this 'three-legged' strategy, a criticism conceded by the head of the Northern Ireland Civil Service, and that policy was characterised by what might by termed bureaucratic segmentation. This suggests that the transforming quality of the agreement of 1998 will be realised if it effects multi-dimensional policy co-ordination rather than simply a recognition that there are different aspects to the 'problem'.

Domestic and international constitutional developments and their impact

Two further developments are worthy of review in an assessment of the evolution of Northern Irish policy. The first is the impact of changes within the British polity; specifically the move towards devolution contemporaneous with the construction of the agreement of 1998. One of the implications of these developments, though not necessarily consciously planned, is that older conceptions of the Union and the claim of integrationists that Northern Ireland should be fully integrated into the United Kingdom look increasingly untenable. At a superficial level, this could be reassuring to Unionists since the 'difference' of Northern Ireland (see p. 153 above) which has informed policy making is not now so self-evident in the context of constitutional reform within the United Kingdom, especially given the east–west relationship embodied in the 'strand three' arrangements.[24] However, as O'Leary has pointed out, the position of Northern Ireland is not directly comparable with that of Wales and Scotland given the federal tendencies of the agreement and the element of process built into it and the Northern Ireland Act 1998 which allow for greater autonomy from the UK than has been accorded to other parts of the Union.[25] Therefore, it seems that the notion of the 'difference' of Northern Ireland remains valid.[26]

The second area for consideration is the influence of the European Union. There is a growing literature on various aspects of the 'European dimension'. This includes discussions of (typically) Nationalist hopes and Unionist fears concerning the erosion of the nation-state which *de facto* bolsters a Nationalist agenda, the possible links between functional and technocratic cross-border co-operation and political change and the potential for the lessening of sectarian antagonisms.[27] The principal issue here, however, is to what extent the process of European integration has influenced British policy makers. The influence of the European dimension has the potential to work in different ways and at different levels. For example, membership of the EU (and its previous incarnations) has bolstered the international standing of both the Irish Republic which may have facilitated the bilateral management of Northern Ireland, and the common membership of the EU of both the UK and the Irish Republic has provided additional forums in which to develop diplomatic links and settle differences.[28] Secondly, is the question of whether the consociational and other structures developed in the 1990s and manifest in the agreement are influenced by the European model. Thirdly, which informs point two, is the extent to which British policy makers have embraced reformulations of sovereignty that have transcended older claims concerning the indivisibility of nation-state sovereignty.[29]

In relation to the latter two points, I would argue a degree of scepticism is needed. While the agreement of 1998 has embedded the bilateral and bi-national elements of managing Northern Ireland more deeply, the acceptance of the principle of Irish involvement and the need for consociational structures is evident in 1973 at the time of accession to the European Community. This implies the difference is of degree rather than kind, although the 'pooling' of sovereignty is now less contentious. There are, as far as I am aware, few statements by British policy makers making direct links between European developments and the management or transformation of Northern Ireland; certainly not to the extent that the Irish government and John Hume have invoked the example. While it may not be conclusive evidence, it is noteworthy that between 1992 and 1997 the bilateral process continued, with the DSD and the Joint Framework Documents, while a 'Eurosceptic' administration was in office. Elizabeth Meehan sounds a note of caution about over-emphasising the role of the EU but does contend, 'that the language and conventions of EU policymaking have helped to open up a space for contending parties to talk about solutions to old problems in a new way – and to act upon that.'[30]

Some commentators see the agreement as heralding the beginning of a post-national phase in Irish politics, in an era when both Unionist and Nationalist communities are interrogating critically ideas of nation, state and identity. It remains to be seen how far this process develops; it does not seem to be the case that such ideas have been propounded by British policy makers. The agreement is geared more to the recognition and accommodation of different national and cultural identities than normatively promoting their supersession or transformation.

Notes

1 B. O'Leary, 'The Conservative stewardship of Northern Ireland 1979–97: sound-bottomed contradictions or slow learning?', *Political Studies* 45(4), 1997.
2 B. O'Leary, 'The Anglo-Irish Agreement: folly or statecraft?', *West European Politics* 10(1), 1987, pp. 15–16.
3 In D. Miller (ed.), *Rethinking Northern Ireland* (Harlow, Addison Wesley Longman, 1998).

4 J. Tonge, review of D. Miller (ed.), *Irish Political Studies* 14, 1999, p. 157.

5 Although successive governments have tried to reassure Unionists by adopting what might be defined as a minimalist pro-Union position by adhering to the consent principle.

6 See FitzGerald cited in O'Leary, 'Conservative stewardship', pp. 674–5; P. O'Malley, *The Uncivil Wars: Ireland Today* (Belfast, Blackstaff, 1983).

7 Cited in O'Leary, 'Conservative stewardship', p. 675.

8 The series *The British General Election of . . .* is published by Macmillan.

9 From various editions of Butler and Kavanagh's studies.

10 Another example is the legal establishment's resistance to changes to some of the Diplock court procedures which the Irish government advocated at the time of the AIA in 1985.

11 See below for a consideration of bipartisanship. The power of the Northern Ireland Secretary of State has often been likened to a quasi-colonial role.

12 A. Greer, 'Policymaking', in P. Mitchell and R. Wilford (eds), *Politics in Northern Ireland* (Boulder, Co., Westview Press, 1999), p. 144.

13 R. Needham, *Battling for Peace* (Belfast, Blackstaff, 1998).

14 P. Bew, H. Patterson and P. Teague, *Between War and Peace: the Political Future of Northern Ireland* (London, Lawrence and Wishart, 1997).

15 P. Dixon, 'A House divided . . .' *Contemporary Record* 9(1), 1995, p. 148, emphasis in original.

16 Bipartisanship also generally informs British foreign policy and tends to be reinforced when service personnel are deployed.

17 This is particularly the case after the signing of the agreement. See *Guardian*, 20 April 1998, *Observer*, 19 April 1998, *Telegraph*, 17 April 1998.

18 O'Leary 'Conservative stewardship' points to the importance of learning in explaining the evolution (and improvement) in policy making under successive Conservative governments.

19 What for some policy makers became the realpolitik of inclusive politics was considered by some MPs and others as appeasement and the rewarding of violence.

20 Mitchell's own account of his role is *Making Peace* (London, Heinemann, 1999). For more on American involvement see P. Arthur, 'American intervention in the Anglo-Irish peace process: incrementalism or interference?', *Cambridge Review of International Affairs* 11(1), 1997; J. Dumbrell, 'The United States and the Northern Irish conflict, 1969–1994: from indifference to intervention', *Irish Studies in International Affairs* 6, 1995 and A. Guelke, 'The United States, Irish Americans and the Northern Ireland peace process', *International Affairs* 72(3), 1996.

21 Callaghan: HC debates vol. 788, col. 48, 13 October 1969.

22 Examples include, 'Northern Ireland Constitutional Proposals', Cmnd 5259, 1973; statements by Carter, a Labour junior minister (HC debates vol. 918, cols 417–18, 29 October 1976), Atkins (HC debates vol. 988, col. 552, 9 July 1980), Prior (HC debates vol. 21, col. 693, 5 April 1982) and the autobiography of Richard Needham.

23 Needham, *Battling for Peace*, p. 320.

24 For a more detailed discussion of this question see E. Meehan, 'The Belfast Agreement – its distinctiveness and points of cross-fertilization in the UK's devolution programme', *Parliamentary Affairs* 52(1), 1999.

25 B. O'Leary, 'The nature of the British–Irish Agreement', *New Left Review* 233, 1999, pp. 84–5.

26 This 'difference' and the notion of 'process' helps to explain why some Unionists are hostile to the agreement and see it as further undermining the

Union. Pro-agreement Unionists accept that the consent principle offers protection and that the unitary state variant of unionism is outmoded.

27 For a review of this literature see E. Meehan '"Britain's Irish question: Britain's European question?" British–Irish relations in the context of European union and the Belfast Agreement', *Review of International Studies* 26, 2000.
28 This point is argued by E. Moxon-Browne, 'The impact of the European Community', in B. Hadfield (ed.), *Northern Ireland: Politics and the Constitution* (Buckingham, Open University Press, 1992).
29 For an optimistic reading of the potential for European developments transcending the nation-state and national identities see G. Delanty, 'Northern Ireland in a Europe of regions', *Political Quarterly* 67(2), 1996.
30 Meehan, 'Britain's Irish question', p. 96.

Appendix:
Northern Ireland Office ministers

Table A1 Conservative administration 1972–74

Secretaries of State	Ministers of State	Under-Secretaries of State
W. Whitelaw (March 1972– December 1973)	Lord Windlesham (March 1972– June 1973)	D. Howell (March 1972– November 1972)
F. Pym (December 1973– March 1974)	P. Channon (March 1972– November 1972)	P. Mills (November 1972– March 1974)
	W. van Straubenzee (November 1972– March 1974)	Lord Belstead (June 1973– March 1974)
	D. Howell (November 1972– March 1974)	

Table A2 Labour administration 1974–79

Secretaries of State	Ministers of State	Under-Secretaries of State
M. Rees (March 1974– September 1976)	S. Orme (March 1974– April 1976)	Lord Donaldson (March 1974– April 1976)
R. Mason (September 1976– May 1979)	R. Moyle (June 1974– September 1976)	J. Concannon (June 1974– April 1976)
	J. Concannon (April 1976– May 1979)	J. Dunn (April 1976– May 1979)
	Lord Melchett (September 1976– May 1979)	R. Carter (April 1976– May 1979)
		T. Pendry (November 1978– May 1979)

Table A3 Conservative administrations 1979–92

Secretaries of State	Ministers of State	Under-Secretaries of State
H. Atkins (May 1979– September 1981)	M. Alison (May 1979– September 1981)	Lord Elton (May 1979– September 1981)
J. Prior (September 1981– September 1984)	H. Rossi (May 1979– January 1981)	P. Goodhart (May 1979– January 1981)
D. Hurd (September 1984– September 1985)	A. Butler (January 1981– September 1984)	G. Shaw (May 1979– January 1981)
T. King (September 1985– July 1989)	Lord Gowrie (September 1981– June 1983)	D. Mitchell (January 1981– June 1983)
P. Brooke (July 1989– April 1992)	Lord Mansfield (June 1983– April 1984)	J. Patten (January 1981– June 1983)
	R. Boyson (September 1984– September 1986)	N. Scott (September 1981– September 1986)
	N. Scott (September 1986– June 1987)	C. Patten (June 1983– September 1985)
	J. Stanley (June 1987– July 1988)	Lord Lyell (April 1984– July 1989)
	I. Stewart (July 1988– July 1989)	R. Needham (September 1985– April 1992)
	J. Cope (July 1989– November 1990)	B. Mawhinney (January 1986– November 1990)
	B. Mawhinney (November 1990– April 1992)	P. Viggers (September 1986– July 1989)
		Lord Skelmesdale (July 1989– November 1990)
		P. Bottomley (July 1989– July 1990)
		Lord Belstead (November 1990– April 1992)
		J. Hanley (November 1990– May 1993)

Table A4 Conservative administration 1992–97

Secretaries of State	Ministers of State	Under-Secretaries of State
P. Mayhew (April 1992– April 1997)	M. Mates (April 1992– June 1993)	Lord Arran (April 1992– January 1994)
	R. Atkins (April 1992– January 1994)	M. Ancram (June 1993– January 1994)
	J. Wheeler (June 1993– April 1997)	T. Smith January 1994– (October 1994)
	M. Ancram (January 1994– April 1997)	Baroness Denton (January 1994– April 1997)
		M. Moss (October 1994– April 1997)

Table A5 Labour administration 1997–

Secretaries of State	Ministers of State	Under-Secretaries of State
M. Mowlam (May 1997– October 1999)	A. Ingram (May 1997–	T. Worthington (May 1997– July 1998)
P. Mandelson (October 1999– January 2001)	P. Murphy (May 1997– July 1999)	Lord Dubs (May 1997– December 1999)
J. Reid (January 2001–		J. McFall (July 1998– December 1999)
		G. Howarth (July 1999–

Bibliography

Newspapers and journals

The Economist
Financial Times
Fortnight
Guardian
Independent
New Statesman
The Times

Official Publications

(Publications are listed chronologically, although there is not a strict chronology when two or more items are published in the same year. Place of publication is London unless stated.)

'Report of the advisory committee on police in Northern Ireland' (Hunt report), Cmd 535, Belfast, 1969.

'Report of the review body on local government in Northern Ireland' (Macrory report), Cmd 546, Belfast, 1970.

'Report of the inquiry into allegations against the security forces of physical brutality in Northern Ireland, arising out of events on 9th August 1971' (Compton report), Cmnd 4823, 1971.

'Review of economic and social development in Northern Ireland: report of the joint review board' (Cairncross report), Cmd 564, Belfast, 1971.

'Violence and civil disturbances in Northern Ireland in 1969' (Scarman report), Cmd 566, Belfast, 1972.

'Report of the commission to consider legal procedures to deal with terrorist activities in Northern Ireland' (Diplock report), Cmnd 5185, 1972.

'Northern Ireland Constitutional Proposals', Cmnd 5259, 1973.

'Report and recommendations of the working party on discrimination in the private sector of employment' (van Straubenzee report), Belfast, 1973.

'Report of the law enforcement commission', Cmnd 5627, 1974.

'The Northern Ireland Constitution', Cmnd 5675, 1974.

'Report of a committee to consider, in the context of civil liberties and human rights, measures to deal with terrorism in Northern Ireland' (Gardiner report), Cmnd 5847, 1975.

'Economic and industrial strategy for Northern Ireland: report by the review team' (Quigley report), Belfast, 1976.

'Review of the operation of the Prevention of Terrorism (Temporary Provisions)

Acts 1974 and 1976' (Shackleton report), Cmnd 7324, 1978.

'Report of the committee of inquiry into police interrogation procedures in Northern Ireland' (Bennett report), Cmnd 7497, 1979.

'The Government of Northern Ireland: a working paper for a conference', Cmnd 7763, 1979.

'The Government of Northern Ireland: proposals for further discussion', Cmnd 7950, 1980.

Committee of Public Accounts, 14th Report, HC 612, 1980.

Industry and Trade Committee, 7th Report, 'Government support for Trade and Industry in Northern Ireland', HC 500, 398(i) and (ii), 1982.

'Review of the operation of the Prevention of Terrorism (Temporary Provisions) Act 1976' (Jellicoe report), Cmnd 8803, 1983.

'Review of the Northern Ireland (Emergency Provisions) Act 1978' (Baker report), Cmnd 9222, 1984.

Committee of Public Accounts, 25th Report, 'Financial assistance to DeLorean Motor Cars Ltd', HC 127(1) and (2), 1984.

'Agreement between the Government of the United Kingdom of Great Britain and Northern Ireland and the Government of the Republic of Ireland', Cmnd 9657, 1985.

Northern Ireland annual abstract of statistics (Department of Finance and Personnel), Belfast, 1986.

SACHR, 'Religious and political discrimination and equality of opportunity in Northern Ireland. Report on fair employment', Cmd 237, 1987.

'An evaluation of the Enterprise Zone experiment in Northern Ireland', Department of Environment (NI), Belfast, 1988.

'Fair employment in Northern Ireland', Cmd 380, 1988.

Committee of Public Accounts, 'Matters relating to Northern Ireland', HC 230, 1989.

Northern Ireland Audit Office, 'Local Enterprise Development Unit: review of performance', HC 5, 1992.

Committee of Public Accounts, 'Northern Ireland Industrial Development Board: selective financial assistance criteria', HC 544, 1993.

'Review of the Northern Ireland (Emergency Provisions) Act 1991', Cmd 2706, 1995.

Northern Ireland Affairs Committee, 1st Report, 'Employment creation in Northern Ireland', HC 37, 1995.

'Government observations on the first report from the Northern Ireland Affairs Committee, session 1994–5, "Employment creation in Northern Ireland HC 37–1"', HC 642, 1995.

SACHR, 'Employment Equality: building for the future', Cmd 3684, 1997.

Northern Ireland Grand Committee, 'Public Expenditure', 18 February 1997.

'Independent Review of Parades and Marches'(North report), Belfast, 1997.

Northern Ireland Audit Office, 'Inward Investment', report by the Comptroller and Auditor General for Northern Ireland, HC 1096, 1998.

Northern Ireland Audit Office, 'The Training and Employment Agency: evaluation and performance', HC 475, 1998.

'The Agreement: Agreement reached in the multi-party negotiations', n.d. (1998).

'Partnership for equality: the Government's proposals for future legislation and policies on Employment Equality in Northern Ireland', Cmd 3890, 1998.

Report of the Independent Commission on Policing for Northern Ireland, 'A New Beginning: Policing for Northern Ireland' (Patten report), 1999.

Northern Ireland Grand Committee, 'Economic development strategy review', 1999.

Northern Ireland Affairs Committee, 'Public Expenditure – inward investment in Northern Ireland', HC 551(I), 1999.

Northern Ireland Affairs Committee, 4th Report, 'The operation of the Fair Employment (Northern Ireland) Act 1989: ten years on', HC 95-I, 1998/99, 1999.

Parades Commission for Northern Ireland, 1st Annual Report, 1998/99, HC 406, 1999.

Official reports (*Hansard*).

Government expenditure plans (various).

Fair Employment Agency/Commission. Annual reports (various).

Industrial Development Board reports (various).

Local Enterprise Development Unit reports (various).

Standing Advisory Commission on Human Rights. Annual reports (various).

Books and articles

Arthur, P., 'The Brooke initiative', *Irish Political Studies,* 7, 1992.

Arthur, P., 'The Mayhew talks 1992', *Irish Political Studies,* 8, 1993.

Arthur, P., 'The Anglo-Irish Joint Declaration: towards a lasting peace?', *Government and Opposition,* 29(2), 1994.

Arthur, P., 'Dialogue between Sinn Fein and the British Government', *Irish Political Studies,* 10, 1995.

Arthur, P., 'American intervention in the Anglo-Irish peace process: incrementalism or interference?', *Cambridge Review of International Affairs,* 11(1), 1997.

Aughey, A., *Under Siege: Ulster Unionism and the Anglo-Irish Agreement,* London, Hurst, 1989.

Aughey, A., 'The party and the Union', in P. Norton (ed.), *The Conservative Party,* Hemel Hempstead, Harvester Wheatsheaf, 1996.

Bardon, J., *A History of Ulster,* Belfast, Blackstaff, 1992.

Barton, B., Relations between Westminster and Stormont during the Attlee premiership', *Irish Political Studies,* 7, 1992.

Bew, P. and P. Dixon, 'Labour party policy and Northern Ireland', in B. Barton and P. Roche (eds), *The Northern Ireland Question: Perspectives and Policies,* Aldershot, Avebury, 1994.

Bew, P. and G. Gillespie, *Northern Ireland: a Chronology of the Troubles 1968-1999,* Dublin, Gill and Macmillan, 1999.

Bew, P., P. Gibbon and H. Patterson, *Northern Ireland 1921-1994: Political Forces and Social Classes,* London, Serif, 1995.

Bew, P. and H. Patterson, *The British State and the Ulster Crisis: From Wilson to Thatcher,* London, Verso, 1985.

Bew, P., H. Patterson and P. Teague, *Between War and Peace: the Political Future of Northern Ireland,* London, Lawrence and Wishart, 1997.

Bloomfield, D., *Political Dialogue in Northern Ireland,* Basingstoke, Macmillan, 1998.

Boyle, K., T. Hadden and P. Hillyard, *Ten Years on in Northern Ireland: the Legal Control of Political Violence,* London, Cobden Trust, 1980.

Canning, P., *British Policy Towards Ireland 1921-1941,* Oxford, Oxford University Press, 1985.

Clarke, L., *Broadening the Battlefield: the H-blocks and the Rise of Sinn Fein,* Dublin, Gill and Macmillan, 1987.

Cochrane, F., *Unionist Politics and the Politics of Unionism since the Anglo-Irish Agreement,* Cork, Cork University Press, 1997.

Connolly, M. and J. Loughlin, 'Reflections on the Anglo-Irish Agreement', *Government and Opposition,* 21(2), 1986.

Cox, W. H., 'Managing Northern Ireland intergovernmentally: an appraisal of the Anglo-Irish Agreement', *Parliamentary Affairs,* 40(1), 1987.

Cox, W. H., 'From Hillsborough to Downing Street – and after', in P. Catterall and S. McDougall (eds), *The Northern Ireland Question in British Politics,* Basingstoke, Macmillan, 1996.

Crossman, R., *The Diaries of a Cabinet Minister: Vol. 3, 1968–70,* London, Hamish Hamilton, 1977.

Cunningham, M., *British Government Policy in Northern Ireland 1969–89: its Nature and Execution,* Manchester, Manchester University Press, 1991.

Cunningham, M., 'Conservative dissidents and the Irish question: the "pro-integrationist" lobby 1973–94', *Irish Political Studies,* 10, 1995.

Delanty, G., 'Northern Ireland in a Europe of regions', *Political Quarterly,* 67(2), 1996.

Dickson, B., 'Creating an effective Human Rights Commission for Northern Ireland', SACHR 24th Report, annex H, HC 265, 1999.

Dingley, J., 'Peace processes and Northern Ireland: squaring circles?', *Terrorism and Political Violence,* 11(3), 1999.

Dixon, P., '"The usual English doubletalk": the British political parties and the Ulster Unionists 1974–94', *Irish Political Studies,* 9, 1994.

Dixon, P., '"A house divided cannot stand": Britain, bipartisanship and Northern Ireland', *Contemporary Record,* 9(1), 1995.

Dixon, P., 'Britain's "Vietnam syndrome"? public opinion and British military intervention from Palestine to Yugoslavia', *Review of International Studies,* 26(1), 2000.

Dumbrell, J., 'The United States and the Northern Irish conflict, 1969–1994: from indifference to intervention', *Irish Studies in International Affairs,* 6, 1995.

Elliott, S., 'The Northern Ireland Forum/Entry to negotiations election 1996', *Irish Political Studies,* 12, 1997.

Elliott, S., 'The referendum and assembly elections in Northern Ireland', *Irish Political Studies,* 14, 1999.

Evans, G. and B. O'Leary, 'Frameworked futures: intransigence and flexibility in the Northern Ireland elections of 30 May 1996', *Irish Political Studies,* 12, 1997.

Evans, G. and B. O'Leary, 'Northern Irish voters and the British–Irish Agreement: Foundations of a stable consociational settlement?', *Political Quarterly,* 71(1), 2000.

Fanning, R., 'The response of the London and Belfast governments to the declaration of the Republic of Ireland 1948–49', *International Affairs,* 58, 1981/82.

Farrell, M., *Northern Ireland: the Orange State,* 2nd edn, London, Pluto, 1980.

Faulkner, B., *Memoirs of a Statesman,* London, Weidenfeld and Nicolson, 1978.

Fisk, R., *The Point of No Return,* London, Andre Deutsch, 1975.

Fisk, R., *In Time of War: Ireland, Ulster and the Price of Neutrality 1939–45,* London, Andre Deutsch, 1983.

FitzGerald, G., *All in a Life,* Dublin, Gill and Macmillan, 1991.

FitzGerald, G., 'What happened to Good Friday?', *London Review of Books,* 2 September 1999.

Follis, B., *A State under Siege: the Establishment of Northern Ireland, 1920–1925,* Oxford, Clarendon, 1995.

Gaffikin, F. and M. Morrissey, *Northern Ireland: the Thatcher Years,* London, Zed Books, 1990.

Gifford, T., *Supergrasses: the Use of Accomplice Evidence in Northern Ireland*, London, Cobden Trust, 1984.

Gillespie, G., 'The Sunningdale Agreement: lost opportunity or an agreement too far?', *Irish Political Studies*, 13, 1998.

Girvin, B., 'The Anglo-Irish Agreement 1985', in B. Girvin and R. Sturm (eds), *Politics and Society in Contemporary Ireland*, Aldershot, Gower, 1986.

Greer, A., 'The Northern Ireland assembly and accountability of government: the statutory committees 1982–86', *Parliamentary Affairs*, 40(1), 1987.

Greer, A., 'Policymaking', in P. Mitchell and R. Wilford (eds), *Politics in Northern Ireland*, Boulder Co., Westview Press, 1999.

Guelke, A., 'The American connection to the Northern Ireland conflict', *Irish Studies in International Affairs*, 11(1), 1984.

Guelke, A., 'The United States, Irish Americans and the Northern Ireland peace process', *International Affairs*, 72(3), 1996.

Haagerup, N. (Rapporteur), 'Report drawn up on behalf of the Political Affairs Committee on the situation in Northern Ireland', European Parliament working document 1–1526/83, 1984.

Harris, R., 'External ownership of industry and government policy: some further evidence from Northern Ireland', *Regional Studies*, 29(1), 1991.

Harvey, S. and D. Rea, *The Northern Ireland Economy with Particular Reference to Industrial Development*, Newtownabbey, Polytechnic Innovation and Resource Centre, Ulster Polytechnic, 1982.

Hayes, M., 'The role of the Community Relations Commission in Northern Ireland', *Administration*, 20(4), 1972.

Hennessey, T., *A History of Northern Ireland 1920–1996*, Basingstoke, Macmillan, 1997.

Hickman, M. J., 'Northern Ireland, the Union and New Labour', in S. Hall, D. Massey and M. Rustin (eds), *Soundings Special: the Next Ten Years*, London, Lawrence and Wishart, 1997.

Hogwood, R., 'The regional dimension of industrial policy', in P. Madgwick and R. Rose (eds), *The Territorial Dimension in United Kingdom Politics*, London, Macmillan, 1982.

Jackson, J., 'The Northern Ireland (Emergency Provisions) Act', *Northern Ireland Legal Quarterly*, 39(3), 1988.

Jarman, N., 'Regulating rights and managing public disorder: parade disputes and the peace process, 1995–1998', *Fordham International Law Journal*, 22(4), 1999.

Jay, R. and R. Wilford, 'An end to discrimination? The Northern Ireland Fair Employment Act of 1989', *Irish Political Studies*, 6, 1991.

Labour Party, 'New Labour: because Britain deserves better', General election manifesto, London, 1997.

Livingstone, S., 'The Northern Ireland Human Rights Commission', *Fordham International Law Journal*, 22(4), 1999.

McAllister, I., 'The legitimacy of opposition: the collapse of the 1974 Northern Ireland Executive', *Eire-Ireland*, 12(4), 1977.

McClements, L., 'Economic constraints', in D. Watt (ed.), *The Constitution of Northern Ireland: Problems and Perspectives*, London, Heinemann, 1981.

McCrudden, C., 'Equality and the Good Friday Agreement', in J. Ruane and J. Todd (eds), *After the Good Friday Agreement: Analysing Political Change in Northern Ireland*, Dublin, University College Dublin Press, 1999.

McCrudden, C., 'Mainstreaming equality in the governance of Northern Ireland', *Fordham International Law Journal*, 22(4), 1999.

McEvoy, K., 'Prisoners, the Agreement, and the political character of the Northern Ireland conflict', *Fordham International Law Journal*, 22(4), 1999.

McGrath, M., 'Extradition: another Irish problem', *Northern Ireland Legal Quarterly*, 34, 1983.

McKittrick, D., *The Nervous Peace*, Belfast, Blackstaff, 1996.

Major, J., *The Autobiography*, London, HarperCollins, 1999.

Mallie, E. and D. McKittrick, *The Fight for Peace: the Secret Story Behind the Irish Peace Process*, London, Heinemann, 1996.

Meehan, E., 'The Belfast Agreement – its distinctiveness and points of cross-fertilization in the UK's devolution programme', *Parliamentary Affairs*, 52(1), 1999.

Meehan, E., '"Britain's Irish question: Britain's European question?" British–Irish relations in the context of European union and the Belfast Agreement', *Review of International Studies*, 26, 2000.

Mitchell, G., *Making Peace*, London, Heinemann, 1999.

Mitchell, P. and G. Gillespie, 'The electoral systems', in P. Mitchell and R. Wilford (eds), *Politics in Northern Ireland*, Boulder, Co., Westview Press, 1999.

Moore, L., 'Policing and change in Northern Ireland: the centrality of Human Rights', *Fordham International Law Journal*, 22(4), 1999.

Moxon-Browne, E., 'The impact of the European Community', in B. Hadfield (ed.), *Northern Ireland: Politics and the Constitution*, Buckingham, Open University Press, 1992.

Needham, R., *Battling for Peace*, Belfast, Blackstaff, 1998.

O'Dowd, L., B. Rolston and M. Tomlinson, *Northern Ireland: Between Civil Rights and Civil War*, London, CSE Books, 1980.

O'Leary, B., 'The Anglo-Irish Agreement: folly or statecraft?', *West European Politics*, 10(1), 1987.

O'Leary, B., 'The Anglo-Irish Agreement: meanings, explanations, results and a defence', in P. Teague (ed.), *Beyond the Rhetoric: Politics, the Economy and Social Policy in Northern Ireland*, London, Lawrence and Wishart, 1987.

O'Leary, B., 'Public opinion and Northern Irish futures', *Political Quarterly*, 63(2), 1992.

O' Leary, B., 'Afterword: what is framed in the Framework Documents?', *Ethnic and Racial Studies*, 18(4), 1995.

O'Leary, B., 'The Conservative stewardship of Northern Ireland 1979–97: sound-bottomed contradictions or slow learning?', *Political Studies*, 45(4), 1997.

O'Leary, B., 'The nature of the British–Irish Agreement', *New Left Review*, 233, 1999.

O'Leary, C., S. Elliott and R. Wilford, *The Northern Ireland Assembly 1982–1986: a Constitutional Experiment*, London, C. Hurst, 1988.

O'Malley, P., *The Uncivil Wars: Ireland Today*, Belfast, Blackstaff, 1983.

O'Neill, M., '"Appointment with history": the referenda on the Stormont Peace Agreement, May 1998', *West European Politics*, 22(1), 1999.

Osborne, R. D., 'Fair employment in Cookstown? A note on anti-discrimination policy in Northern Ireland', *Journal of Social Policy*, 11(4), 1982.

Power, P., 'The Sunningdale strategy and the northern majority consent doctrine in Anglo-Irish relations', *Eire-Ireland*, 12(1), 1977.

Prior, J., *A Balance of Power*, London, Hamish Hamilton, 1986.

Purdie, B., 'The friends of Ireland: British Labour and Irish nationalism 1945–49', in T. Gallagher and J. O'Connell (eds), *Contemporary Irish Studies*, Manchester, Manchester University Press, 1983.

Purdie, B., *Politics in the Streets*, Belfast, Blackstaff, 1990.

Rees, M., *Northern Ireland: a Personal Perspective*, London, Methuen, 1985.

Roper, S. and R. Thanki, 'Innovation 2000: an *ex ante* assessment of Northern Ireland's research and development strategy', *Regional Studies*, 29(1), 1995.

Rose P., *How the Troubles came to Northern Ireland*, Basingstoke, Macmillan, 2000.

Rowthorn, R., 'Northern Ireland: an economy in crisis', *Cambridge Journal of Economics*, 5, 1981.

Rowthorn, R. and N. Wayne, *Northern Ireland: the Political Economy of Conflict*, Cambridge, Polity Press, 1988.

Ruane, J. and J. Todd, *The Dynamics of Conflict in Northern Ireland: Power, Conflict and Emancipation*, Cambridge, Cambridge University Press, 1996.

Ruane J. and J. Todd, 'The Belfast Agreement: context, content, consequences', in J. Ruane and J. Todd (eds), *After the Good Friday Agreement: Analysing Political Change in Northern Ireland*, Dublin, University College Dublin Press, 1999.

Scorer, C. and D. Hewitt, *The Prevention of Terrorism Act: the Case for Repeal*, London, NCCL, 1981.

Sheehan, M., 'Government financial assistance and manufacturing investment in Northern Ireland', *Regional Studies*, 27(6), 1993.

Sim, J. and P. Thomas, 'The Prevention of Terrorism Act: normalising the politics of repression', *Journal of Law and Society*, 10(1), 1983.

Simpson, H., 'The Northern Ireland Housing Executive', *Housing Review*, 22(3), 1973.

Stalker, J., *Stalker*, London, Harrap, 1988.

Sunday Times Insight Team *Ulster*, London, Andre Deutsch, 1972.

Taylor, P., *Stalker*, London, Faber and Faber, 1987.

Thatcher, M., *The Downing Street Years,* London, HarperCollins, 1993.

Tomlinson, M., 'Walking backwards into the sunset: British policy and the insecurity of Northern Ireland', in D. Miller (ed.), *Rethinking Northern Ireland*, Harlow, Addison Wesley Longman, 1998.

Tonge, J., review of Miller (ed.) 1998 in, *Irish Political Studies*, 14, 1999.

Walker, C., 'Police and community in Northern Ireland', *Northern Ireland Legal Quarterly*, 41, 1990.

Walker, C., 'The bombs in Omagh and their aftermath: the Criminal Justice (Terrorism and Conspiracy) Act 1998', *Modern Law Review*, 62(6), 1999.

Weir, S., 'The Keynesians across the water', *New Society,* 9 June 1983.

Wilford, R., 'Epilogue', in P. Mitchell and R. Wilford (eds), *Politics in Northern Ireland*, Boulder, Co., Westview Press, 1999.

Index

Note: 'n' after a page reference indicates a note number on that page.